D0301480

Tudor Histories of the English Reformations, 1530–83

Tudor Histories of the English Reformations, 1530–83

THOMAS BETTERIDGE

Ashgate

Aldershot • Brookfield USA • Singapore • Sydney

Published by
Ashgate Publishing Limited
Gower House
Croft Road
Aldershot
Hants GU11 3HR
England

Ashgate Publishing Company
Old Post Road
Brookfield
Vermont 05036–9704
USA

British Library Cataloguing in Publication Data

Betteridge, Thomas
   Tudor Histories of the English Reformations, 1530–83
   (St Andrews Studies in Reformation History)
   1. Reformation—England—Sources.
   I. Title.
   274.1'6

Library of Congress Cataloging-in-Publication Data

Betteridge, Thomas.
   Tudor histories of the English Reformations, 1530–83/Thomas Betteridge.
      (St Andrews Studies in Reformation History)
   Includes bibliographical references and index.
   ISBN 1–84014–281–2 (alk. paper)
      1. Reformation—England—Historiography. 2. Great Britain—History—Tudors, 1485–1603—Historiography. 3. England—Church History—16th century—Historiography. I. Title. II. Series.
   BR377.B48   1999
   274.2'06'072—dc21   98–54195
                                                                  CIP

ISBN 1 84014 281 2

This book is printed on acid free paper

Typeset in Sabon by Manton Typesetters, 5–7 Eastfield Road, Louth, Lincs, LN11 7AJ and printed in Great Britain

Contents

St Andrews Studies in Reformation History

*The Shaping of a Community: The Rise and Reformation of the
English Parish c. 1400–1560*
Beat Kümin

*Seminary or University? The Genevan Academy and
Reformed Higher Education, 1560–1620*
Karin Maag

Marian Protestantism: Six Studies
Andrew Pettegree

Protestant History and Identity in Sixteenth-Century Europe
(2 volumes) edited by Bruce Gordon

*Antifraternalism and Anticlericalism in the German Reformation:
Johann Eberlin von Günzburg and the Campaign against the Friars*
Geoffrey Dipple

*Reformations Old and New: Essays on the Socio-Economic
Impact of Religious Change c. 1470–1630*
edited by Beat Kümin

Piety and the People: Religious Printing in French, 1511–1551
Francis M. Higman

The Reformation in Eastern and Central Europe
edited by Karin Maag

John Foxe and the English Reformation
edited by David Loades

The Reformation and the Book
Jean-François Gilmont, edited and translated by Karin Maag

Acknowledgements

This study started life as a doctoral dissertation at the University of East Anglia. During the course of its completion I have incurred numerous debts, intellectual and personal, from friends and colleagues. With Tom Webster I have had many long and informative discussions on early modern religion. I am extremely grateful to Tom Freeman for his generosity in sharing with me his unrivalled knowledge of John Foxe and *Acts and Monuments*. I have gained a great deal from the suggestions and comments made by a large number of people who have read parts of this study or listened to my ideas. I would therefore like to thank the following for their generous support: David Aers, Janice Allan, John Arnold, Justine Ashby, Patrick Collinson, Colin Davis, John Guy, David Scott Kastan, John N. King, David Lawton, Kate Lyon, Damien Nussbaum, Andrew Pettegree, Diane Purkiss, Mark Perrott, Val Purton, Emma Rees, Sarah Salih, Greg Walker and Peter Womack. I would like to thank the library staff at UEA for their tolerance and professionalism. This study would not have been completed without the funding I received from the British Academy in the form of a post-graduate studentship.

This book is dedicated to my father.

Abbreviations

BIHR	*Bulletin of the Institute of Historical Research*
EETS	Early English Text Society
EHR	*English Historical Review*
ELH	*English Literary History*
ELR	*English Literary Renaissance*
HJ	*Historical Journal*
JEH	*Journal of Ecclesiastical History*
JMRS	*Journal of Medieval and Renaissance Studies*
MLQ	*Modern Language Quarterly*
MLR	*Modern Language Review*
MP	*Modern Philology*
PMLA	*Publications of the Modern Language Association*
P & P	*Past and Present*
SCJ	*Sixteenth Century Journal*
SEL	*Studies in English Literature*
STC	Short Title Catalogue of Books Printed in England, 1475–1640
TRHS	*Transactions of the Royal Historical Society*

Introduction

In 1551 Robert Crowley published an allegorical history of the Henrician and Edwardian Reformations, *Philargyrie of Greate Britayne*.[1] This text is an exemplary mid-Tudor history of the process of reformation. It tells the story of Philargyrie, a gold-eating giant, and his two 'religious' henchmen, Hypocrisie and Philaute. Crowley's poem goes on to describe how the English people, when their misery became too much to bear, 'gan to crye / To god almyght / For them to fyght'.[2] It is the act of responding to this cry of supplication, and defeating Philargyrie, that is reformation in this text. This process of reform is instigated, however, not by the monarch but by Truth who mediates between the people and the king.

> But then toke trueth
> Pitie and ruth
> And to the kynge he went
> And sayd syr kynge
> Amende this thynge
> Thy realme else wylbe shent[3]

Having listened to Truth's lecture, the king

> For feare gan sprynge
> Unto the Bible boke
> And by and by.
> Ryght reuerntly
> That swerde in hand he toke
> No wyght, quoth he
> Shall spared be
> That doth my flocke oppresse[4]

Despite this image of royal action, however, the final lines of Crowley's poem depict the actual enactment of reformation as being in the hands of figures like Truth, who take the king's commands out into the commonwealth and put them into action. In this text reformation is produced by the voice of Truth speaking within a public arena and making the king respond. Indeed, it is only the advent of Truth that enables the appearance of royal power within the world of the poem. The space in which Philargyrie operates, the commonwealth or country,

---

[1] Robert Crowley, 'Philargyrie of Greate Britayne', ed. John N. King, *ELR* 10 (1980), pp. 46–75, STC 6089.5.
[2] Ibid., p. 73.
[3] Ibid., p. 73.
[4] Ibid., p. 74–75.

has no place for the king who seems to have no knowledge of what is happening in his realm until informed by a voice, Truth, speaking from a position between the people and the monarch. This space, between royal power and the people, is the public sphere in mid-Tudor histories of the English Reformations. It is the reform and ordering of this space that is reformation in these texts. Indeed it is often the claim to be the voice of the public, to be able to play the role of Truth, that provides the textual motivation and authority of Tudor histories and historians of the English Reformations.

The Henrician, Edwardian, Marian and Elizabethan regimes all used historical discourses and narratives to claim legitimation for the religious changes they introduced; they all had their own historians to write *the* history of *the* English Reformation. In the shifting religious and political landscape of the period 1530–70, however, these histories were constantly being overtaken by events. Indeed the repeated attempts by Tudor writers to produce a complete and finished history of the English Reformation was itself a product of this instability. In these terms Christopher Haigh's comment that, 'If Reformation is to be understood as it happened in England it must be broken up, or deconstructed' is clearly apposite.[5] The English Reformations as historical events were written by Henrician, Edwardian, Marian and Elizabethan historians in order to legitimate the religious policies of the monarch or government of the day.

This book examines Tudor histories of the English Reformations written in the period 1530–83. The Introduction situates these histories within the context of mid-Tudor culture and in particular in terms of modern understandings of the period's historical, religious and political discourses. Chapter 1 discusses the representation of the Henrician Reformation in *Halle's Chronicle* and John Bale's *King Johan*. In subsequent chapters this book goes on to address the issues reflected in Bale's editions of the *Examinations of Anne Askewe*, examines in detail the almost wholly neglected history writing of Mary Tudor's reign and finishes with a discussion of the Elizabethan editions of John Foxe's *Acts and Monuments*. In the process of working chronologically through the Reformation historiography of the period 1540–63 this book explores the ideological conflicts that mid-Tudor historians of the English Reformations addressed, and the differences as well as the similarities, often cutting across doctrinal differences, that existed between their texts.

---

[5] See Christopher Haigh, *English Reformations: Religion, Politics, and Society under the Tudors* (Oxford, 1993), pp. 12–21.

History, chronicles and the apocalypse

Tudor histories of the English Reformations have had an important influence on the modern understandings of religious change in England during the sixteenth century. At the same time the bulk of the texts this study is concerned with have largely been neglected by modern critics writing on Tudor historiography. This has had two extremely negative effects. It has led to a partial and reduced understanding of the nature of Tudor history writing and it has also left unquestioned the status of these works within modern accounts of religious change in Tudor England. Mid-Tudor Reformation historiography has had an important influence on twentieth-century understandings of the English Reformations, setting a historical agenda within which modern historians are still working. In order to avoid reflecting back on these works an understanding of religious change in sixteenth-century England whose salient points they themselves helped determine, it is necessary to look at them afresh as individual histories producing textual meaning before the advent of *the* English Reformation.

The most influential and authoritative account of developments in Tudor history writing is F.J. Levy's *Tudor Historical Thought*.[6] This text, despite its relative age, is largely accepted as the orthodox version of developments in Tudor historiography and is, as Annabel Patterson has recently commented, 'to date our definitive account of sixteenth-century historiography'.[7] An over-simple but nonetheless essentially accurate summation of Levy's account of Tudor historiography would be that it tells its reader the story of the teleological and implicitly progressive journey of Tudor history writing from the precocious modernity of Thomas More's *The History of Richard III, King of England*,[8]

---

[6] F.J. Levy, *Tudor Historical Thought* (San Marino, California, 1967). Also see Judith Anderson, *Biographical Truth: The Representation of Historical Persons in Tudor and Stuart Writing* (New Haven, 1971); A.G. Dickens and J.M. Tonkin, *The Reformation in Historical Thought* (Oxford, 1985); Levi Fox (ed.), *English Historical Scholarship in the Sixteenth and Seventeenth Centuries* (London, 1956); F.S. Fussner, *The Historical Revolution: English Historical Writing and Thought, 1580–1640* (London, 1962); F.S. Fussner, *Tudor History and Historians* (New York, 1970); John Kenyon, *The History Men: the Historical Profession in England since the Renaissance* (London, 1983); Joseph M. Levine, *Humanism and History: Origins of Modern Historiography* (Ithaca, 1987); Mary McKisack, *Medieval History in the Tudor Age* (Oxford, 1971); J.W. Thompson, *A History of Historical Writing* (Gloucester, Mass., 1967).

[7] Annabel Patterson, 'Rethinking Tudor Historiography', *South Atlantic Quarterly*, 92 (1993), pp. 185–208, p. 207.

[8] Thomas More, 'The History of Richard III, King of England', in *The Complete Works of St. Thomas More*, ed. Daniel Kinney, 15 vols (New Haven, 1986), vol. 15, pp. 313–485.

through the medieval muddle of the mid-Tudor chronicles and on to the final achievement of modern history writing in Francis Bacon's *The History of the Reign of King Henry the Seventh*.[9] This view of developments in Tudor historiography has, however, recently been criticized by a number of historians. For example David Womersley has commented that:

> Not the least paradoxical aspect of this narrative [of Tudor historiography] ... was its disparagement and neglect of virtually all the historical writing which the men of the sixteenth century themselves considered to be of the first importance, and which they were prepared to buy in large quantities and at high prices.[10]

Levy's account of Tudor historiography relies on a number of historical and methodological assumptions. In particular, it embodies a potentially simplistic understanding of the status of history as a discourse. Indeed many recent accounts of Tudor historiography share this view of 'history' constructing it as an unproblematic, almost self-explanatory, term. This creates a situation in which the status of texts as historical within such studies is not explicitly addressed. This theoretical naiveté has also led to modern conventions of history writing being applied to sixteenth-century texts to judge their historical truthfulness or modernity as a basis for evaluating their worth. Such an approach to Tudor historiography is clearly potentially distorting. Ultimately it is based on an unreflective understanding of the status of history as a discourse.

For reasons of brevity, and also lucidity, this study will not discuss in detail the theoretical status of history as a discourse.[11] Instead the following paragraph will briefly sketch out how history as a concept will be understood in this work. History is the production of truth-claiming representations of the past. In the process of producing these images historical texts articulate understandings of historical causation that in turn express ideas about cultural authority and social *telos*. History is not, however, the past. History is the production of a representation of a past which constructs itself, at the moment of its articulation, as the image of the past. Michel de Certeau writes that:

> Historiography (that is, 'history' and 'writing') bears within its own name the paradox – almost an oxymoron – of a relation established between two antinomic terms, between the real and

---

[9] Francis Bacon, *The History of the Reign of King Henry the Seventh*, ed. F.J. Levy (New York, 1972).

[10] David Womersley, 'Sir Thomas More's History of King Richard III; a new theory of the English texts', *Renaissance Studies*, 7 (1993), pp. 272–90, pp. 289–90.

[11] For the debate over the theoretical status of history see Keith Jenkins (ed.), *The Postmodern History Reader* (London, 1997).

discourse. Its task is one of connecting them and, at the point where this link cannot be imagined, of working *as if* the two were being joined.[12]

History, as part of the process of its production, papers over or fills the gap between the past and its own pasts through the paradoxical process of writing the truth of its representation of the past as beyond itself, as beyond its own textuality. This creates a situation in which every time a historical work deploys a metaphor or metonym, and implicitly refers to its own textuality, it marks out the gap separating its past from the past. Nancy F. Partner points out that:

> No assemblage of 'evidence', however large, can reproduce the past point for point and so the trope of metonymy, which extrapolates a whole thing from its contiguous part, is the organising concept and argument of even the dryest and most cautious historical construct.[13]

The past as the object of historical analysis is the necessary prerequisite of history as a discourse. Yet this process of objectification means that the pasts that history produces can never be more than partial and incomplete images of the past.[14]

Within this understanding of history the differences between various periods of history writing are less ones of truthfulness than of textual organization and form. Mid-Tudor culture permitted a far more diverse set of textual strategies to be used when writing history than are presently allowed; whereas now it is effectively impossible to write academic or 'serious' history in the form of a play or a poem, this was not the case during the sixteenth century. The images of the past expressed in, for example, John Bale's morality play *King Johan*,[15] John Foxe's apocalyptic drama *Christus Triumphans*,[16] or Miles Hogarde's allegorical

---

[12] Michel de Certeau, *The Writing of History*, trans. Tom Conley (New York, 1988), p. xxvii.

[13] Nancy F. Partner, 'Making up lost time: Writing on the writing of history', *Speculum*, 61 (1986), pp. 90–117, pp. 105–6.

[14] De Certeau comments that:

> founded on the rupture between a past that is its object, and a present that is the place of its practice, history endlessly finds the present in its object and the past in its practice. Inhabited by the uncanniness that it seeks, history imposes its laws upon the faraway places that it conquers when it fosters the illusion that it is bringing them back to life.

De Certeau, *The Writing of History*, p. 36.

[15] John Bale, 'King Johan', *The Complete Plays of John Bale*, ed. Peter Happé, 2 vols, (Cambridge, 1985), vol. I.

[16] John Foxe, *Two Latin Comedies by John Foxe The Martyrologist; Titus et Gesippus, Christus Triumphans*, ed. intro. and trans. John Hazel Smith (Ithaca, 1973).

poem *The assault of the sacrame[n]t of the Altar*,[17] clearly construct themselves as truthful. Even when Tudor historians deploy the kind of narrative structures used in modern historical discourses as, for example, John Proctor does in his *The historie of wyates rebellion, with the order and maner of resisting the same*,[18] they tend to buttress such narratives with allegorical figures or passages in order to universalize their meaning. This use of a variety of textual forms by Tudor historians has, unfortunately, meant that some sixteenth-century works of history have been left out of accounts of Tudor history writing simply because of their textual form; they do not 'look' modern. The tendency in some accounts of Tudor historiography to privilege one textual form, narrative, and one method of production, by a named individual author, reduces the scope of such accounts and undermines their historical accuracy. In particular, as Andrew Hadfield has recently pointed out, the use of a simple opposition between modern and medieval history writing as an explanatory tool in accounts of Tudor historiography is often problematic. Hadfield comments that:

> It is a myth that in the 'Middle Ages' 'historians' wrote only chronicles and were incapable of sorting out data, were incapable of being sceptical regarding the reliability of certain source material, could not interpret the material they used in a historical manner and believed that societies had always been fundamentally the same because God had ordained them that way.[19]

The assertion of a fundamental and meaning-producing division between early modern and medieval history writing has often led to a situation in which Tudor texts that do not share the conventions of modern history writing are condemned as irredeemably old-fashioned.

The problems caused by an anachronistic application of modern or humanist[20] notions of what is good history to sixteenth-century texts

---

[17] Miles Hogarde, *The assault of the sacrame[n]t of the Altar* (London, 1554), STC 13556.

[18] John Proctor, *The historie of wyattes rebellion, with the order and maner of resisting the same* (London, 1554), STC 20407.

[19] Andrew Hadfield, *Literature, Politics and National Identity: Reformation to Renaissance* (Cambridge, 1994), pp. 12–13. See also Lee Patterson, 'Critical Historicism and Medieval Studies', in Lee Patterson (ed.), *Literary Practice and Social Change in Britain 1380–1530* (Berkeley, 1990), pp. 1–14; Antonia Gransden, *Historical Writing in England Vol. 2: 1307 to the Early Sixteenth Century* (Ithaca, 1982).

[20] Although it is beyond the scope of this study to discuss in detail the humanist concept of history one should note that it was more complex then is sometimes suggested. In particular, humanist representations of the past need to be understood as an integral part of the humanist endeavour. Slavoj Žižek comments that:

> the new '*zeitgeist*' [humanism] had to constitute itself by literally *presupposing itself in its exteriority*, in its external condition (in antiquity). In

are particularly pertinent in terms of explaining the modern scholarly disregard of chronicles, the dominant form of mid-Tudor history writing. This neglect of chronicles as a genre of history writing is invariably based on a construction of them as, in some sense, inherently old-fashioned. They lack authors (they have compilers), coherence (they are disordered) and modernity (they are medieval). As texts they simply have not got what it takes. F.J. Levy, for example, is constantly dismissive about the integrity of mid-Tudor chronicles. He claims that, 'the most striking fact about any of these chronicles is the amount of random information they contain.'[21] He goes on to comment: 'Up to a point, chronicles developed by accretion.'[22] What seems to concern Levy most about chronicles is that they do not have proper authors and that therefore they assemble themselves without order or deliberation.[23] This construction of chronicles, however, produces a situation in which important questions regarding the nature of Tudor Reformation historiography are obscured. For example in the *A breuiat cronicle contaynynge all the kinges from Brute to this daye*,[24] the Henrician Reformation of the early 1530s is represented by the following entries:

> This yere [1534] the kinge was by due proces of the law diuorsed from lady Katherine his brothers wife, and he maryed Lady Anne Boleine, which was crowned Quene on whitsonday.[25]
>
> ...
>
> This yere was borne the Ladye Elizabeth at Grenewetch, on the euen of the Natiuitie of our Lady.[26]

---

other words, it was not sufficient for the new *'zeitgeist'* retroactively to posit these external conditions (the antique tradition) as 'its own', it had to (presup)pose itself as already-present in these conditions.

Žižek's argument here illustrates the importance when discussing humanism of separating its pasts from its past. Slavoj Žižek, 'Identity and Its Vicissitudes: Hegel's "Logic of Essence" as a Theory of Ideology', in Ernesto Laclau (ed.), *The Making of Political Identities* (London, 1994), pp. 40–75, p. 59.

[21] Levy, *Tudor Historical Thought*, p. 167.

[22] Ibid., p. 168.

[23] For some of the problems associated with applying modern understandings of authorship to historical texts within intellectual history and literary criticism see Michel Foucault, 'What is an Author', trans. Josué V. Harari, in *The Foucault Reader*, ed. Paul Rabinow (London, 1991), pp. 101–20.

[24] *A breuiat cronicle contaynynge all the kinges from Brute to this daye* (Canterbury, 1551?), STC 9968.

[25] Ibid., I.ii (3)–I.ii (3v).

[26] Ibid., I.ii (3v).

> This yere [1535] was a Nunne called the holy mayde of Kente, two
> monkes, and two fre[r]es and a preest hanged and headed for
> treason, blasphemy, and ypocresye.[27]

> ...

> This yere was the Bishop of Rome with all his false usurped power
> abbolished quite out of the Realme.[28]

Was the writer of this text aware that there was a potential conflict
involved in placing the king's divorce before the banishment of the
Pope's jurisdiction from England? Certainly this issue caused considerable problems for historians like Edward Halle, whose account of the
Henrician Reformation appears designed to avoid producing precisely
such a stark understanding of the chronology of divorce and the break
with Rome. Does the *breuiat chronicle*'s representation of the process of
the Henrician Reformation relate to the image of King John it contains?
Of John the *breuiat cronicle* states:

> This kinge contemned the bishop of Romes aucthoryte, whiche if
> he had done of conscience and for religions sake, as he semed to do
> for couetousnes, and of a frowarde minde, undoubtedlye he had
> bene worthy hye commendacion. By his cowardnes and slothful
> necligence the signorye of Englande greatlye decayed.[29]

This image of King John is an amalgamation of the Protestant understanding of him as a prototype godly monarch and the Catholic view of
him as a tyrant. *A breuiat cronicle* presents itself as a simple mimetic
recording of the principal events of each king's reign. Within this structure an author implicitly has no role and yet the text's representation of,
for example, King John clearly undermines this claim to be unauthored.
Indeed the combination in this text of an account of the Henrician
Reformation with a representation of King John, one that draws on the
same view of John as Bale did in his play *King Johan*, suggests that the
writer of this text had a historical agenda, the existence of which
fundamentally undermines Levy's model of chronicle production.

Levy is right, however, to suggest that chronicles do often articulate a
claim to authority based on their unmediated contemporaneous recording of significant events. In a reversal of modern ideas of what
authoritative texts should look like, early modern chronicles deny their
status as authored and base their truthfulness precisely on this lack of
an author. Ironically it is what makes these texts appear old-fashioned
in the eyes of some twentieth-century readers that made them authorita-

---

[27] Ibid., I.ii (3v).
[28] Ibid., I.ii (4).
[29] Ibid., b.ii (5v)–b.ii (6).

tive during the sixteenth century. For example, *The Chronicle of Queen Jane and of two Years of Queen Mary*[30] contains the following entries:

> The (*blank*) daie of June the galluses taken down in London.
> The same daye the crosse begon to be new gilted agayn.
> This moneth master Thomas Bridges toke apon him the lewetenaunt-ship of the Tower.
> The ix. day of June the quene removed to Richmond.
> The xth day a gon shot at Polles.[31]

In a reversal of the modern privileging of the author as a source of authority, this chronicle presents its writer as a mere cipher who simply records significant events within a basic chronological framework. Its claim to express the truth of the past is based on its lack of author; time passes, events happen, the chronicle is written, history is produced. Hayden White has suggested that this structure is typical of chronicles and that it accounts for their tendency not to conclude but instead simply to grind to a halt.[32] To conclude a chronicle, in terms of the conventions of the genre, would imply a collapse of the text's source of authority, its embodiment of the passing of time. It is perhaps a desire to prevent this generic hiatus that explains the addition of new conclusions to printed chronicles throughout the Tudor period.[33] For example, Robert Fabyan's *The New Chronicles of England and France*[34] is given a number of new endings. The final entry of the 1559 edition reads:

> The .viii. daye of Maye, the queenes hyghnes [Elizabeth] rode to the parliament, and gaue her roial assent to all such actes as there

---

[30] *The Chronicle of Queen Jane and of two Years of Queen Mary*, ed. John Gough Nichols (Camden Society, o.s. 48, 1850).

[31] Ibid., p. 76.

[32] Hayden White comments that:

> the chronicle ... does not so much conclude as simply terminate; typically it lacks closure, that summing up of the 'meaning' of the chain of events with which it deals that we normally expect from the well-made story. The chronicle typically promises closure but does not provide it – which is one of the reasons why the nineteenth-century editors of the medieval chronicles denied them the status of genuine 'histories'.

Hayden White, 'The Value of Narrativity in the Representation of Reality', in *The Content of the Form: Narrative Discourse and Historical Representation* (Baltimore, 1987), pp. 1–25, p. 16.

[33] At the same time one should note that the relation between the printed versions of medieval chronicles and the manuscripts on which these versions were based was a potentially problematical one. See D.R. Woolf, 'Genre into Artifact: the Decline of the English Chronicle in the Sixteenth Century', *SCJ*, 19 (1988), pp. 321–54.

[34] Robert Fabyan, *The New Chronicles of England and France, named by himself the Concordance of Histories*, ed. Henry Ellis (London, 1811).

were made, with high thankes to al the estates, for their greate
trauaile and diligence therein. Whose highnes Iesus preserve.[35]

One should note, however, that this final entry illustrates the potential
problems of White's argument. Chronicles do often base their claim to
authority on the basis of their unmediated embodiment of past events;
however, the person who wrote this continuation to Fabyan's chronicle,
Richard Grafton, was making an explicit political and doctrinal point
in claiming that 'al estates' welcomed the acts passed by Elizabeth's first
Parliament. He was deploying the genre conventions of chronicles, in
particular their claim to be a simple mimetic record of the passing of
time, to represent as truthful his own partial view of the past.

The use, and the subversion, of the chronicle genre to write history
was a common polemical strategy throughout the period 1530–63 in
Tudor Reformation historiography. For example from 1530 there was a
constant production of chronicles that had as their topic the corruption
of the papacy.[36] *A breve Cronycle of the Byshope of Romes Blesyng*[37]
opens with the typically Protestant claim that:

> Who lyst to loke about
> May i[n] Cronicles soon fi[n]de out
> What sedes the Popyshe rout
> In England hath sowen
> Because the tyme is shorte
> I shall bryvely reporte
> And wryte in dewe sorte
> Therein what I haue knowen.[38]

The writer of this piece is simultaneously representing chronicles as
unadorned repositories of the truth of the past and claiming the role of
author in bringing to the reader's attention those parts of this truth that
it is necessary to know. This authorial claim, however, runs contrary to
the generic claim of chronicles to be authoritative texts because of their
status as unmediated records of past events – because they lack authors.

Robert Crowley, in his 'Continuation' to *An Epitome of Cronicles ...
continued to the Reigne of Quene Elizabeth by Robert Crowley, Thomas
Copper and Thomas Languet*,[39] also exploits the conventions of the

---

[35] Ibid., p. 723.

[36] For example, *The Sum of the Actes and decrees made by diverse bishops of rome*, trans. T. Gydson (1538), STC 21307a.5 and *A mustre of scismatyke byshoppes of Rome, otherwyse naming them selves popes, moche necessarye to be redde of al the kynges true subiectes* (London, 1534?).

[37] T. Gibson, *A breue Cronycle of the byshope of Romes blessynge* (1548?), STC 11842a.

[38] Ibid., no pagination.

[39] Robert Crowley, *An Epitome of Cronicles ... continued to the Reigne of Quene*

chronicle genre to produce a polemical ordering of recent events. *An Epitome of Cronicles* is a traditional chronicle until it reaches the reign of Mary Tudor. At this point Crowley uses the conventions of the chronicle form to stress the extent of the Marian persecution. He achieves this by ignoring the generic specific reasons why fifteenth- and sixteenth-century chronicles adopted different approaches to the trials and punishment of heretics. While medieval chronicles invariably record such events Tudor chronicles often only refer to the trials of prominent people or to specific notorious cases. This difference of approach relates directly to the status of chronicles as repositories of significant events. In a time when persecutions for heresy become 'normal' they cease to be the concern of the chronicle writer. Crowley, however, subverts this convention. His 'Continuation' contains such entries as:

> The .rrbi. daye of this moneth, there was bourned at Leycester a marchantes seruant.
>
> ...
>
> The rrr. daye there were .iii. burned at S.Edmundes burye.[40]

Listing such martyrdoms was not the norm in pre- or post-Marian chronicles. Typically such works simply list the main clerical martyrs and refer to their artisan comrades as 'divers others'.[41] Crowley's subversion of the chronicle form as part of a historical Protestant agenda utilizes the genre's conventions to allow him to make the doctrinal point that the act of martyrdom transcends the hierarchical social order. He subverts the genre of chronicle history writing to make his account of the Marian persecution meaningful.

The radicalism of Crowley's move is reflected by the furious response it provoked in one of the original editors of *An Epitome of Chronicles*, Thomas Cooper.[42] The latter brought out his own updated version of

---

Elizabeth by Robert Crowley, Thomas Cooper and Thomas Languet (London, 1559), STC 15217.5.

[40] Ibid., G.ggg.2.

[41] For an example of a more typical representation of the Marian persecution see Fabyan, *The New Chronicles of England and France*, p. 717.

[42] Thomas Cooper, *Coopers Chronicle* (London, 1560), STC 15218. J.W. Martin comments on these two texts that:

> The contrast in treatment of the Marian years ... is very sharp. Cooper, more in accord with earlier parts of the *Chronicle*, devotes much more attention to continental events and on the English scene deals only with important figures. Crowley's account focuses almost entirely on England and gives much more space to the burning of Protestants from all levels of society

J.W. Martin, *Religious Radicals in Tudor England* (London, 1989), p. 159.

this chronicle in 1560. In this text Cooper claims that Crowley's 'Continuation' contained five hundred faults. Cooper's text also adopts a far more conventional approach to the Marian persecution, representing it through such entries as:

> The Byshops in Englande styll continued to burne men for matters of religion: So that this yere in diverse places were executed to the number of .67. of ther aboute of which .11. were women.[43]

For Cooper it is the fact of persecution, and not the individual moments of martyrdom, that is important. In these terms he is clearly working within the conventions of Tudor chronicle writing. In Crowley's 'Continuation', however, each martyr has an individual entry; all are equal in the eyes of God and the historian. The meaning of Crowley's text is located at the point at which its form, its genre and its writer's polemical agenda interact. The facts of the Marian persecution, in this text, have meaning in terms of Crowley's subversion of the conventions of chronicle writing.

The genre conventions of chronicle writing were also put under pressure in Tudor Reformation historiography due to the tendency of mid-Tudor writers to use apocalyptic images and themes to produce historical meaning.[44] It is a mistake, however, to view apocalyptic discourse as simply a tool that Tudor historians applied to the past to produce history. Instead one should see the relationship between history and apocalypse as dynamic but also unstable. While mid-Tudor writers constantly asserted that history was meaningful because of the apocalypse, and the apocalypse might be understood by studying the past, in practice in their texts the relation between history and apocalypse is often obscure and sometimes conflicting.

These issues are reflected in the highly influential *Carion's Chronicle*[45] which claimed to contain 'all that is nedefull to be knowen, concernyng thynges done in tymes passed'.[46] This 'nedefull' refers to the text's status as a repository of useful historical lessons designed to help

---

[43] Cooper, *Chronicle*, B.iii (1).

[44] There have been a number of authoritative works on Tudor apocalyptic thought. See Richard Bauckham, *Tudor Apocalypse* (Oxford, 1978); Paul Christianson, *Reformers and Babylon: English Apocalyptic Visions from the Reformation to the Eve of the Civil War* (Toronto, 1978); Katherine R. Firth, *The Apocalyptic Tradition in Reformation Britain: 1530–1645* (Oxford, 1979).

[45] *Carion's Chronicle: The Thre Bokes of Chronicles and Carion gathered wyth great diligence of the beste athours: Whereunto is added an appendix by John Funcke*, trans. G. Lynne (London, 1550), STC 4626. For a discussion of this text's place within Protestant historiography see Avihu Zakai, 'Reformation, history, and eschatology in English Protestantism', *History and Theory*, 26 (1987), pp. 300–18.

[46] *Carion's Chronicle*, *ii.

princes govern virtuously. It also, however, relates to its ability to confirm those details of the past necessary to understand eschatological Biblical prophecies. History has an order and it is this order that *Carion's Chronicle* is written to express. Indeed without a knowledge of this order the reading of histories is worthless:

> He that wyll reade hystoryes to profyt the same must comprehende all the thymes sence the foundacyon of the worlde into a certayne order.[47]

Carion's Chronicle claims to contain all history that must be known in order to understand the apocalyptic structure of history and its relation to the three ages of the world, those of Abraham, Moses and Christ. Yet this claim is undermined in the English edition of the text through the addition of a continuation. The order that *Carion's Chronicle* claimed to contain is complete, except it needs to be continuously added to in order to remain in this state of completion. In terms of the relationship between the chronicle form in which it is written and the apocalyptic ordering of history that it offers its reader, this text will require constant revision in order to maintain its promise to contain all that is necessary to understand Biblical prophecy. The writer of the bulk of the text points out:

> It is greatly necessary to overlaye all these thynges [the histories of the eastern empires and their relation to Elias's prophecy], and often to consyder them, that the order of all tymes and histories may be knowen aryght.[48]

For the order of history to be 'knowen aryght' it is necessary for it to be complete, and completion in terms of the ideas expressed within *Carion's Chronicle* can only be achieved at the end of history, indeed in a space beyond history. An apocalyptic chronicle is therefore in some senses a contradiction in terms, the textual conventions of the latter undermining the doctrine of the former. Ultimately apocalyptic doctrines and images require a linear narrative in which the ending and the beginning are implicitly articulated at once and are mutually self-sustaining, indeed self-validating.[49] This structure effectively made the writing of complete apocalyptic histories impossible until the day that such histories would no longer have meaning, until the day when history was over and Christ had come into his own. These issues were of particular relevance to Tudor Reformation historiography since in the period 1530–63 there were at least four major explicit enactments

---

[47] Ibid. *b.(1v)
[48] Ibid. Cc.iiii. (v)
[49] See White, 'The Value of Narrativity in the Representation of Reality', p. 21.

of religious reform, all of which drew on apocalyptic images to assert their legitimacy and permanency.[50] This multiplicity of claims, however, clearly potentially undermined the legitimating potential of apocalyptic discourse in terms of the political actions of mid-Tudor monarchs. How many times could similar, albeit doctrinally opposed, events be legitimated as apocalyptic?

These problems, implicit in the relation between historical and apocalyptic discourses, are made explicit in John Foxe's historical drama, *Christus Triumphans*. This play is an allegorical history of the Church. It tells the story of the Church's foundation, its corruption by the Papacy, and finishes with its rescue in the arms of its bridegroom, Christ. This final apocalyptic event in which Christ comes into his Church, however, does not, and indeed given the historical nature of Foxe's text cannot, take place within the play itself. The final lines of the text contain the absolute promise of Christ's appearance but not its fulfilment. They are spoken by a Chorus of Virgins waiting for the arrival of their bridegroom.[51]

> The poet has shown what he could. And he earnestly advises you not to be unprepared, lest the bridegroom, when he comes reject you as you sleep. The time is perhaps not long, ... Meantime be warned, be on your guard with prudence, I pray. And do applaud.[52]

Foxe's play as apocalyptic drama knows how it will end and as history it knows that this ending is yet to happen. In these terms it expresses in an explicit fashion the ultimately antinomic relationship between history and apocalypse. Indeed the binary oppositions contained within apocalyptic paradigms of good and evil, Christ and Antichrist, themselves positively encouraged such an understanding of the relation between history and apocalypse. The apocalypse as the truth of history, albeit an incomplete and partially hidden one, made history the untruthful field over which this truth was played out: only when the bridegroom appeared would the truth of Foxe's history be complete.

---

[50] While the use of apocalyptic images by apologists for the Henrician, Edwardian and Elizabethan religious settlements is well known, one should note that those writing in support of Mary Tudor's policies were equally capable of drawing on this imagery to support their cause.

[51] Foxe here is referring to Matthew 25.v.1–13. 'The Parable of the Ten Virgins'. His command to the audience to be prepared for the coming of the bridegroom is designed to ensure that there will be no foolish virgins in the audience of his play. Indeed the end of Foxe's text itself places the audience in a state of preparedness that effectively marks them, in terms of the parable, as wise virgins.

[52] John Foxe, *Two Latin Comedies by John Foxe The Martyrologist; Titus et Gesippus, Christus Triumphans*, p. 371.

It is for this reason that Bale's attempt to articulate an implicitly supportive relationship between history and apocalyptic thought was a profoundly problematic one. His claim that

> [The Book of Revelation] is a full *clearance* to all the chronicles and most notable histories which hath been wrote since Christ's ascension, opening the true natures of their ages, times and seasons[53]

implies an almost iconoclastic relation between chronicles and the scriptural truth that opens them up and clears them away. Bale himself, however, pointed out, 'Yet is the text [Revelation] a light to the chronicles, and not the chronicles to the text.'[54] It is this hierarchical relation between Scripture and history that relates the differences between Bale's *The Image of Both Churches: Being an exposition of the most wonderful book of Revelation of St. John the Evangelist* and his play *King Johan* directly to the status of the latter as history rather than exegesis.[55] In *The Image of Both Churches* Bale's discourse is motivated by a working-through of the Biblical text to provide a sentence by sentence interpretation. Whatever the considerable problems involved in this undertaking Bale could at least assert that the status of the text he was glossing was stable and fixed.[56] When he wrote *King Johan*, however, he could make no such claims to coherence or completeness. All he had were other men's accounts of the past that were themselves, in his eyes, of dubious veracity because of their monkish provenance. Bale's solution to this problem was to turn to the apocalypse and Scripture to create the truth of his history. However, as has been suggested, the appearance of apocalyptic imagery in a work of history radically undermines the truthfulness of the historical text by introducing an inherently ahistorical, if not anti-historical, truth into its midst. In other words, once an event becomes apocalyptic it implicitly becomes not of history and, in a sense, drops out of a historical discourse;

---

[53] John Bale, 'The Image of Both Churches: Being an exposition of the most wonderful book of Revelation of St. John the Evangelist', in *Select Works*, ed. Henry Christmas (Cambridge, 1849), pp. 249–640, STC 1296.5, p. 253 [emphasis added].

[54] Ibid., p. 253.

[55] Alec Ryrie comments:

> History, for Bale and those of a similar stamp, could illustrate, explain and amplify Scripture, but it could never be authoritative in its own right.

Alec Ryrie, 'The Problems of Legitimacy and Precedent in English Protestantism, 1539–47', in Bruce Gordon (ed.), *Protestant History and Identity in Sixteenth-Century Europe: The Medieval Inheritance*, 2 vols (Aldershot, 1996), vol. I, pp. 78–92, p. 78.

[56] Or at least it is constructed as stable by Bale in the process of producing the exegesis of it.

it becomes scriptural.[57] Bale's glosses on the Book of Revelation have a relation to the truth that his historical works can never achieve.[58]

There is therefore a conflict between the textual motivation of texts which had as their intention the constructing of truthful images of the past and those for which the aim was to express or mediate the truth of Scripture. While the latter were dealing with a fixed, inherently coherent, ordered aspect of the universal, absolute truth,[59] the formers' subject was implicitly disordered, incoherent and contingent. Apocalyptic imagery can be read as a sign that marks the point at which the absolute, universal truth of Scripture enters the contingent, worldly historical text through metaphor and metonym. As such it signifies a moment of crisis, even of failure, within the historical text. It marks the point at which the truth of history, and the authority of the historian, had to be validated by a discourse that was beyond, indeed antinomic, to history itself; a truth that made history redundant – the truth of Scripture.

The use of apocalyptic imagery in sixteenth-century Tudor Reformation historiography has a function that is inseparable from the way these histories as texts produce their meaning. One cannot distil apocalyptic discourse from these texts and relate the result of one's labour to the thoughts of a sixteenth-century writer. Texts do not hold or express the ideas and thoughts of an author; they produce meaning.[60] Analysing how a text generates meaning rather than, for example, focusing on an author's ideas as one's object of study, enables one to ask different, although not inherently better, questions. Instead of repeating the orthodox forms of intellectual history and asking how does a work, or a collection of texts, express an author's ideas one can ask how does this

---

[57] This was particularly so in the case of martyrdom when at the actual moment of witness bearing the narrative of history collapsed and the martyr became part of the trans- or even anti-historical truth of God's teaching. On martyrdom see Origen, *Prayer, and Exhortation to Martyrdom*, trans. John J. O' Meara (London, 1954).

[58] Indeed there is a constant pressure in Christianity, and therefore among early Tudor Protestant writers, to construct a dynamic in which history is equated with the world and lies while Scripture, its opposite, embodies a trans-historical truth. The most sophisticated discussion of this problem is probably that of St Augustine. See R.A. Markus, *Saeculum: History and Society in the Theology of St. Augustine* (London, 1970). See also Margaret W. Ferguson's discussion of Augustine's view of language and its relation to history in Margaret W. Ferguson, 'Saint Augustine's region of unlikeness: the crossing of exile and language', *Georgia Review*, 29 (1975), pp. 844–64.

[59] Although it was precisely the exact content of this truth that fuelled the religious controversies of the sixteenth century.

[60] For the status of texts and textuality see Pierre Macherey, 'The Problem of Reflection', *Substance*, 15 (1976), pp. 6–20 and Roland Barthes, 'Theory of the Text', trans. Ian McLeod, in Robert Young (ed.), *Untying the Text: A Post-Structuralist Reader* (London, 1990), pp. 31–47.

text produce meaning? How does this text construct its author? How does this text relate to its moment of articulation? The methodology implicit in these questions does tend to produce a set of readings as isolated moments of analysis divorced from a predetermined teleological or narrative structure. There is, however, a compelling argument that such a methodology is necessary, indeed vital, when studying Tudor Reformation history writing. These works have had a seminal influence on modern understandings of the English Reformations. To read them within the context of the history of *the* English Reformation is to perform a potentially tautological gesture, reflecting back on them their concerns and silences. One needs instead to treat them as individual texts, as part of the process that was the English Reformations.

Identity, Protestantism and history

This discussion of the histories, chronicles and texts relates directly to the status of 'Protestantism' within accounts of Tudor historiography as a self-evident, indeed normative, label. However, Protestantism's status as a movement that obsessively claimed an inherent exclusivity and integrity, while in the process of making this claim revealing its fractured and culturally antagonistic basis, makes this use of the term inherently distorting. It relies on papering over the extent to which what it meant to be a Protestant in the sixteenth century was a source of conflict and anxiety. On social identities in general Ernesto Laclau comments that:

> The key term for understanding this process of construction is the psychoanalytic category of *identification*, with its explicit assertion of a lack at the root of any identity: one needs to identify with something because there is an originary and insurmountable lack of identity.[61]

The subject position of Protestant, as the object of desire within a process of identification, needs to be understood as an unstable social identity that people were constantly striving to attain but never fully or finally achieving. Understanding Protestantism in these terms demands a reversal of the questions usually asked of Protestant texts. Instead of asking, 'how does this text's Protestantism affect or determine its meaning? how does this Protestant writer express his or her beliefs?' one should ask, 'what is Protestantism in this text? how does this text

---

[61] Ernesto Laclau, 'Introduction', in Ernesto Laclau (ed.), *The Making of Political Identities* (London, 1994), pp. 1–8, p. 3.

construct its writer as a Protestant author?' The production of a concept 'Protestantism' as a normative historical signifier, as in such formulations as the 'Protestant' view of the past, seems almost designed to avoid asking these kind of questions and it has certainly led to a failure to understand the uncertain and fragile nature of Protestantism as a social identity in the period 1520–70. It has also led to an exaggeration of the effects of the doctrinal changes in this period on Tudor culture and a simultaneous neglect of the continuities that transcended these developments.[62]

This study is not directly concerned with the Protestantization of England between 1520–80[63] but it is necessary, before embarking on a discussion of Tudor Reformation historiography, briefly to discuss the status of Protestantism as a social identity in this period. Such a discussion, however, is potentially problematic if premised on the necessity of producing a unified, coherent conceptualization of early and mid-Tudor Protestantism given the uncertainty, shared by its opponents and its adherents, as to its true character in this period.[64] Mid-Tudor culture found itself locked in a paradoxical situation in which all its members agreed on the ultimate source of authority, the Bible, while being unable to agree on the material or practical substance of this authority.[65] This cultural crisis was addressed by Tudor writers through the production of endless authoritative orderings and listings of religious beliefs and practices that, in their proliferation and repetition, themselves reflect the very uncertainty that they were designed to dispel.[66] When one, as a historian or a literary critic, produces a definition

---

[62] For example, while it is a commonplace that the English Reformations, and in particular Henry VIII's attack on Rome, turned to history in an effort to produce legitimation there was nothing inherently 'Protestant' in this discursive move. It was as true of the Marian Reformation as it was of the Edwardian or the Elizabethan.

[63] For two contradictory histories of this process see A.G. Dickens, *The English Reformation* (London, 1989) and Haigh, *English Reformations* (Oxford, 1993).

[64] For the difficulty involved in defining heresy during the Henrician period see Greg Walker, 'Heretical sects in pre-Reformation England', *History Today*, 43 (May 1993), pp. 42–8. Mark Greengrass has pointed out that similar problems occurred in France at the onset of the Reformation. See Mark Greengrass, *The French Reformation* (Oxford, 1987), pp. 10–11.

[65] Bruce Gordon makes an important point when he comments that:

> Terms such as Church, authority, nation and even reformation itself were variously and often in contradictory ways used in the sixteenth century.

Bruce Gordon, 'The Changing Face of Protestant History and Identity in the Sixteenth Century', in Bruce Gordon (ed.), *Protestant History and Identity in Sixteenth-Century Europe: The Medieval Inheritance*, 2 vols (Aldershot, 1996), vol. I, p. 7.

[66] John Bossy makes an essential point in terms of the sixteenth century when he suggests that both Protestantism and post-Tridentine Catholicism produced similar cul-

of sixteenth-century religious identities that claims certainty or even coherence there is a danger that what one is in practice reproducing is a textual strategy that was itself part of the agenda of mid-Tudor writers. In particular, modern attempts to define Protestantism are often in danger of repeating, albeit in a different form, a textual ordering of Protestant beliefs similar to that constantly performed by such writers as William Tyndale or John Bale. From its inception Protestantism demanded the production of texts that claimed authority in terms of setting down or fixing what was and was not truthful religious teaching. To produce a list or ordering of Protestant beliefs that constructs itself as universal and coherent, *as* Protestantism, is to repeat a gesture that was a cause and not a result of the Protestant endeavour. This gesture, like the similar one in humanist discourse, was predicated on the existence of a disorder that was inherently other, of the past and, initially, papist. It is therefore essential, as it is with humanism, to separate the pasts of Protestantism from Protestantism's past.[67] At one level Protestantism was the production of textual orderings of religious practices and beliefs that, in a paradoxical move, defined themselves against an other, a papist past, that was a product of, and not a cause of, their own moment of articulation. Within this schema Protestantism is the creation of an idealized social identity dependent on an understanding of papistry as its other. Without papists there can be no Protestants. And, of course, there can be no papists without Protestants.

This understanding of Protestantism has important implications in terms of the beliefs that are traditionally viewed as distinctively Protestant and their use as explanatory tools within accounts of sixteenth-century cultural developments. For example, in traditional accounts of Protestant beliefs the principle of 'by Scripture alone', *scriptura sola,* is invariably stressed as central.[68] Privileging this

---

tural results in terms of the ordering and organizing of religious practices through the textual fixing of the liturgy and other Church rituals. See John Bossy, *Christianity in the West: 1400–1700* (Oxford, 1985), p. 103. Gerald Strauss has also recently commented on the importance of order as a concept to Protestant and Catholic German writers. See Gerald Strauss, 'The Idea Of Order in the German Reformation', in *Enacting the Reformation in Germany: Essays on Institution and Reception* (Aldershot, 1993), pp. 1–16.

[67] Clearly this is what revisionist historians have been attempting to achieve with their emphasis on the popularity and vitality of the pre-Reformation Church. See Eamon Duffy, *The Stripping of the Altars: Traditional Religion in England 1400–1580* (New Haven, 1992). However, for an important critique of Duffy's view of fifteenth-century religion see David Aers, 'Altars of power: Reflections on Eamon Duffy's *The Stripping of the Altars: Traditional Religion in England 1400–1580*', *Literature and History*, n.s. 3/2 (1995), pp. 90–105.

[68] For a simple and insightful discussion of this concept see Alister McGrath, *Reformation Thought: An Introduction* (Oxford, 1993), pp. 132–58.

principle as an idealized component of what it meant to be a Protestant, is however, fraught with difficulties. One problem associated with the use of this concept to define Protestantism is that of reconciling it with the behaviour of such Protestant writers as John Bale who were capable, in the same text, of proclaiming their attachment to *scriptura sola*, attacking the papists for their neglect of it and blatantly misquoting Scripture in order to score a polemical point.[69] Does this make Bale a 'bad' Protestant? Certainly if the term 'Protestant' is to have meaning it must be applicable to a writer like Bale who viewed himself, and was represented by his opponents, as a typical Protestant. Unfortunately the privileging of *scriptura sola* as one of the signifiers of Protestantism even occurs in modern studies which acknowledge that it was a problematic concept for mainstream Protestantism. Often one encounters a structure in which the problems caused by *scriptura sola* are accepted in terms of Protestantism while being ignored when it is used by the modern historian to repeat the Protestant attack on the 'churchly' religion of the late medieval Church. The distinction between mainstream magisterial Protestantism and Catholicism in terms of the relation between Church, Scripture, authority and the social order was one of degree and not kind.

Another problem with the use of 'by Scripture alone' to define Protestantism is this doctrine's actual stability and meaning. At this point one should note that the text of the Bible itself effectively undermines this principle due to its contradictory and frankly incoherent nature.[70] Indeed this problem was made worse during the course of the sixteenth century with the proliferation of Biblical texts that represented themselves as authoritative. G.R. Evans has commented that:

> It is a supreme irony that it was at the time when *Scriptura sola* became a reforming slogan that it became unprecedentedly difficult to point unequivocally to the Sacred Page and say, 'That is Holy Scripture'.[71]

There is, however, perhaps more than irony at work in this paradoxical situation. The polemical use of the principle of *scriptura sola* not only itself effectively produced this very difficulty but also created the possibility of its solution. To articulate the principle of 'by Scripture alone' in

---

[69] For a discussion of Bale's cavalier attitude to the meaning and text of Scripture see Rainer Pineas, 'Some polemical techniques in the nondramatic works of John Bale', *Bibliotheque d'Humanisme et Renaissance*, 24 (1962), pp. 583–8.

[70] For a discussion of the Bible as a text see David Lawton, *Faith, Text and History: the Bible in English* (Hemel Hempstead, 1990).

[71] G.R. Evans, *Problems of Authority in the Reformation Debates* (Cambridge, 1992), p. 56.

a situation in which the status of Scripture is itself a source of cultural conflict is to place oneself beyond this conflict, to claim the role of validator and authorizer of Scripture.

This point needs stressing because far too often Protestantism is still constructed as an attempt to produce an inherently truthful translation of the Bible or even as an attempt to democratize Scripture. These representations of Protestantism are clearly anachronistic. At no stage did mainstream or magisterial Protestants wish the *real* ploughman (let alone woman) to have the same access to Scripture and its interpretation as they reserved for themselves. Euan Cameron points out, 'the reformers did not translate for the sake of pure detached scholarship'. Cameron goes on to comment that:

> Once the Bible had been corrected, translated, and interpreted, then (and only then, one might say!) it was offered to the people. Since the reformers appealed to Scripture as their source of authority, they represented themselves to their audience as proclaiming the 'truths' of Scripture, instead of the inventions and fictions of the Roman Church.[72]

This structure is given exemplary expression in William Tyndale's work, *The Obedience of a Christian Man*,[73] in which Tyndale advocates Scripture as the only interpretative tool necessary to understand Scripture itself. He writes:

> One Scripture will help to declare another. And the circumstances, that is to say, the places that go before and after, will give light unto the middle text. And the open and manifest Scriptures will ever improve the false and wrong exposition of the darker sentences.[74]

One wonders how, within this hermeneutic structure, one decides which passages are 'open and manifest' and which 'dark'? Indeed Tyndale's theory of textual interpretation is entirely tautological, as within the circle of Scripture as the truth of Scripture there is no point from which one can start one's explication of the text; there is no place for any texts to speak the truth of Scripture which are not scriptural. One must ask, if only Scripture can be used to interpret Scripture then what is the status of Tyndale's own text in this process? In practice, however, *The Obedience*

---

[72] Euan Cameron, *The European Reformation* (Oxford, 1991), p. 141.

[73] William Tyndale, 'The obedience of a Christian man', in *Doctrinal Treatises and Introductions to Different Portions of the Holy Scriptures*, ed. Henry Walter (Cambridge, 1848), pp. 127–344, STC 24446. To use Tyndale as an example of Protestant thought is rather ironic given that, as Patrick Collinson has recently pointed out, 'the label "Protestant" had not been invented when Tyndale first translated the New Testament'. See Patrick Collinson, 'William Tyndale and the Course of the English Reformation', *Reformation*, 1 (1996), pp. 72–97, p. 76.

[74] Tyndale, *The Obedience*, p. 250.

of a Christian Man embodies an argument that Scripture is self-interpreting in terms of producing an authoritative truth while enacting a claim to be an authoritative text itself. Ironically it sustains this claim to authority, in the face of its non-scriptural status, on the basis of its articulation of the principle of *scriptura sola*. John N. King comments that, 'Although he advocated individual reading and interpretation, Tyndale still channelled his readers' interpretation through his textual apparatus.'[75] Scripture might be able to interpret itself but only within the textual space created by Tyndale's authoritative text stating its right to be self-interpreting.

At the same time Tyndale's advocacy of 'by Scripture alone' also acts as the authorizing source, and the reason, for his polemical attack on his opponents.[76] Undoubtedly *The Obedience of a Christian Man* does advance the principle of 'by Scripture alone', but it does so within a polemical framework that implicitly undermines the radical implications of this idea at the very moment of its articulation. This potentially fractured use of the principle *scriptura sola* is far from unique to Tyndale's text. As Euan Cameron points out:

> 'Scripture alone' needs to be understood in a particular, technical light. Protestantism was neither crudely fundamentalist, nor radically democratic in offering the Scriptures to the people without restraint ... 'Scripture alone' was hand-maiden both to their [the Protestants] polemic and to their theory of salvation.[77]

Given this potentially conflicting understanding of *scriptura sola*, as simultaneously an authoritative and a polemical concept, it is perhaps not surprising to find that, as Alister E. McGrath has suggested, there was a considerable movement within magisterial Protestantism over its status. McGrath comments that:

> The magisterial Reformation initially seems to have allowed that every individual had the right to interpret Scripture; but subsequently it became anxious concerning the social and political consequences of this idea.[78]

---

[75] John N. King, *English Reformation Literature: The Tudor Origins of the Protestant Tradition* (Princeton, 1982), p. 47.

[76] In this context one should note that, as Quentin Skinner suggests, the production of the first authorized version of the Bible in English can be regarded as at least partly a result of Thomas Cromwell's highly organized propaganda campaign in support of the Royal Supremacy during the 1530s. This is not to deny, as Skinner also points out, that this move may have been motivated by Cromwell's religious beliefs, rather it illustrates that the polemic was not a subsidiary unimportant part of Protestantism but was one of its driving forces. See Quentin Skinner, *The Foundations of Modern Political Thought. The Age of Reformation*, 2 vols (Cambridge, 1992), vol. II, p. 98.

[77] Cameron, *European Reformation*, p. 144.

[78] McGrath, *Reformation Thought*, p. 155.

Protestantism did represent itself as a return to the pure Word of God. In terms of intellectual history and literary criticism, however, it is clearly inappropriate and misleading to use the concept of 'by Scripture alone' as a trans-historical, coherent belief, the articulation of which defines a text, or a person, as Protestant. In particular, this use of the term evaporates from it both its status as a polemical tool and the strains that it produced within Protestantism.

This discussion is not seeking to deny that Protestantism was a highly significant cultural movement that had a profound impact on the lives of many in sixteenth-century Western Europe. Its intention is the more modest one of flagging the problems associated with the production of a homogenized and coherent set of beliefs that can be easily grouped together under the label Protestantism. In particular, the unstable nature of Protestantism as a social identity throughout the sixteenth century means that to use this term to explain cultural change, and specifically the move from the medieval into the modern, is historically perilous and often anachronistic.

These points are particularly salient when one is discussing Tudor Reformation historiography.[79] English Protestants were quick to turn to the past to provide legitimation but this move was a potentially difficult one.[80] As Richard Bauckham points out, 'History for Tudor Protestants was a problem as well as an inspiration, a quest for self-explanation as well as a quarry for theological polemics.'[81] The past was both a challenge and a provocation for English Protestants, a land that needed to be colonized and tamed so that it would, or at least could, reflect back at them their own image.[82] One of the earliest texts to construct itself as expressing a model of Protestantism and of its other, a papist past, was *A Proper Dyalogue Betweene a Gentillman and a Husbandman: Eche complaynynge to other their miserable calamite through the ambicion of the clergye*.[83] This text is in two

---

[79] Indeed, as Bruce Gordon points out, Protestant historical thought was fluid throughout the sixteenth century. See Bruce Gordon, 'The Changing Face of Protestant History and Identity in the Sixteenth Century', p. 3.

[80] This potentially problematic turn to the history is consistently made by Tudor Reformation apologists because there is invariably a relation in their texts between the stability of the past and the naturalness of the existing social order. To ignore or even attack the authority of the past was an extremely radical move, completely valid in terms of Christianity, Catholic or Protestant, but not at all useful if one wished to defend the existing social order. There are, moreover, texts which do not turn to the past to validate religious change.

[81] Bauckham, *Tudor Apocalypse*, p. 113.

[82] For a general discussion of the writing of history by English Protestants see Glanmor Williams, *Reformation Views of Church History* (London, 1970).

[83] 'A Proper Dyalogue Betweene a Gentillman and a Husbandman: Eche complaynynge

parts, a verse dialogue between two explicitly sixteenth-century characters which frames an extract from a Lollard text.[84] The verse dialogue
contains an anti-clerical critique of the decayed state of the commonwealth with a historical account of how this decay came about. The
Husbandman tells the Gentillman that:

> Fyrst whan englonde was in his floures
> Ordred by the temporall gouernoures
> Knowenge no spirituall iurisdiccion.
> Than was ther in eche state and degre
> Haboundance and plentuous prosperite
> Peaceable welthe without affliccion.[85]

The fall from this Eden was, according to the Husbandman, the result
of the clergy gaining worldly dominion so that through their charges
and extortions the commonwealth was brought low. The Husbandman
then goes on to advocate to the Gentillman that they should travel to
London, where a Parliament is sitting, to seek redress. The Gentillman,
however, is doubtful of the wisdom of this course given the lessons that
history can teach regarding those who have resisted the clergy in the
past. He tells the Husbandman:

> Whosoeuer will agaynst them contende
> Shall be sure of a mischefe in the ende
> Is he gentellman lorde or kynge.
> And that vnto kynge Iohn I me reporte
> With other princes and lordes a great sorte
> Whom the cronycles expresse by name.
> Whiles they were a lyue they did them trouble
> And after their deathe with cruelnes to double
> They ceased not their honour to diffame.[86]

Despite this historical knowledge of the past behaviour of the clergy the
Gentillman then goes on to reproduce the clergy's own reported claim
that it is only recently that the people have turned against them. The

---

to other their miserable calamite through the ambicion of the clergye', in *English Reprints*, ed. E. Arber, 30 vols (London, 1871), vol. 28, STC 1462.3. For a recent discussion
of the probable writer of this text see Douglas H. Parker, '*A proper dyalogue betwene a
gentillman and a husbandman*: the question of authorship', *Bulletin of the John Rylands
Library*, 78 (1996), pp. 63–75.

[84] In terms of the veracity of this extract as a Lollard text Anne Hudson has suggested
with reference to the reprinting of such fifteenth-century works during the Tudor period
that '... all the evidence points to a remarkable conservatism in the sixteenth-century
handling of ... medieval material'. Anne Hudson, '"No Newe Thyng": The printing of
medieval texts in the early reformation period', in *Lollards and Their Books* (London,
1985), pp. 227–48, p. 245.

[85] *A Proper Dyalogue Betweene a Gentillman and a Husbandman*, p. 138.

[86] Ibid., p. 145.

Husbandman, however, will have none of this, telling the Gentillman that:

> By seynt mary syr that is a starcke lye
> I can shewe you a worcke by and by
> Against that poynte makinge obiection.
> Which of warrantyse I dare be bolde
> That it is aboue an hundred yere old
> As the englishe selfe dothe testifye.[87]

The Gentillman immediately asks the Husbandman to read this interesting piece to him, which he proceeds to do. The reader of the text is then confronted with an apparently genuine piece of Lollard prose, albeit, in textual terms, only 'heard' through the voice of the Husbandman. The reading of this piece has such an effect on the Gentillman that he immediately promises to act on what he has heard. He tells the Husbandman that his new knowledge of the existence of such works, and the possibility of more of them coming to light, will produce reform in the commonwealth:

> Nowe I promyse the after my iudgement
> I haue not hard of soche an olde fragment
> Better groundyd on reason with Scripture.
> Yf soche auncyent thynges myght come to lyght
> That noble men hadde ones of theym a syght
> The world yet wolde chaunge perauenture
> For here agaynst the clergye can not bercke
> Sayenge as they do thys is a newe wercke
> Of heretykes contryued lately.
> And by thys treatyse it apperyth playne
> That before oure dayes men did compleyne
> Agaynst clerkes ambycyon so stately.[88]

The dialogue ends inconclusively with a discussion of the role of the temporal authorities, implicitly the Gentillman, in carrying out the clergy's bidding by burning people who accuse them of being oppressive.

The structure of this piece creates a dynamic in which the words of the Husbandman and the Gentillman, the verse dialogue, and the Lollard treatise are simultaneously homogenized within a text and differentiated in terms of status and authority. The Lollard text is effectively buried within the dialogue; it is at the heart of the dialogue and is simultaneously differentiated from it by its form (it is in prose) and its language (according to the Husbandman it is written in 'antique' English). This distancing of the Lollard treatise from the dialogue creates a

---

[87] Ibid., p. 149.
[88] Ibid., p. 165.

narrative structure which functions, at one level, to appropriate the fifteenth-century work as a part of the sixteenth-century text. Within this structure the Lollard text functions as an authorizing fragment of the past that needs to be framed by the polemic contained within the dialogue to have meaning. This structure embodies a claim for authority by the dialogue's author based on his ability to use a fifteenth-century text to motivate and justify sixteenth-century religious polemics. To be a Protestant in terms of this text is to be able to perform this authorial role, to be able to produce a text that welds together through a literary device a fragment of the past, a historical account of clerical oppressions and a call for a religious reform. This text enacts the production of a Protestant identity through the articulation of a historical narrative based on an appropriation of artefacts and testimonies from the past that are then, in a tautological move, deployed to validate the status of this very identity.

This structure is repeated throughout the sixteenth century in texts written to articulate a historical understanding of what it was to be a Protestant. In the process the fragility of this identity is revealed as writer after writer performs the tautological gesture of proving that his or her understanding of what it means to be a Protestant can be confirmed by 'finding' it in the past. An example of this structure is the way in which John Foxe in the 1570 edition of *Acts and Monuments*[89] narrates the persecution of Lollards in the diocese of Lincoln during the early years of the sixteenth century. To recount these events Foxe, and his printer John Daye, produce a table illustrating the progress of Bishop Longland's persecution of the Amersham Lollards. This table gives the names of the accusers, the accused and the details of the crimes the latter are accused of; most of these 'crimes' take the form of words and sayings attributed to the accused. The table represents the persecution in such a way as to create the impression that if the Church had gone on looking, more and more Lollards would have been found. As each of the accused identifies a number of new offenders so the number of Lollards constantly increases. The reader is given the illusion that they are themselves following, almost taking part in, the persecutory process. Foxe, however, has already framed this table for the reader. He has effectively produced the meaning of the persecution before textually it has taken place. Foxe writes:

> Foure principall pointes they [the Lollards] stoode in agaynste the Churche of Rome, in pilgrimage, adoration of saintes, in readying

---

[89] John Foxe, *The Ecclesiastical History, Contaynyng the Actes and Monumentes of Thynges passed in euery Kynges tyme in this realme especially in the Church of England principally to be noted* (London, 1570), STC 11223.

Scripture bookes in Englishe, and in the carnall presence of Christes body in the Sacrament'.[90]

It may be that many Lollards did indeed reject these practices and insist on their right to read the Scriptures in English; however, one must ask whether it is purely coincidence that Foxe's principal areas of doctrinal conflict between the Lollards and the 'Church of Rome' create a situation in which most, if not all, Elizabethan Protestants could happily view these Lollards as their natural religious forerunners. It is important to note that at this stage in the narrative the reader has no way of judging the accuracy of these 'principall pointes'. At the end of the table Foxe draws up another list of the items with which these Lollards were charged. In the process he separates the belief or crime from the named individual accused in the table. Foxe's rhetorical framing of this Lollard table encourages the reader firstly to look out for the 'foure principall' points of Lollard doctrine already suggested; the table then allows one to experience the process of the inquisition; while the final summing up of the opinions for which the Lollards were charged separates belief from individual again. In the process the specificity of the accusation against old Father Bartlet, its basis in a moment of non-magisterial religious radicalism, disappears:

> For the other day there came a man to him as he was threshyng, and said, God speede father Bartlet, ye worke sore, yea said he, I threshe God almighty out of the straw.[91]

Clearly, at one level, this is a reference to the Lollard rejection of transubstantiation. These words, however, have a different meaning as part of Foxe's Elizabethan construction of Lollardy than they do coming from the lips of old Father Bartlet while he works in the fields. Foxe's history takes the raw material of the past, the words of the martyrs and their persecutors, presents them to the reader and then refines them down to a number of principal points.[92] In the process Foxe makes the words of such people as 'old father Bartlet' the authorizing, truthful fragment of the past that nonetheless requires his historical work and polemical framing to be meaningful in the present.[93] As in *A Proper Dyalogue*, in *Acts and Monuments* a Protestant identity is being articulated and asserted on the basis of this identity's appearance in a

---

[90] Ibid., p. 945.

[91] Ibid., p. 947.

[92] Dr John Arnold has pointed out to me that in these terms Foxe's text reproduces a central component of inquisitorial discourse.

[93] This is not to imply that Foxe's intentions were to ignore or distort the words of people like 'old father Bartlet'. See Chapter 4 for a more in-depth discussion of Foxe's historiography.

past that is itself the product of Protestantism. The Protestant historian produces pasts in which, not surprisingly, he finds himself.

The status of Protestantism as a dynamic unstable social identity makes it problematic to use it as a normative peg or anchor to secure readings of the sixteenth-century texts. It is not the nature of the term itself that is at issue but the function it often performs within modern accounts of Tudor culture. To deploy 'Protestantism' or, for very similar reasons, 'humanism', as that which in one's account of Tudor historiography produces a break with the past or the onset of modernity is to rewrite these cultural identities as one's own and to produce texts that are Protestant and humanist. To move beyond this dynamic it is necessary to produce literary critical and historical questions that transcend the tautological process of constructing the meaning of a text by using its own self-validating structures.

Politics, counsel and publicness

Tudor histories of the English Reformations are profoundly political texts. Despite this, however, as a genre they have largely been neglected by intellectual historians writing on sixteenth-century political thought. This is extremely unfortunate since these texts implicitly, and often explicitly, articulate clear understandings not only of the events they describe but also of how reform and renewal can and should take place within the Tudor polity. At the same time, however, it is undoubtedly true that as histories they tend not to draw on the classical traditions and humanist vocabulary that have recently been recognized as having a seminal importance on Tudor political thought.[94] In these terms one could argue that they are not really intellectual enough to be discussed alongside such canonical works as Thomas Starkey's *A Dialogue Between Reginald Pole and Thomas Lupset*, or William Tyndale's *The Obedience of a Christian Man*.[95] Despite this lack of intellectual clout, however, Tudor histories of the English Reformations address many of the same issues as the texts that play a central role in modern accounts of Tudor political thought. In particular, the question of counsel and its relation to the reform of the commonwealth is often central to these histories. Indeed, in a sense, one can see these historical texts as repre-

---

[94] See John Guy, 'The Henrician Age', in J.G.A. Pocock, assisted by Gordon J. Schochet and Lois G. Schwerver (eds), *Varieties of British Political Thought 1500–1800* (Cambridge, 1993), pp. 13–46, p. 14.

[95] Thomas Starkey, *A Dialogue Between Reginald Pole and Thomas Lupset*, ed. Kathleen M. Burton (London, 1984).

senting, and enacting, the very issues theorized by such text's as Starkey's *Dialogue*.[96]

The debate over counsel and its central part within Tudor political theory has recently been subjected to a large degree of historical scrutiny. John Guy has suggested that:

> Whether expressed in Court, Council, or Parliament, it was counsel that made the exercise of royal power legitimate. ... In the humanist-classical tradition, counsel was linked directly to virtue, since it was the dictates of virtue that impelled the king to act according to the common good.[97]

It is not the aim of this study to go over the ground covered by such scholars as Guy. Moreover it is not the intellectual or theoretical status of counsel that Tudor histories of the English Reformations are concerned with but its practice. In a sense one could see these texts as providing an antidote to the tendency that Guy has noted within recent studies of counsel in which discussion of classical themes and rhetorical strategies is privileged at the expense of analysing the meaning of counsel itself as a concept within the Tudor polity. Guy comments that:

> 'Counsel' was neither in itself a neutral concept nor even one suited intrinsically to the orderly conduct of politics. It subsumed competing moral and political values which stimulated at best intellectual debate, at worst political ideology. The politics of 'counsel' were in this sense the unceasing politics of discourse.[98]

Counsel, as presented in such works as Sir Thomas Elyot's *Of the Knowledge which Maketh a Wise Man*,[99] John Skelton's *Magnyfycence*[100] or William Tyndale's *The Obedience of a Christian Man*, is profoundly dynamic and public. It is necessary both to the functioning of the polity and to the psychological health of the monarch.[101] Counsel's enemies are constructed in these texts as inherently private, working in the dark of the polity and the monarch's mind, corrupting the public functioning

---

[96] On Starkey's *Dialogue* see T.F. Mayer, *Thomas Starkey and the Commonweal; Humanist Politics and Religion in the Reign of Henry VIII* (Cambridge, 1989).

[97] John Guy, 'Tudor monarchy and its critiques', in John Guy (ed.), *Tudor Monarchy* (London, 1997), pp. 78–109, p. 80.

[98] John Guy, 'The rhetoric of counsel in early modern England', in Dale Hoak (ed.), *Tudor Political Culture* (Cambridge, 1995), pp. 292–310, p. 293.

[99] Sir Thomas Elyot, *Of the Knowledge which Maketh a Wise Man*, ed. Edwin Johnston Howard (Oxford, Ohio, 1946), STC 7668.

[100] John Skelton, 'Magnyfycence', in *Four Morality Plays*, ed. Peter Happe (London, 1979), pp. 211–311.

[101] See F.W. Conrad, 'The problem of counsel reconsidered: the case of Sir Thomas Elyot', in Paul A. Fideler and T.F. Mayer (eds), *Political Thought and the Tudor Commonwealth: Deep structure, discourse and disguise* (London, 1992), pp. 75–107, p. 75.

of counsel and therefore the health of the commonwealth through flattery, sophistry and private machinations.

Tudor histories of the English Reformations are also concerned with the reform and order of the public space of counsel. They constantly discuss the corruption, purgation and restoration of this site of efficacious counsel. Indeed these histories invariably represent themselves as part of this reforming process, part of the public counsel that the monarch should, and indeed is bound, to hear. The writers of these texts also invariably present themselves as a public voice calling for reform, valorized by its publicness and the extent to which it speaks for the commonwealth as a whole. At the same time, however, there is a separation between the place of public counsel, the voice of the historian as that of the public, the polity and the commonwealth. This symbolic space, which is neither polity nor commonwealth, and which marks a gap between monarch, subject and country, can be usefully understood as a Tudor public sphere.[102]

The public sphere as imagined in mid-Tudor histories is a symbolic space related to but distinct from the polity and the commonwealth. To have the right to speak in this culturally valorized space, however, one had to be, or realistically aspire to be, part of the polity: one had to be a potential or actual magistrate.[103] Indeed the concept of the public sphere as imagined in these mid-Tudor histories is only meaningful for members of the polity since its articulation specifically created a gap between one's position within the body politic and one's status as a subject. It was from this symbolic space, from the position of the public, that it was possible for these historical texts to express understandings of the process of reformation that were different from, and potentially critical of, those of the government.

This symbolic space is exploited to its full in the radical Protestant Marian text *Certayne Questions Demanded and asked by the Noble*

---

[102] See Jürgen Habermas, *The Structural Transformation of the Public Sphere: An Inquiry into a Category of Bourgeois Society*, trans. Thomas Burger, with the assistance of Frederick Lawrence (Cambridge, 1992). Habermas has on a number of occasions insisted that his study is only concerned with a liberal public sphere. Despite this, however, there have been a number of attempts to push back the date at which one can speak of a public sphere in terms of English political *praxis*. See David Lawton, 'Dullness and the fifteenth century', *ELH*, 54 (1987), pp. 761–99, and David Zaret, 'Religion, science and printing in the public spheres in seventeenth-century England', in Craig Calhoun (ed.), *Habermas and the Public Sphere* (Cambridge, Mass., 1993), pp. 212–35.

[103] This dependence on being a part of the polity before one could be a member of the public is precisely the point at which a Tudor public sphere most radically differs from Habermas' model of a liberal public sphere. In the latter, to be of the public was not to be of the state while in the former one could only be of the public if one were a part of the polity.

Realme of Englande, of her true naturall chyldren and Subietes of the same.[104] In this work the reader is presented with a set of provocative questions. These questions are intended to produce in the reader answers critical of Mary's rule on the basis of a difference between monarch and country. The first two questions are:

> Ite[m] whether ther be two kynd of tresones, one to the kynges parsone, [and] a nother to the body of the relme or not, [and] whether the boddy of the rellme, may pardone the committed treason unto the parsone of the prince, and a gayne whether the Prynce may pardo[n] treason done to [the] body of the releme? Ite[m] whether a Prince can betray hys own realme, or not?[105]

Later on the pamphlet asks the even more potentially radical question, 'whether the Realme of England belong to the Quene, or to her subietes'.[106] In the process of posing these questions *Certayne Questions* creates a separation between Mary and Englande. This text constructs itself as the voice of Englande and asks questions specifically designed to make its hearers experience a gap between their status as subjects to the queen and their membership of a larger community, that of the Englande's 'naturall' subjects.[107]

This is not to suggest, however, an inherent conflict between monarchy and public in mid-Tudor texts. In particular, mid-Tudor histories invariably constructed the crown's proper position as being the cynosure of the public sphere. Indeed the public's potential as critical of the monarch was predicated in mid-Tudor histories on the weak nature of the Tudor public sphere, on an acceptance that the proper, natural, role of the public was to advise, counsel and not to insist.[108] The emergence of an image of a strong public in Tudor historical writing, one that demanded to be heard

---

[104] *Certayne Questions Demanded and asked by the Noble Realme of Englande, of her true naturall chyldren and Subietes of the same*, attributed to Myles Hogherde (Zurich?, 1555), STC 9981.

[105] Ibid., A.ii.

[106] Ibid., A.iiii (v).

[107] For the radicalizing effects of Mary's rule on English Protestant political theory see Gerry Bowler, 'Marian Protestants and the idea of violent resistance to tyranny', in Peter Lake and Maria Dowling (eds), *Protestantism and the National Church in Sixteenth Century England* (London, 1987), pp. 124–43: Jane Dawson, 'Revolutionary conclusions: the case of the Marian exiles', *History of Political Thought*, 11 (1990), pp. 257–72.

[108] Nancy Fraser has argued that one should distinguish between publics which construct themselves as weak because their 'deliberative practice consists exclusively in opinion formation and does not also encompass decision making' and strong publics whose ' … discourse encompasses both opinion formation and decision making'. See Nancy Fraser, 'Rethinking the public sphere: a contribution to the critique of actually existing democracy', in Craig Calhoun (ed.), *Habermas and the Public Sphere* (Cambridge, Mass., 1993), pp. 109–42. p. 134.

and heeded, was the sign that the commonwealth was in need of reform and that the public sphere had ceased to function properly. Indeed, mid-Tudor histories often contain a claim on behalf of their writers to be able to perform this role, to be the people, speaking as the voice of a strong public, who can restore the public sphere to its proper natural weak state.

At the same time the concept of a public and a public sphere required that of a non-public against which to define itself; a private that was antinomic to the proper functioning of the public sphere and which produced disorder, corruption and social upheaval.[109] This private other of the public is associated in mid-Tudor history writing with inappropriate linguistic productivity, the undermining of counsel and the subversion of royal power. It is variably represented by images of the grotesque body and of the lower bodily stratum as signs of the corruption and distortion of the public sphere by the private.[110] Representations of the private in Tudor historical texts also express an understanding of those qualities that members of the public must renounce in order to be of the public. Not surprisingly there was a symbolic relationship between these two classes of private other, so that, for example, while the presence of images of the grotesque body in the public sphere was a sign of political corruption, a man's physical body was constructed as a possible source of corruption within the public man. This private constantly appears in mid-Tudor Reformation historiography. It represents the corrupt pre-Reformation state and justifies the emergence of a strong public calling for reform, often embodied in the voice of the

---

[109] As Jean Bethke Elshtain has suggested:

> Images of public and private are necessarily, if implicitly, tied to views of moral agency; evaluations of human capacities and activities, virtues, and excellence; assessments of the purposes and aims of alternative modes of social organisation ... Those silenced by power – whether overt or covert – are not people with nothing to say but are people without a public voice and space in which to say it.

Jean Bethke Elshtain, *Public Men, Private Woman: Women in Social and Political Thought* (Oxford, 1981), p. 4 and p. 15. The failure to appreciate that the idea of an articulate citizen as represented in sixteenth-century magisterial texts depended on its other, the non-articulate non-citizen, is a crucial weakness in Arthur B. Ferguson's otherwise insightful study, *The Articulate Citizen and the English Renaissance* (Durham, 1965).

[110] The idea of a grotesque body and its role in early modern culture is discussed in depth by Mikhail Bakhtin in his seminal work, *Rabelais and His World*, trans. Hélène Iswolsky (Bloomington, 1984). One should note, however, that while the grotesque body in these mid-Tudor histories shares the same characteristics as that discussed by Bakhtin – it is gross, consuming, decaying, out of proportion – it lacks the regenerative status that the grotesque body, according to Bakhtin, has in the work of such writers as Rabelais. For a further discussion of Bakhtin's ideas see Peter Stallybrass and Allon White, *The Politics and Poetics of Transgression* (London, 1986).

historian. Its symbolic violent purgation from the polity and commonwealth is reformation in these texts.

These issues can be briefly illustrated with reference to two early
Reformation texts, Sir Thomas Elyot's *Pasquil the Plaine* and Simon
Fish's *The Supplication of Beggars*. Although neither of these texts have
traditionally been viewed as histories, Elyot's work can be usefully read
as a disguised history of the Henrician Reformation while Fish's consistently deploys historical examples to buttress its polemic.

The Supplication of Beggars is an incitement to reformation based on
the assumption which sustained all magisterial histories of the English
Reformations that history and the existing hierarchical social order
were inherently mutually sustaining: history produced and protected an
ordered society and *vice versa*. The *Supplication* repeatedly compares
the present weakened state of England with the power and wealth of
the land before the clergy, in Fish's words, became 'sturby lobies' and
'bloudsuppers'. For example Fish claims that:

> The danes nether the saxons yn the time of the auncient Britons
> shulde neuer haue ben abill to haue brought theire armies so farre
> hither ynto your lond to haue conquered it if they had had at that
> time suche a sort of idell glotons to finde at home. The nobill king
> Arthur had neuer ben abill to haue caried his armie to the fote of
> the mountaines to resist the coming downe of lucius the Emperoure
> if such yerely exaction had ben taken of his people.[111]

Fish goes on to lament,

> Oh the greuous shipwrak of the comon welth, which yn auncient
> time bifore the coming yn of these rauinous wolues was so prosper-
> ous: that then there were but fewe theues.[112]

The *Supplication*, however, is far more than a simple attack on the
clergy's wealth and life-style. Its claim to be a supplication is simultaneously borne out by the tone of Fish's narrative voice and implicitly
undermined by the practical motivation of the text. The narrator of
Supplication speaks for the beggars but his role is to tell Henry what is
going on in his realm and show him how to reform his country and
return it to its earlier glory. The emphasis in the text on asking Henry
questions that have answers implicit in the text itself makes *Supplication* a lesson that is bound to be effective. For example, it asks Henry:

> whate remedy: make lawes ageynst theim. I am yn doubt whether
> ye be able: Are they not stronger in your owne parliament house

---

[111] Simon Fish, *The Supplication of the Beggars*, ed. Edward Arber (London, 1878),
STC 10883, p. 5.
[112] Ibid., p. 8.

then your silfe? whate a nombre of Bisshopes, abbotes, and priours
are lordes of your parliament?[113]

Supplication, however, as has been suggested, does not leave the answers to these questions to chance but goes on to refer to history, in the
loosest possible sense, to illustrate the truth of its view of the power of
the clergy. This structure positions *Supplication*'s readers in the same
symbolic space as its narrator implicitly occupies, alongside royal power,
commenting on it but not being part of it. Fish's text is an act of
supplication spoken from a position between the monarch and his
subjects. Although it is explicitly addressed to Henry VIII its ideal
reader is someone who recognizes himself as a proper person to have
views, even to have answers to the text's questions. In effect, *Supplication* is an attempt to produce a strong public centred on the king and
based on the need to 'reform' the clergy's corrupt power.

The nature of the clergy's corruption is also understood in *Supplication*
in terms of their undermining of the relation between monarch, polity
and commonwealth. One of the central charges Fish levels against the
clergy is that to protect their ill-gotten gains they constantly step between
the monarch and his people, producing disobedience and rebellion. *Supplication* asks what the clergy do with all their wealth and argues that
they do 'nothing but exempt theim silues from th[e] obedience of your
grace. Nothing but translate all rule power lordishippe auctorite obedience and dignitie from your grace vnto theim'.[114] Fish's work constantly
represents the clergy as corrupting the social order through their raven-
ous begging, undiscriminating lechery and bottomless greed. It consistently
emphasizes the linguistic disorder the clergy produce through their multiplicity of names, beliefs and practices. By associating the clergy with
inappropriate textual production Fish's work implies that the clergy 'fill
up' the public sphere with disordered, meaningless and corrupting words.
Fish lists the clergy's numerous different orders and roles and equates this
multiplicity of clerical offices to the clergy's consumption of a disproportionate amount of the country's resources.[115]

---

[113] Ibid., p. 8.

[114] Ibid., p. 6.

[115] Protestant 'sects' perform an identical symbolic polemical function in Catholic
texts. Indeed in William Barlow's *A Dialogue Describing the Originall Ground of these
Lutheran Faccyons, and Many of their Abuses*, this relation between orders and sects is
made explicit. Wyllyam tells his partner in the dialogue that makes up the majority of
Barlow's text that:

> I certyfe you that ye maye fynde mo divers sectes of erronyous opynyons
> among them [German 'Lutherans'] in one cytie beyond [the] sea: than be
> sondrie orders of religious people in all Englande'.

> These [ydell beggers and vacabundes] are ... the Bisshoppes,
> Abbottes, Priours, Deacons, Archedeacons, Suffraganes, Prestes,
> Monkes, Chanons, Freres, Pardoners and Somners. And who is
> abill to nombre this idell rauinous sort whiche ... haue begged so
> importunatly that they haue gotten ynto theyre hondes more then
> the therd part of all youre Realme ...[116]

There is a symbolic relation between the space occupied by this list of
offices and the clergy's status as owners of a third of the realm. This list
represents the clergy as producers of empty words that simply consume
textual space and drive out the truth. *Supplication*'s emphasis, in explicitly sexual terms, on the unproductive nature of the clergy's lives as
chaste men who only 'produce' bastards relates directly to this production of linguistic disorder. The protean quality of the clergy's language,
its disproportionate, disrupting nature, is matched by *Supplication*'s
representation of them as possessing grotesque, consuming, insatiable
bodies. Fish claims that the clergy spend all their time, when not sub-
verting royal authority, trying to seduce wives and daughters. He argues
that if the clergy continue abstaining from marriage then, 'all the realme
at length ... shall be made desert and inhabitable.'[117] Fish's text appears
here to contradict itself; the clergy's false chastity leads to the production of bastards and yet if their behaviour continues the country will
end up devoid of people. This apparent contradiction, however, relates
directly to the unproductive nature of the clergy's status within the
country, their role as producers of endless empty words, their profitless
consumption of resources and their bastards. The clergy produce, consume and speak but the end result is sterility, waste and nonsense.
Driving this grotesque body off stage, restoring order to language, is
reformation in Fish's work. *Supplication*'s aim is to provoke its reader,
nominally the king but in practice an anti-clerical strong public, into
undertaking this reform. Fish, the voice of the truth speaking between
the monarch and his subjects, calls for reformation in a voice that
demands to be heard.

Stephen Gardiner, in his introduction of the 1553 Preface to William
Barlow's *A Dialogue Describing the Originall Ground of these Lu-
theran Faccyons, and Many of their Abuses*, uses imagery similar to
Fish's in order to represent his doctrinal enemies. Gardiner writes that:

> verye playnlye here is shewed theyr [the Lutherans] monstruous
> maners and mutabilitie, theyr cankered contencions, and horrible

---

William Barlow, *A Dialogue Describing the Originall Ground of these Lutheran Faccyons,
and Many of their Abuses*, ed. John Robert Lum (London, 1897), STC 1461, p. 121.

[116] Fish, *Supplication*, p. 3.

[117] Ibid., p. 7.

ipocrisy, their develyshe devyses, and bytter blasphemye, with infinite lyke reliques of that raylynge relygion, wherby the christian
reader shall ryghte well perceaue, what fylthy frute buddeth out of
this frantike fraternitie and synfull Synagoge of Sathan, infernallye
inuented, to seduce symple soules.[118]

I have quoted Gardiner at length here since this passage's polemic is
partly based on its textual enactment of the disorder of the Lutherans.
This text argues that Protestantism produces a disordered, discordant
anti-religion and performs this polemic through its description of
Lutherans in repetitive punning couplets. Gardiner constructs an image
of his doctrinal enemies that associates them with the production of a
changeable, shifting language whose meaning is unstable and discordant. In these terms Gardiner's Lutherans and Fish's clergy have identical
effects on language. And the role that Gardiner articulates for himself,
and for William Barlow, is also identical to that which Fish claims in his
tract, that of the voice of truth exposing in public the lies and corrupt
practices of the Lutherans/clergy.

Sir Thomas Elyot's *Pasquil the Plaine*[119] is in many ways a very
different text to either those of Fish or Gardiner.[120] Like *Supplication*,
however, one of the main concerns of Elyot's text is the reform and
ordering of a Henrician public sphere. In effect *Pasquil* is a critique of
the Henrician Reformation based on its insufficiently public nature.
Elyot's work discusses the nature of counsel and compares two forms of
corrupt counsel, flattery and private, with the honest, plain public
speaking of Pasquil. In the process of making this comparison this text
also incites its readers to read in an informed active way, to follow
Pasquil's lead and penetrate the private, and therefore inherently corrupt, machinations that produced the Henrician Reformation. In *Pasquil*
private counsel leads to public disorder and tyranny. John Guy comments that in Elyot's text, 'Ambition and private causes rather than love
for the commonwealth have turned the world upside down. Virtue has
become vice, vice virtue, faith is turned to heresy.'[121] In a realm of
private counsel, according to Elyot, 'after noone is tourned to fore

---

[118] Barlow, *A Dialogue*, p. 25.

[119] Sir Thomas Elyot, 'Pasquil the Playne', in *Four Political Treatises* (Gainesville,
Florida, 1967), pp. 41–100, STC 7672.

[120] For a discussion of the humanist influences on *Pasquil* see Alistair Fox, 'Sir
Thomas Elyot and the Humanist dilemma', in Alistair Fox and John Guy (eds), *Reassessing the Henrician Age: Humanism, Politics and Reform, 1500–1550* (Oxford, 1986),
pp. 52–73.

[121] John Guy, 'The King's Council and political participation', in Alistair Fox and John
Guy (eds), *Reassessing the Henrician Age: Humanism, Politics and Reform, 1500–1550*
(Oxford, 1986), pp. 121–47, p. 139.

noone … '.[122] Pasquil's world has marked similarities with that created by the vices in such plays as John Skelton's *Magnyfycence* or Bale's *King Johan*. It also reflects directly, however, and perhaps precisely,[123] the nature of the regime that pushed through the royal divorce and the break with Rome. It is clear from this text that, for Elyot, the disasters of the Reformation were the result of a collapse of counsel and a failure of publicness at the heart of the polity.[124]

In Pasquil's world, that of the Reformation Parliament, honesty is the preserve of a graven image, a statue, while the court is full of time-servers like Gnatho and silent, but deadly counsellors/confessors like Harpocrates. Indeed Harpocrates's combination of these two roles is viewed by Elyot, as it was by his doctrinal enemies like William Tyndale, as inherently contradictory. While Harpocrates is silent in public, when he should be warning his king of the dangers of his policies, in the privacy of the confessional he can give false counsel made more persuasive by his role as confessor. Pasquil argues that:

> if in the secrete tyme of confession wherin confessours have aboue all men most largeste lybertie to blame and reproue, he shulde eyther dissemble the vyces that he knoweth in his mayster, or els forbere to declare to him the enormitie of suche capytall synnes as he hath confessed.[125]

He goes on to assert the power of public speech to reform diseases of the body and soul.

> And what indeuour maye be in sylence? Wherefore speche is not onely profitable but also of necessite muste be vsed in healing the diseases both of the soule [and] also the bodie.[126]

Pasquil is dismissive of the idea of counsellors who keep their mouths shut as the commonwealth heads for disaster. Indeed if counsellors spoke the truth then there would be no need for Pasquil to do so, and people would not have to listen to a stone statue 'sittinge in the citie of Rome'.[127] In this text Elyot explicitly equates private counsel with

---

[122] Elyot, *Pasquil*, p. 65.

[123] See Guy, 'The King's Council and political participation', p. 139 for a discussion of this point.

[124] See F.W. Conrad, 'The problem of counsel reconsidered: the case of Sir Thomas Elyot'. Conrad writes (p. 100):

> Elyot seems to have believed that had more inferior governors openly rebuked Henry's lechery before it became habitual, the course of English history might have been different.

[125] Elyot, *Pasquil*, p. 67.

[126] Ibid., p. 95.

[127] Ibid., p. 42.

corruption; while the flattery of Gnatho works in public, it is his master Harpocrates who is the real perverter of the polity.[128]

Pasquil the Plaine is, therefore, at one level an oppositional history of the religious changes of the 1530s. Elyot's text contains both a critique of these changes on the basis of their status as the product of the oxymoronic combination of private counsel and a claim by its writer to be able to restore publicness to these events, to play the role of Pasquil. Elyot's text presents itself as the record of Pasquil's annual counselling and truth-telling session, a yearly public exposure of private lies and deceits and in the process advocates the need for a Pasquil/Elyot in post-Reformation England to restore the public sphere by making public the private causes of Henry's religious policies. Pasquil represents a strong public, the voice of the truth, speaking in public and insisting on being heard and acted on. Pasquil is also, however, a lesson in reading and the proper role of the public man of virtue. When Harpocrates suggests to Pasquil that if he spoke privily he would do more good, Pasquil rejects his advice out of hand.

> *Pasquil.* ... my playnnes is so well knowen that I shall neuer come vnto priuie chamber or galeri.
> *Harpocrates.* Sens thou profitest so lyttel, why arte thou so busy.
> *Pasquil.* To thintent that men shall perceiue, that theyr vices, which they think to be wonderfull secrete be knowen to all men.[129]

This passage produces a choice between 'priuiness' and truth and effectively invites its reader to side with the latter. Indeed to read Elyot's text purposefully and to understand its construction of the Henrician Reformation is to penetrate the privy chamber or gallery. It is to be located outside the court but reflecting on it from a position of power and authority based upon its status as public.[130] Elyot's use of a graven image residing in Rome to make this point emphasizes the extent to which his attack on Henry's rule relates directly to the monarch's religious policies, their basis in corrupt private counsels and their failure to be sufficiently public.

Tudor Reformation historiography was centrally concerned with the proper ordering of the relation between monarch and commonwealth. It reflected this concern through its use of images of the public and the

---

[128] It is interesting to note that the latter's position, and devious behaviour, is identical to that rumoured of Bishop Longland, who, it was claimed, acted as Wolsey's agent in planting the 'levitical scruple' in Henry VIII's conscience during the royal confession. See J.J. Scarisbrick, *Henry VIII* (London, 1988), pp. 152–3.

[129] Elyot, *Pasquil*, p. 99.

[130] This anti-court subject position clearly resembles that articulated by Sir Thomas Wyatt in such satires as *Mine Own John Poins*.

public sphere. This was perhaps inevitable given the ambiguous status of the Henrician Reformation. Was it an act of the monarch? of Parliament? or the people? was it a secular event or a religious one?[131] G.R. Elton has commented that:

> From the moment that Henry VIII entered upon his breach with the papacy and thus opened the door to the Reformation, all political debate – all issues of domestic and foreign policy – acquired an ideological component in addition to its normal character as conflicts for power.[132]

Tudor Reformation historiography was constituted out of these conflicts. In describing and attempting to explain reformation as a process it reflected the legitimation crisis produced by the events of the 1530s.[133] In these terms, Tudor histories of the English Reformations can be seen as the symbolic sites for the playing out of the political issues discussed in theory in those Tudor texts explicitly concerned with the theoretical organization of the polity: history acted while theory only talked.

---

[131] John Guy has pointed out that the passing of the acts which established Henry's role as Supreme Head of the Church was a three-way compromise among the grandiose claims of the king himself, the concerns of the clergy and the role of Parliament. See John Guy, *Tudor England* (Oxford, 1991), pp. 133–4.

[132] Geoffrey Elton, 'Tudor Government: The Points of Contact', in *Studies in Tudor and Stuart Politics and Government*, 4 vols (Cambridge, 1983), vol. III, pp. 3–57, p. 55.

[133] J.G.A. Pocock has recently argued that the ambiguous nature of the Henrician Reformation, and the tensions it produced, created much of the conflict in the English polity during the period 1530 to 1688. See J.G.A. Pocock,' A discourse of sovereignty: observations on the work in progress', in Nicholas Phillipson and Quentin Skinner (eds), *Political Discourse in Early Modern Britain* (Cambridge, 1993), pp. 377–428.

CHAPTER ONE

John Bale, Edward Halle
and the Henrician Reformation

> Where by divers sundry old authentic histories and chronicles it is
> manifestly declared and expressed that this realm of England is an
> empire, and so hath been accepted in the world, governed by one
> supreme head and king having the dignity and royal estate of the
> imperial crown of the same, unto whom a body politic, compact of
> all sorts and degrees of people divided in terms and by names of
> spirituality and temporality, be bounden and owe to bear next to
> God a natural and humble obedience ...
>
> The Act of Appeals (1533)[1]

The Henrician Reformation from its advent claimed legitimacy on the
basis of history and social order: authentic histories declared the naturalness of a body politic ruled by one supreme head. This famous
extract from the prologue to the Act of Appeals is, however, riddled
with rhetorical sleights of hand and doctrinal tension. What did it mean
to claim that history declared the status of England as an empire?
Whose and what history made this declaration? And in what way was
the monarch's supreme headship next to God? Despite all their asser-
tions and proclamations apologists for the Henrician Reformation never
could finally or even satisfactorily answer these questions. This failure
is marked in their texts by moments of polemical collapse and textual
hiatus. In particular, Tudor Reformation historiography constantly found
itself confronted with three key issues: who or what made Reformation
happen? Was it a secular or spiritual event? And what was its historical
status?

These issues were made more pressing, and more problematical, due
to the presence of images of publicness and public spheres in magisterial
Tudor histories of the English Reformations. The act of speaking for the
public and arguing that the public sphere had been corrupted and
needed reform, took on explicit, and potentially dangerous, political
meanings within a historical discourse. If purgation of the public sphere
was a religious historical event did this mean that membership of the
public was equally historical or religious? Two radical possibilities are

---

[1] Geoffrey Elton, *The Tudor Constitution* (Cambridge, 1972), p. 344.

embodied in this question, that magisterial status itself was historical and, even more subversively, that one was authorized to speak in public, not on the basis of social position, but in terms of the sanctity of one's relation to God. Magisterial Tudor historians had to find ways of explaining the process of Reformation that avoided foregrounding these issues. Their histories had to represent the emergence of a strong reforming public in ways that protected the prevailing political and social order, and in particular the status of the monarch.

These issues determined the content and form of Tudor Reformation historiography from the moment that Henry VIII enacted his break with Rome. This chapter briefly examines a number of early Henrician defences of the Royal Supremacy. It discusses the production in these texts of images of a Henrician public sphere explicitly centred on the king. It then goes on to look at the way publicness as a concept is used by William Tyndale to sustain his right to adopt an authoritative prophetic voice within the commonwealth. The second part of the chapter examines the representations of the Henrician Reformation contained in Edward Halle's *Chronicle* and John Bale's *King Johan*. It discusses the way these texts reflect the potential conflict between the magisterial and religious understandings of the process of Reformation within the context of an imagined mid-Tudor public sphere.

Publicness, polemic and the Henrician Reformation

During the early 1530s a plethora of texts were produced by government apologists defending Henry's divorce and his attack on the English Church. In many of these works ideas of publicness and history were deployed to whip up support for the actions of the Henrician regime. One should note, however, that this turn to history was neither inevitable nor unproblematic. It was fuelled by a desire to deny the novelty of royal policies and to provide textual motivation for representations of the Henrician Reformation as inherently supportive of the social order.[2]

A Glasse of the Truthe[3] was one of the earliest tracts issued as part of the propaganda campaign the government instituted in the 1530s,

---

[2] For the historical sources used by Henry VIII and his counsellors see G.D. Nicholson, 'The nature of and functions of historical argument in the Henrician Reformation', PhD Thesis (Cambridge, 1977).

[3] 'A Glasse of the Truthe', in *Records of the Reformation: the Divorce*, ed. Nicholas Pocock, 2 vols (London, 1870), vol. II, pp. 385–421, STC 11918. See also Steven W. Haas, 'Henry VIII's Glasse of Truthe', *History*, 64 (1979), pp. 353–62; Richard Rex, 'The crisis of obedience: God's Word and Henry's Reformation', *HJ*, 39 (1996), pp. 863–94.

initially to justify Henry's divorce and later, in the second half of the decade, to support the Royal Supremacy.[4] G.R. Elton comments that 'The *Glass of Truth* is a successful piece of propaganda – readable, clear, lively, short enough but seemingly full of meat.'[5] *A Glasse* is written in the form of a dialogue between a Divine and a Lawyer.[6] The narrative motivation of this discussion is to put forward Henry's position on his marriage and divorce. One should note, however, that the form of *A Glasse* is not coincidental to the argument that it contains, rather it is fundamental to its polemical thrust. *A Glasse* constructs itself as a simple dialogue between two concerned members of the polity. It explicitly bases its authority, as a text, on its status as a dialogue, on the extent to which its form enacts and produces the truth of the king's great matter. As a dialogue *A Glasse* is at one level an image of a public sphere. It claims to embody a public dispute whose publicness and dialogical qualities are the basis of its textual authority.

The Prologue to *A Glasse* discusses the status of the dispute between the Divine and Lawyer that makes up the bulk of the text. This prologue opens with an apology to its readers telling them that:

> You shall have here, gentle readers, a small Dialogue between the Lawyer and Divine: wherin, if there lack such eloquence, such drift of arguments and conveyance of reasons, as peradventure were requisite, and as ye shall desire: yet we shall most entirely pray you, that where we be not sufficient to supply the same, to content yourself with this our rudeness, declaring the pure truth alone, which you shall be right sure to find in this poor treatise.[7]

Although these claims to 'dullness' and lack of eloquence are entirely conventional this does not prevent them from also being significant. *A Glasse* presents itself as a piece of clumsy plain writing that nonetheless contains the truth. Indeed it is precisely this plainness that guarantees the status of the text's truth. *A Glasse* constructs itself as requiring active readers, people who are prepared to find the truth. The plainness of the text, its rudeness, ensures that the discriminating reader will

---

[4] For a discussion of this propaganda campaign see Geoffrey Elton, *Policy and Police: the Enforcement of the Reformation in the Age of Thomas Cromwell* (Cambridge, 1972), pp. 171–216.

[5] Ibid., p. 177. Virginia Murphy has recently echoed Elton's views and has repeated his stress on the readability of *A Glasse*. See Virginia Murphy, 'The literature and propaganda of Henry VIII's first divorce', in Diarmaid MacCulloch (ed.), *The Reign of Henry VIII: Politics, Policy and Piety* (London, 1995), pp. 135–58, p. 157.

[6] On Tudor dialogues see K.J. Wilson, *Incomplete Fictions: The Formation of English Renaissance Dialogue* (Washington, 1985), and Roger Deakins, 'The Tudor prose dialogue: genre and anti-genre', *SEL*, 20 (1980), pp. 5–23.

[7] *A Glasse*, p. 385.

discover the truth of the text and, therefore, of Henry's great matter. The prologue to *A Glasse* contains a representation of the tract's ideal reader that the dialogue form of the main body of the text then reinforces and sustains.

As a dialogue the central section of *A Glasse* allows its reader to experience the production of meaning, the slow but inevitable emergence of the truth of government policy. Indeed the very title of this tract, *A Glasse of the Truthe*, points to its status as a text that is a reflection of the truth, a produced image. The dialogue form of the text allows the reader the pleasure of seeing the truth emerge during the course of a witty exchange. For example the text opens with the following discussion.

> *The Lawyer*. Me seemeth it is wisely and truly said, that the right way is ever the nearest way; and likewise the plain way most sure to try all manner of truth by.
> *The Divine*. I think that it be true which you speak; but you speak so obscurely, that I wot nere what you mean thereby.[8]

The irony of this exchange, in which a lawyer paraphrases Scripture and a divine thinks it is true but is not sure because he finds the words obscure, and its combination of the polemic with the comic, is typical of *A Glasse*. It creates a situation in which the reader is being invited through humour to participate in the dispute on the side of the Lawyer. *A Glasse* incites its reader to share the Lawyer's humour and therefore to accept his discourse as their own. In the process it places its reader within the dialogue as active party in the dispute.

Later in the tract during a discussion over the Pope's power to dispense 'law divine' the following exchange occurs.

> *The Divine*. ... yet one thing I must know your will in ere that I proceed any farther.
> *The Lawyer*. What is that, I beseech you?
> *The Divine*. Marry, sire, this is it, whether you will that I should shew you what the old ancient doctors do say, or what the moderns, which somewhat flattereth the Pope's authority, saith; other else declare you mine opinion, taketh out of both, which I trust shall not be far from the truth?
> *The Lawyer*. The ancient doctors' and many also of the moderns' opinion hath been declared herein in many other books ... But is there, say you, difference amongst other of their opinions?[9]

Typical of *A Glasse* is the way this exchange is motivated by a series of pre-answered questions. The main polemical point of this passage is to

---

[8] Ibid., p. 388.
[9] Ibid., p. 399.

construct those writers who claim that the Pope can dispense with 'law divine' as modern and untrustworthy. By establishing that there is a difference between the views of the ancients and moderns before the Lawyer explicitly asks if there is one, the reader is encouraged to become a knowing participant in the debate.

The dialogue form of *A Glasse* invites a form of active reading and constructs such readers as a potential public sphere. Membership of this symbolic space is, however, restricted to those readers whose reading of *A Glasse* produces the same truth as that of the text overall: one can only be of *A Glasse*'s public sphere if one agrees with governmental policy. At the same time the public sphere imagined in this tract is confined to those within the country who have the right and duty to be concerned with the future of the commonwealth. The prologue points out that while the king's concern for a heir is simply human, and is restricted to his lifetime, the effects of a doubtful succession will be far greater for the intended audience of *A Glasse*.

> if we well consider, [it] is much more our hindrance than his [Henry's]; for his lack of heirs male is a displeasure to him for his lifetime ... But our lack shall be permanent so long as the world lasteth, except that God provide ...[10]

The 'we' and 'our' in this passage refers to the readers of *A Glasse*; members of the polity concerned with matters of state, and implicitly with social order, but not part of the inner circle of royal government.[11] *A Glasse*, however, does not address them as individuals but as a collective readership whose possession of the truth of the king's cause is fundamental to the proper functioning of the polity. The dialogue form of this tract constitutes its readers as a public by making them responsible for reading between the lines of the text in order for them to become part of a glass of truth.[12]

Within the symbolic public sphere represented in *A Glasse* history has a specific legitimating role. Like other sites of early modern authority, the truth of history, in this tract's terms that it supports Henry's position, is

---

[10] Ibid., p. 386.

[11] John Guy has described the Henrician polity as being made up of a number of concentric circles. One could argue that the ideal readers of *A Glasse* are both the members of the third circle of government, the king's 'local' men, and their neighbours. In effect, this text could therefore be seen as an attempt to symbolically extend the outer reaches of the royal affinity to all those capable of reading *A Glasse* and producing its truth i.e. the justice of Henry's policy towards his marriage with Catherine of Aragon. See John Guy, *Tudor England* (Oxford, 1991), p. 167.

[12] In these terms the intended audience of *A Glasse* is similar to that of *Pasquil the Playne*. Indeed the kind of active reading incited by *A Glasse* is also identical to that encouraged by Elyot's work.

unearthed in the process of the debate between the Lawyer and the Divine. Throughout *A Glasse* references to the past, to the ancient writers and history are viewed as authoritative. This valorization of the historical past was, however, neither inevitable nor necessarily useful for Henry and his apologists. As many of Henry's opponents pointed out in purely quantitative terms history, and in particular the clear acceptance of papal authority by earlier English monarchs, was squarely on the side of the papacy. Indeed *A Glasse* often seems to refer to the past as authoritative almost without discrimination. In one of its more specific references to history it uses the example of Wycliffe to prove that those who argue that Levitical Law is human are heretics. Recounting the condemnation of Wycliffe's teachings by the Council of Constance it states that:

> it may evidently appear now that this matter [the status of Levitical Law] is not disputable, but already judged and concluded, since it is determined that he shall be taken for a very heretic that holdeth or upholding disputeth the contrary.[13]

This representation of Wycliffe's teaching, however, is not simply of interest because it illustrates the un-Protestant nature of *A Glasse*. One should also note the status of disputation in this passage. Wycliffe's teachings are properly condemned and this condemnation is lawful and authoritative because they have already been discussed by a proper public body of men and found heretical. The status of Wycliffe's teaching, as represented in *A Glasse*, is placed outside the discussion between the Lawyer and Divine in a space beyond dispute. What is perhaps most significant here, however, is not the literal accuracy of *A Glasse*'s construction of Wycliffe's views, or its outrageous implication that the Pope is a Wycliffite, but its representation of the past itself as authoritative. In particular, it is significant that this authority is here explicitly equated with the law. History is located in this text as a site of truth beyond its own textuality, but requiring the framing of *A Glasse* to have this authority brought into the public arena and made active.

A Glasse concludes with a passage that follows the end of the dialogue and which sums up the purpose of the text overall.

> And thus this little treatise shall make his end, praying the readers, that if anything be amiss in it, to arrecte it rather to lack of discretion than of good will; and though peradventure, in opening the cause, some be indirectly touched farther mayhap than pleaseth them, we humbly desire them to reckon that if we could have, by our simple wits, devised any other way so plainly and truly to have opened this cause, we would much rather have done it than thus.[14]

---

[13] *A Glasse*, p. 396.
[14] Ibid., p. 419.

Again the reader is encouraged to read through or around the inadequacies of the text in order to appreciate the truth, and justice, of Henry's policies. It is interesting that this passage implies that the degree of knowledge in terms of the king's causes that *A Glasse* is 'indirectly' offering its readers may be regarded by some of them as inappropriate. The text apologizes for involving its readership in matters of high policy. It regrets the necessary of its existence and of the public sphere whose emergence it incites. *A Glasse* reflects an acceptance within Henry's government that the royal divorce needed to be supported by those in, and just beyond, the outer rings of the polity and that these people would probably rather not have been burdened with this demand for political involvement.[15]

The Henrician public sphere as imagined in *A Glasse* is further developed in a later tract, *A litel treatise ageynste the mutterynge of some papistes in corners*.[16] In many respects this text builds directly on *A Glasse*. It too constructs its ideal readers as members of a public sphere produced in order to create a space within which royal policies can be enacted and actively understood. To be of the public, as imagined in *A litel treatise*, is to support the policies of the king. One difference, however, between *A Glasse* and *A litel treatise* is that while the former is largely written as a dialogue the latter is addressed directly to the reader. These different textual forms, however, have less impact on the experience of reading these two tracts then one might expect. As has been suggested, the dialogue form of *A Glasse* foregrounds the production of meaning, it makes its readers experience the process of becoming

---

[15] J.P. Genet has recently suggested that the kind of political participation and involvement in government that *A Glasse* enacts and attempts to incite in its readership was fundamental to the growth of the state witnessed in Europe during the sixteenth century. Genet writes:

> The final conclusion is that the modern state itself comes into being when kings need the support of their subjects and when subjects concede to royal demands through representative institutions. In its essence, this is a rediscovery of politics, in the original sense of the word ... though in a context quite different from that of the Greek *polis*. An institutionalised dialogue between rulers and subjects is an indispensable component of the system, and political theory (which is no longer pure theology), a literature of protest, political discourse and ceremonies – all the elements of the system of political communication – have their precise origins in that transformation.

J.P. Genet, 'Which state rises?', *Historical Research*, 65 (1992), pp. 119–33, p. 132.

[16] 'A litel treatise ageynste the mutterynge of some papistes in corners', in *Records of the Reformation: the Divorce*, ed. Nicholas Pocock, 2 vols (London, 1870), vol. II, pp. 539–52., STC 19177. Richard Rex suggests that it is in this text that the full panoply of Henrician anti-papal rhetoric first appears. See Rex, 'The crisis of obedience: God's Word and Henry's Reformation'.

part of a glass of truth, a Henrician public sphere. In *A litel treatise* a different structure produces a similar type of ideal reader. Replacing the dialogue form of *A Glasse* in this text the reader is incited to read actively, to become part of a public sphere, against an imagined form of private malign reading. This text is written explicitly to oppose a form of reading/writing, 'muttering', that is inherently disruptive, disordered and private. Without the 'mutterynge of papists in corners' there would be no need for *A litel treatise*.

This private other of the public discourse embodied in *A litel treatise* is consistently represented as manifesting characteristics identical to those that *The Supplication of Beggars* associated with the clergy. The papists, as they mutter in their corners, fill up the realm with lies, smoke and useless words. In *A litel treatise* this process is related directly to the way the papists have distorted history. The text asks its readers to:

> behold how the favourers of blind abusion would fain blow abroad smoky and misty reasons to dark and dim men's eyes withal. They say it was merry before such matters were moved, but they tell not what time it was, with whom, nor wherin it was merry. And if they mean that the nobility and commons of this realm of Englande had more riches and greater plenty of food ... and lived in much more wealth ... then let them consider that this was before the Pope and his clergy were grown so great, so strong and mighty, and to so huge possessions and riches as they welde at this day ...[17]

A litel treatise is written precisely in order to provide its readers with the tools necessary to penetrate the 'smoky and misty' reasons of the papists. Its narrative motivation is the revelation and, therefore, defeat of the lies of the papists. Indeed this text's authority is based on the moment of revelation it embodies – its role in making papistry public.

A litel treatise is an incitement for the emergence of a strong public, one capable of taking on and vanquishing the lies of the papists that have filled up and blocked the proper functioning of the polity. It provides the motivation and the tools necessary for this public to form and for it to take action. Once the muttering has been stopped and the smoke has cleared, however, *A litel treatise*, and the strong public whose emergence it incited its readers to embody, will no longer be necessary.

This strong public, moreover, is not conceived as opposed to or detrimental to royal power. *A litel treatise* constructs Henry as the exemplary member of a public sphere that is defined by its opposition to papistry. It argues that the papacy only achieved its position of

---

17 *A litel treatise*, pp. 548–9.

power because 'the noble princes themselves were unlearned, and could not judge in such matters [i.e. the status of the Pope] but they gave alway credence to the false, subtle and sly persuasions of the Pope and his bolsterers'.[18] A litel treatise goes on to commend Henry, and his council, for their great labour in searching out the truth. It claims that:

> if they themselves had not by their diligent study sought out his
> [the Pope's] false fraud, the Popish forme should never have been
> reformed, nor it should never have been known that the Pope is
> but a bishop in his own diocese.[19]

A litel treatise is an attempt to spread the 'learning' of Henry and his council out into the polity as a whole. To accept the argument of this text, to position oneself within its codes of articulation against its papist enemies, is, in effect, to become part of an temporarily expanded royal council. It is to share in the fruits of the labours of Henry, and his counsellors, and also, by implication, to accept the truth and justice of their policies. Not to do so, to deny the validity of their arguments would, in terms of A litel treatise, make one a muttering papist, a producer of smoky reasons and malicious rumours.

One can relate the models of publicness articulated in such tracts as A Glasse and A litel treatise directly to those deployed throughout the work of William Tyndale. The Obedience of a Christian Man,[20] for example, contains a model of publicness that its writer explicitly compares with an image of the privateness of the papists almost identical to that expressed in A litel treatise. Tyndale argues, in this text, that in a well-ordered commonwealth the public representation of power is marked by singularity and is exclusively centred upon the monarch. It was this singularity that Tyndale claimed the papists had distorted and undermined. Throughout The Obedience he portrays the papist clergy to be, in private, out of the public gaze, corrupting the workings of the polity.

> In all their [the clergy's] doings, though they pretend outwardly the
> honour of God or a commonwealth, their intent and secret counsel
> is only to bring all under their power, and to take out of the way
> whosoever letteth them, or is too mighty for them.[21]

Tyndale argues that the clergy encourage the monarch to surrender to the desires of his body and to become a slave to his lusts, a tyrant.

---

[18] Ibid., p. 544.

[19] Ibid., p. 544.

[20] William Tyndale, 'The Obedience of a Christian Man', in Doctrinal Treatises and Introductions to Different Portions of the Holy Scriptures, ed. Revd Henry Walter (Cambridge, 1848), pp. 127–344, STC 24446.

[21] Ibid., p. 338.

A king that is soft as silk, and effeminate, that is to say, turned into the nature of a woman, – what with his own lusts, which are as the longing of a woman with child, so that he cannot resist them, and what with the wily tyranny of them that ever rule him – shall be much more grievous unto the realm than a right tyrant. Read the chronicles, and thou shalt find it ever so.[22]

The clergy's corrupt prompting gives the monarch a lustful, demanding feminine body. In the process they make the monarch a beast. Such a monarch is clearly incapable of ruling with wisdom and reason. Indeed the image of the monarch's body as grotesque, as the meaning of a kingship, is the representation of tyrannical government in mid-Tudor texts.

The clergy's role as the distorters and perverters of the proper ordering of society extends in Tyndale's work from the corruption of the court to their use of the privacy of the confessional to subvert and undermine the proper relationship between husband and wife, master and servant. On the behaviour of the clergy at court Tyndale writes:

If any of the nobles of the realm be true to the king, and so bold that he dare counsel him that which should be to his honour and for wealth of the realm; they will wait a season for him, as men say; they will provide a ghostly father for him. God bring their wickedness to light! There is no mischief whereof they are not the root; nor bloodshed but through their cause ...[23]

He goes on to extend this critique of the clergy to the relationship between husband and wife writing that, because of the information gleaned during confession:

The wife is feared, and compelled to utter not her own only, but also the secrets of her husband; and the servant the secrets of his master.[24]

Like the vices in a morality play, the papist clergy turn the natural order upside down; they 'make' wives rule their husbands, servants order masters and the king a woman. This dynamic model of the corruption of the public sphere by the private behaviour of the clergy takes place within Tyndale's entirely conventional view of the social order.[25] *The Obedience* opens with a set of hierarchical pairs, children and elders, wives and husbands, servants and masters, subjects and rulers in which the former has a God-given obligation to give complete obedience to

---

[22] Ibid., p. 180.

[23] Ibid., p. 239.

[24] Ibid., p. 337.

[25] One should note that within Tyndale's Lutheran model of humanity the order of society is always in danger of disruption through humanity's fallen state.

the latter. Tyndale offers the reader a choice between this conventional, magisterial, model of the social order and one corrupted and privatized by the clergy's machinations.

At the same time, however, the status of the hierarchical social order that Tyndale advocates in this text as natural and proper is undermined by aspects of the religious teaching that his work contains. At one point Tyndale tells his readers to, 'Seek Christ in your children, in your wives, servants and subjects'. He goes on to argue that these are all worldly titles and that, 'In Christ we are all one thing, none better than another, all brethren'.[26] Tyndale's thought is potentially incoherent at this point. He wishes to privilege a traditional model of the social order as natural while simultaneously undermining the status of this order in terms of Christ's teaching. *The Obedience* contains a doctrinal conflict that was to bedevil magisterial Protestantism: the authorizing Word of God should be open to all but simultaneously the true meaning of the Scripture was predetermined by the natural normative status of the traditional, hierarchical, social order.[27] For the non-magisterial to appear in public was, in Tyndale's polemic, a sign of papistry. Tyndale's use of an image of an ordered public sphere as the sign of a godly[28] commonwealth effectively makes godliness dependent on publicness. In the process Tyndale's text denies the possibility of a godly public sphere that was also not a magisterial one. Tyndale would, perhaps, claim that there is a absolute difference between secular and spiritual authority.[29] Such a separation,

---

[26] Tyndale, *The Obedience*, p. 200.

[27] There is no inherent incompatibility between a religious discourse and that of publicness; a discourse can be in the public sphere but not of it. It is precisely this distinction, however, that is undermined by Tyndale's use of a magisterial image of the public sphere as a validating principle in terms of scriptural interpretation.

[28] In this context 'godly' or 'godliness' refer to discourses and identities that valorized explicitly Christian teachings before other discourses, for example the magisterial. Of course it was quite possible, indeed it was often felt essential, that magistrates should be both magisterial and godly. It is also possible in this context to speak of godly Catholics as well as Protestants.

[29] Indeed the pressure of events and the need to make abstract theories applicable to the situation in England rapidly produced a watering down of even this basic element of Luther's teachings. Francis Oakley comments that:

> By the years 1534–5 Barnes, and in some measure Tyndale too, had come to envisage the king's authority as minister of God as extending now beyond the temporal to encompass the spiritual. That is to say, they had moved from their own earlier Lutheran emphasis on the strict separation of the temporal and spiritual realms and in a direction more congenial to the propagandists of the royal supremacy.

Francis Oakley, 'Christian obedience and authority, 1520–1550', in J.H. Burns, with the assistance of Mark Goldie (ed.), *The Cambridge History of Political Thought, 1450–*

however, is more apparent than real. If lawful or legitimate authority inherently produces a hierarchical social order through the exclusion from the realm of the public of all those who should not have a voice, then the space for spiritual authority, and its nature, is severely curtailed. In particular, it is clear from Tyndale's work that any claim to spiritual authority that explicitly subverted the hierarchical structure of society would be inevitably suspect.

These issues relate directly to the way Tyndale uses history in his writings. Glanmor Williams has pointed out the importance history played in Tyndale's work. He comments that, 'In all [Tyndale's] mature writings it is impossible not to detect his profound awareness of the implications of history.'[30] This was particularly true of *The Practice of Prelates*,[31] a text which Williams suggests inaugurated an original interpretation of medieval English history.[32] In *The Practice of Prelates* Tyndale relates the model of publicness articulated in *The Obedience* directly to history. As Williams suggests, he constructs a narrative of papal corruption of the Church that emphasizes its private, secret and devious nature. Tyndale writes that:

> to see how our holy father came up, mark the ensample of an ivy tree: first it springeth out of the earth, and then awhile creepeth along by the ground till it find a great tree. Then it joineth itself beneath alow unto the body of the tree, and creepeth up a little and a little, fair and softly. And at the beginning, while it is yet thin and small, that the burden is not perceived, it seemeth glorious to garnish the tree in the winter, and to bear off the tempests of the weather. But in the mean season it thrusteth roots into the bark of the tree, to hold fast withal; and ceaseth not to climb up, till it be at the top and above all. And then it sendeth his branches along by the branches of the tree, and overgroweth all, and waxeth great,

---

1700 (Cambridge, 1994), pp. 159–92, p. 177. The above discussion of the relationship between the status of the temporal and the spiritual in terms of scriptural interpretation suggests that in 1528, when *The Obedience* was published, there was already a potential for this slippage between the two realms.

[30] Glanmor Williams, *Reformation Views of Church History* (London, 1970), p. 23.

[31] William Tyndale, 'The Practice of Prelates', in *Expositions and Notes*, ed. Henry Walter (Cambridge, 1849), pp. 237–344, STC 24465.

[32] Williams argues that:

> In his *Practice of Prelates* Tyndale offered what was, at the time, a highly original interpretation of the relations between Church and state in medieval England ... Reduced to its simplest terms, Tyndale's line was that the history of medieval England was the history of a long and sustained conspiracy on the part of Anti-Christ as represented by the popes and their minions ... to reduce the kings of England to submissive puppets.

Williams, *Reformation Views of Church History*, p. 27.

heavy, and thick; and sucketh the moisture so sore out of the tree and his branches, that it choaketh and stifleth them. And then the foul stinking ivy waxeth mighty in the stump of the tree, and becometh a seat and a nest for all unclean birds, and for blind owls, which hawk in the dark, and dare not come at the light.[33]

This portrayal of the papal usurpation of temporal power, Tyndale's similitude of the Pope, makes the historian's proper role the stripping of papist ivy from the tree of secular rule: the truth of history demands making public the Pope's devious and secretive path to temporal power. In a similar fashion to *A litel treatise*, this structure makes the status of the truth directly depend on un-truth, on the 'foul' stinking ivy that the Protestant historian must expose. While in *A litel treatise* to be of its public was not to be a muttering papist, in Tyndale's text a public voice is articulated whose motivation and authority is based on the exposure of the historical process by which the papacy usurped temporal power.

The Practice of Prelates, like *A Glasse* and *The Obedience*, embodies an image of a public that is inherently magisterial and whose opponents are subverters of the hierarchical social order. The process of bringing to light the growth of the ivy, the papal usurpation of temporal power, is directly associated with this magisterial public. *The Practice of Prelates* implicitly argues that the historical exposure of the Pope's acquisition of temporal power is inherently supportive of the existing social order. The narrative motivation of this text is recounting the foul deeds of the Pope and his henchmen in their subversion of royal power. The reader of this text is, therefore, positioned as inherently opposed to this behaviour and is invited to view himself, in the process of reading the work, as acquiring a privileged historical knowledge of the Pope's usurpation. This knowledge is, however, centred not on the king and his council, as it effectively is in *A litel treatise*, but is instead explicitly claimed by Tyndale himself.[34] It is this knowledge, and the authority that it gives him, that allows and validates Tyndale's authorial voice, one that speaks for the public and demands that the king listen.

---

[33] Tyndale, *The Practice of Prelates*, p. 270.

[34] Rudolph P. Almsy comments that:

> Although Tyndale may believe that any individual, even a king, can understand Scripture through its own authority, Tyndale's performance [in *The Practice of Prelates*] belies this easy notion. He elevates himself as the authority – indeed, as the prophet of God – whose reading of the Old Testament must be accepted.

Rudolph P. Almsy, 'Contesting voices in Tyndale's *The Practice of Prelates*', in John A.R. Dick and Ann Richardson (eds), *William Tyndale and the Law*, Sixteenth Century Essays and Studies, 26 (1994), pp. 1–10, p. 3.

History functions in Tyndale's work as the ground or site for the playing out of the battle between the forces of good and evil, the true believers and papists, publicness and privateness. Unlike later Tudor historians writing within the same tradition, however, Tyndale's use of history is relatively unambitious. Not for Tyndale the kind of grand apocalyptic narratives that Bale and Foxe spent so much time working on. Katherine Firth comments that, 'In [Tyndale's] case ... the argument from history came from sets of examples and not from any theory of progressive revelation or development.'[35] Tyndale uses history in much the same way as the writers of *A Glasse* or *A litel treatise*. He refers to the past as an object, a site of examples of papist tyranny and corruption. Indeed Tyndale goes further than these two works when he argues that the non-appearance of historical facts can also be read as a mark of papistry. Tyndale asks his readers to:

> Take an example of [the Prelates'] practice out of our own stories. King Harold exiled or banished Robert archbishop of Canterbury; for what cause, the English Polychronicon specifieth not: but if the cause were not somewhat suspect, I think they would not have passed it over with silence.[36]

Tyndale's history is entirely the tool of his performance of the role of the voice of the public. It is his voice that makes the past meaningful, that draws the examples and fills in the gaps. Tyndale's notorious condemnation of Henry's divorce of Catherine is part of this performance.[37] In *The Practice of Prelates* the events of the early 1530s are presented as part of a continuum of papist plotting designed to cause civil dissent and war. Tyndale claims that Henry's marriage to Anne Boleyn will result in a disputed succession to the English throne. He writes that:

> our prelates have utterly determined that this marriage that is between the king and the queen must be broken; and so is the princess disinherited, and the king of Scots next to the crown. And we may fortune to find one at home, which, because he is near at hand, would look to step in before him; and it may chance thereto

---

[35] Katherine R. Firth, *The Apocalyptic Tradition in Reformation Britain: 1530–1645* (Oxford, 1979), p. 25.

[36] Tyndale, *The Practice of Prelates*, p. 294.

[37] Patrick Collinson comments that:

> In *The Obedience of A Christian Man* William Tyndale had instructed the mind and conscience of Henry VIII, not privily but in print, for all the world to see and, if it chose, to draw the most critical of conclusions.

Patrick Collinson, 'De Republica Anglorum: Or History with the politics put back', in *Elizabethan Essays* (London, 1994), pp. 1–29, p. 21.

> that another yet will look to come in ... peradventure, the third
> born at home may make friends likewise; yea, and so forth.[38]

Tyndale's prophecy of the likely effects of Henry's divorce make it of a piece with other historical moments when the machinations of the prelates produced strife. The status of Tyndale's voice in *The Practice of Prelates* as the public denouncer of the plots of the prelates is here extended into the future. Tyndale the historian becomes Tyndale the prophet. Indeed his criticism of the royal divorce is for Tyndale what validates his narrative voice as prophetic in this text.[39]

At the end of *The Practice of Prelates* Tyndale addresses his kingly and magisterial audience directly and warns that:

> none obedience, that is not love, can long endure; and in your
> deeds can no man see any cause of love: and the knowledge of
> Christ, for whose sake only a man would love you, though ye were
> never so evil, ye persecute. Now then, if any disobedience rise, are
> ye not the cause of it yourselves?
> Say not but that ye be warned![40]

Tyndale here is assuming the voice of a strong public. *The Practice of Prelates* draws on history to prove that the commonwealth is in danger and that the prelates have corrupted the functioning of the public sphere.[41] The strong public required to restore order is the narrative motivation of the text and its emergence is enacted in Tyndale's assumption of a prophetic voice speaking the lessons of history in public and demanding that they be heeded.

Despite the similarities between the images of publicness and public spheres in these four texts there is, however, a clear difference between Tyndale's works and those written to defend the Henrician Reformation. While the latter construct the monarch as an exemplary member of the imagined public that they represent, Tyndale's works are directed from the position of a strong public addressing the monarch. *A Glasse* and *A litel treatise* embody representations of public spheres explicitly united around Henry. *The Obedience* and *The Practice of Prelates*

---

[38] Tyndale, *The Practice of Prelates*, p. 333.

[39] Patrick Collinson has recently discussed the status of this prophetic 'voice' as ' ... part of the original thrust of the Reformation'. See Patrick Collinson, 'Biblical rhetoric: the English nation and national sentiment in the prophetic mode', in Claire McEachern and Debora Shuger (eds), *Religion and Culture in Renaissance England* (Cambridge, 1997), pp. 15–45, p. 20.

[40] Tyndale, *The Practice of Prelates*, p. 344.

[41] Tyndale is quite explicit that this corruption is not a thing of the medieval past. He writes that: 'In king Henry the seventh's days the cardinal Morton and the bishop Fox delivered unto the king's grace the confessions of as many lords as his grace lusted.' Ibid., p. 305.

contain images of public spheres whose cynosure is the monarch but whose emergence is motivated by the failure of government, by the corruption of the commonwealth by the papists. In the government-inspired texts the moment of reform has already passed and the purpose of these works is to rally support for these events. The public spheres these texts imagine are, therefore, weak, concerned only with the validation and not the instigation of reformation. Tyndale's texts are calls for reform, addressed directly to the king. They contain images of strong publics, whose emergence is motivated by the papist's corruption and disorder, and whose voice insists, indeed demands, to be heard.

Halle's *Chronicles* and the public sphere in history

Edward Halle's *The Union of the Two Noble and Illustrious Families of Lancaster and York*[42] is an exemplary piece of Tudor history writing in terms of its form and content. It is also one of the first historical attempts to make sense of the Henrician Reformation. Halle's *Chronicle* contains similar images of publicness and public spheres as those articulated in *A Glasse* and *A litel treatise*. The potential conflict that this use of the discourse of publicness causes in such texts as *The Obedience*, between spiritual and secular authority, is, however, also reflected in Halle's work.

As has been suggested, there was a symbolic relation between images of the public sphere in mid-Tudor texts and the place of history in early modern culture. The place of the public alongside but apart from royal power is analogous to the position that de Certeau has suggested history as a discourse occupied during the sixteenth century. He writes that:

> located in the vicinity of political problems – but not in the place where political power is exercised – historiography is given an ambivalent status ... it is at once the discourse of the master and that of the servant – it is legitimized through power and drawn from it, in a position where, withdrawn from the scene, as a master thinker, the technician can replay the problems facing the prince.[43]

---

[42] Edward Halle, *The Union of the Two Noble and Illustrious Families* (London, 1548), STC 12723.

[43] Michel de Certeau, *The Writing of History*, trans. Tom Conley (New York, 1988), p. 8. For a specific discussion of a Tudor piece of history as exemplifying a notion of a public sphere see Annabel Patterson, *Reading Holinshed's Chronicles* (Chicago, 1994), pp. 20–21. For a different view of the relation between royal power and history see Keith Thomas, *The Perception of the Past in Early Modern England* (London, 1983); D.R. Woolf, 'The power of the past: history, ritual and political authority in Tudor England', in Paul A. Fideler and T.F. Mayer (eds), *Political Thought and the Tudor Commonwealth: Deep Structure, Discourse and Disguise* (London, 1992), pp. 19–49.

Although this comment is addressed to the kind of history produced by such writers as Machiavelli, this understanding of the place of history is applicable to such Tudor historians as Halle. Mid-Tudor histories often dealt with contemporary events in which the role of the monarch was central. For example, in Halle's account of the revolt over the Amicable Grant, the behaviour of Cardinal Wolsey, and implicitly that of Henry VIII, is reflected on and criticized because of its lack of publicness. Equally important, however, in terms of the relation between the discourse of publicness and that of history, is their identical expression of a magisterial understanding of the existing social order as natural and God-given. These points are reflected in Halle's construction of history in the introduction to his *Chronicles* and his use of the discourse of publicness to sustain the view that true history explicitly defended the existing magisterial social order.

In the preface to his *Chronicles* Halle constructs his role not as the maker of historical meaning but as a simple archivist unearthing facts that were in danger of being lost to oblivion. Halle's history is initially represented as being entirely motivated by the desire to protect the past from being swallowed up by the darkness of oblivion.

> Obliuion the cancard enemie to Fame and renoune the suckyng serpe[n]t of auncient memory, the dedly darte to the glory of princes, and the defacer of all conquestes and notable actes ...[44]

Halle's text enacts the defeat of Oblivion by bringing the past into the public domain in order to protect it from the ravages and corruption of this enemy of fame.

Halle's construction of Oblivion relates it directly to the representation of the private in the work of such Henrician writers as Elyot, Bale and Tyndale. Oblivion, for Halle, is imagined as monstrous and subversive; it is related to the 'suckyng serpe[n]t', the destroyer of famous kings, to darkness and evil, to the pit into which the 'great' tyrants Nero and Caligula fell. It is also represented as continually on the move, constantly threatening the deeds of great men and wiping them from the pages of history. Halle writes:

> every nacio[n] was desirous to enhaunce lady Fame, and to suppresse that dedly beast Obliuio[n]. For what diuersitie is betwene a noble prince [and] a poore beggar, ye a reasonable man and a brute beast, if after their death there be left of them no remembrance or token. So that euidently it appereth that Fame is the triumphe of glory, and memory by litterature is the verie dilator and setter furth of Fame.[45]

---

[44] Edward Halle, *Halle's Chronicle*, collated with the editions of 1548 and 1550 (London, 1809), p. v.

[45] Ibid., p. v.

Producing the same effects as Tyndale's papists, Halle's Oblivion levels social distinctions and creates a disordered, upside-down world, in which a king and a beggar are equal. Similarly Halle's history, like Tyndale's public polemic, drives Oblivion off the historical stage and restores order, or rather an order.

> writyng is the keye to enduce vertue, and represse vice: Thus memorie maketh menne ded many a thousand yere still to live as though thei wer present; Thus Fame triumpheth vpon death, and renoune vpon Obliuion, and all by reason of writyng and historie.[46]

Halle's history performs the same reforming function as Tyndale's public exposure of the private behaviour of the papists. Like Elyot's Pasquil it makes the private public and in doing so enacts its expulsion from the public sphere.

There is, however, a potential hiatus between Halle's assertion of the power of his writing to protect against Oblivion and social disorder and his acceptance, also contained in this preface, that his text cannot include all the events of the last 150 years: it cannot be the past. Halle's history opens with an admission of defeat, of its writer's relative powerlessness to make sense from all the material he has at hand.

> what miserie, what murder, and what execrable plagues this famous region hath suffered by the deuision and discencion of the renoumed houses of Lancastre and Yorke, my witte cannot comprehende not my toung declare nether yet my penne fully set furthe.[47]

Despite the conventionality of this announcement of failure, and its status as a rhetorical device stressing the degree of the disorder that the writer was going to discuss, there is a conflict between it and Halle's earlier justification of his history as a defence against the power of Oblivion. Halle's commitment to the naturalness of the existing social order creates a hiatus in his text between his role of historian and that of member of the magisterial class. As the former he is aware of his limitations: as the latter he cannot have any.

Halle's history is predicated on a potential crisis at its centre. It claims authority on the basis of its ability to fix down and destroy Oblivion while simultaneously admitting that ultimately the chaos of the past is beyond its control. At the same time this conflict is contained within the main section of Halle's work by the narrative thrust of the text. The

---

[46] Ibid., p. vi..

[47] Ibid., p. 1. There is a level at which such an announcement of failure at the opening of a text is an entirely conventional move; however, this does not prevent it also being a significant one, in particular in relation to a work of history.

story of England's slow descent into civil war and tyranny and its rescue by the Tudors expresses and performs Halle's historical agenda. In particular, the reigns of Henry VI, Edward IV, Richard III and Henry VII illustrate the dangers of allowing the agents of Oblivion on to the historical stage and enact their banishment from this space. Halle's history wins a victory over Oblivion by exposing its effects in the past, through such disruptive figures as Joan of Arc, Margaret of Anjou and Richard III. It marks and certifies their defeat at the public hands of history. It is a commonplace that Halle's history was at one level a pæan to the Tudors. In his *Chronicles* the realms of Henry VII and even more of his son, Henry VIII, are moments of order, of the defeat of Oblivion. The reader of Halle's account of the first years of Henry VIII's rule is regaled with detailed descriptions of the public display of royal power. Tournaments, masques and battles are all part of the public representation of the king's lordship and Halle's history at this point is aligning itself with the view that Henry's kingship was above all public and therefore virtuous.

This understanding of Henry VIII's rule as virtuous because it is public is, however, not fixed or permanent in Halle's writing. His history shows the need for continual vigilance in order to protect and ensure the continuing public nature of Henry's kingship. Halle's account of the revolt over the Amicable Grant is exemplary in these terms.[48] It displays the movement from the corrupt, implicitly private, behaviour by the king's counsellors, in particular Wolsey, through the emergence of the aberration of a strong public, one provoked by the initial corruption, to a conclusion in which order is restored and the strong public disappears. In the process Halle's history maintains its status as magisterial while discussing an episode that could easily appear subversive of the existing political order.

The events of 1525 are of central importance to an understanding of Henrician government and the English Reformations.[49] The revolt against the Amicable Grant was arguably the only completely successful rebellion during the rule of the Tudor dynasty.[50] Perhaps fewer people participated in it than in the Pilgrimage of Grace and perhaps it was less

---

[48] Halle's discussion of the Evil May Days is also interesting and, as Annabel Patterson has recently suggested, far from unproblematically supportive of the behaviour of royal government. See Patterson, *Reading Holinshed's Chronicles*, pp. 196–9.

[49] For an insightful account of the Amicable Grant see G.W. Bernard, *War, Taxation and Rebellion in Early Tudor England: Henry VIII, Wolsey and the Amicable Grant* (Brighton, 1986).

[50] Although it should be noted that in an important sense Mary Tudor came to the throne as the result of a successful rebellion, one that drew on similar if not identical legitimating discourses as did the protest over the Amicable Grant.

dangerous to the regime than Wyatt's revolt; the fact remains that in 1525, and not in 1536 or 1554, people successfully rejected royal demands and forced a complete change of policy. For Halle these events are clearly potentially problematical. How does one explain a revolt, a refusal of obedience, in such a way that it becomes a reinforcement of the very power/authority that it has just denied? His answer is to use the discourse of publicness so that the revolt becomes not an eruption of disorder but a part of the order that is the public.

Halle presents the refusal to pay the Grant as an intensely public and explicitly political event. G.W. Bernard points out that:

> The framework that supports Hall's account of the Amicable Grant is constitutional. For Hall, the Amicable Grant was regarded as an illegal extra-parliamentary demand which, if allowed, would have led to government by commission and the subversion of English liberty.[51]

The public act of resistance embodied in the refusal to pay the grant is not, however, in Halle's text directed against the king but at his counsellors, particularly Wolsey. Halle claims that the latter's behaviour was implicitly, perhaps deliberately, designed to 'plucke the peoples hartes from the kyng'.[52] The whole debate over the legality of the Amicable Grant is framed by the discourse of publicness with Wolsey playing the role of distorter of the public sphere and his opponents the role of those desiring to restore it to its proper dimensions. This creates a situation in which debates over the grant result in the production of two alternative models of the public sphere, one in which Wolsey, and by implication the king, issues orders that are then acted on, and the other in which the public is far more directly involved in legitimating royal policy.

These two conflicting models of the public sphere are effectively expressed during a discussion between Wolsey and the city council. The latter bases its rejection of Wolsey's demands on two points: that a law passed in the reign of Richard III made such benevolences as the Amicable Grant illegal and that men, in fear or in order to curry favour, would grant money in private that they or their dependants could not afford to pay.

> Then was it answered to the Cardinall, by a counsailer of the citee, that by the lawe there might no suche beneuole[n]ce be asked, nor men so examined, for it was contrary to the statute made the first yere of kyng Richarde the thirde, also some persones commyng before your grace [the Cardinal], maie for feare graunt that, that all daies of their life they shall repent, and some to wynne your

---

[51] Bernard, *War, Taxation and Rebellion in Early Tudor England*, p. 151.
[52] Halle, *Chronicles*, p. 698.

> fauor, will graunt more then they bee able to paie of their awne, and so ronne in other mennes debtes, so that by dredfull gladness, and fearefull boldness, men shall not be masters of themselfes, but as menne dismaied, shall graunt that that their wifes and children shall sore rewe.[53]

Wolsey replies to this councillor that he is amazed that any person would refer to the reign of Richard III, a usurper and tyrant, for a legal precedent. He is then told:

> And it please your grace ... although he [Richard] did euil, yet in his tyme wer many good actes made not by hym onely, but by consent of the body of the whole realme, whiche is the parliament.[54]

The councillor here is expressing an image of the body politic that transcends the vagaries of royal dynasties, claiming that although Richard III was a tyrant the body politic of which he was the pre-eminent member could still pass authoritative laws. This councillor is drawing on the idea of the king's two bodies in order to resist having his, and his fellow councillors', relation to the king reduced to the level of the individual. While Wolsey wishes to restrict public discussion and interview the city aldermen on their own this councillor, and the council as a whole, insist on acting as a collective body.

The process that the cardinal envisages is one in which each individual alderman would come before him and subscribe to raise specific sums of money. In effect he is attempting to treat the aldermen as simultaneously private individuals and public office holders. Wolsey, in this exchange, is depicted as seeking to isolate the area of debate so that agreeing to pay the grant relates directly to the individual alderman's loyalty to Henry VIII. It is for this reason that he needs to deny the validity of any argument based on precedent. The councillors are obviously keen to avoid at all costs such a collapse of personal and public roles. As their spokesman makes clear it is their status as representatives of a larger body, their membership of an entity that transcends them as individuals that allows, indeed demands, that they reject the cardinal's claims.

> The Maior did wisely not to assent to graunt to any thyng for although he and the Aldermen had assented, the common counsaill would never have assented.[55]

The aldermen insist on their right to be treated as members of a weak public and in the process of articulating this claim implicitly lay claim to be members of a strong public produced by Wolsey's unlawful behav-

---

[53] Ibid., p. 698.
[54] Ibid., p. 698.
[55] Ibid., p. 699.

iour. Were it not for the cardinal's corrupt attempt to collapse their public and private roles it would not have been necessary for them to assume the potentially dangerous status as a strong public – speaking in public and demanding to be acted upon.

It is not only within the confines of the City of London, however, that Halle depicts the resistance to the Amicable Grant as drawing on the language of publicness. In the countryside the commons also rose in protest. The Duke of Norfolk, according to Halle, raised a great power to confront the rebels, but before attacking them sought to know the reasons for their rebellion.

> and of his [Norfolk] noblenes he sent to the co[m]mons, to knowe their intent, which answered: that they would liue and dye in the kynges causes, and to the kyng be obedient: when the duke wist that he came to the[m], and then all spake at once, so that he wist not what they meant.[56]

Halle here constructs the commons within the genre conventions of the morality play in which they are invariably loyal but disordered and needing firm leadership. They also need, in such plays as Bale's *King Johan* or Nicholas Udall's *Respublica,* someone to speak for them, to make their words carry weight in the public sphere. This relationship between Halle's image of the commons and that found in some morality plays also directly shapes the ensuing dialogue between Norfolk and the leader of the rebels.

> Then he [Norfolk] asked who was their Captain, and bad he should speke: then a well aged manne of fiftie yeres and aboue, asked licence of the Duke to speake, which grau[n]ted with good will. My lorde saied this man, whose name was John Grene, sithe you aske who is our capitain, for soth his name is Pouertie, for he and his cosyn Necessitie, hath brought vs to this dooyng, ...[57]

Halle's commons represent themselves as characters from a morality drama; their entry into the public sphere is allegorical – they enter not as individuals but as literary tropes. It is not John Grene the individual who speaks for the commons but Poverty and Necessity, both signs of the failure of the public sphere to be sufficiently public and therefore to produce a well-ordered commonwealth. Norfolk's sympathetic response, in Halle's account, reflects the acceptable nature of the performance of these roles by the commons. Their rebellion is effectively mediated and made safe through their acceptance that the presence of their voices within the public sphere was an aberration, a sign of corruption.[58]

---

[56] Ibid., p. 699.
[57] Ibid., p. 699.
[58] It is precisely the breakdown of this kind of negotiation and debate that Richard

Halle's account of the common's revolt against the Amicable Grant, and Norfolk's response to it, illustrates the way the discourse of publicness can be used by mid-Tudor writers to mediate moments of ideological tension in their texts. The appearance of the people or commons as voices in the public sphere is consistently constructed by Halle in his *Chronicles* as an aberration and as a sign of decay and corruption within the commonwealth. At the same time, however, it could be desirable, within the discourse of publicness, for the people, as a whole, to speak in public in order to expose a truth that is being suppressed. The presence of the commons as speaking subjects in Halle's text is a mark of Wolsey's corruption of the polity and the common-wealth. It also, however, provides the justification for the emergence of a strong public to restore order; a restoration whose main sign of success would be the disappearance of the commons from the public domain. Indeed, in Halle's text, it is only as symbolic figures that the people can have an acceptable voice within the public sphere. The belly could speak to the head as the belly but not as the head, and certainly not in order to deny its status as the belly.[59]

Halle goes on to suggest that Henry claimed to have no knowledge of the Amicable Grant and that, 'The kyng was sore moved, that his subietes were thus stirred ... '.[60] Drawing on the discourse of publicness, Halle's Henry accuses Wolsey and the council of not acting in a suffi-ciently public manner. Blame for this disastrous policy, however, shifts from Wolsey to the king's council as a whole and is finally evaporated away in the general restoration of order personified in Henry's perform-ance of the role of caring merciful king, pardoning the rebels and

---

Morrison in his tract, *A Remedy for Sedition*, claims is the hallmark of sedition. He writes that:

> Surely in time of sedition, laws [lose] their voices; or to say better, in such rageous outcries of soldiers, and braying of horses, cluttering and jangling of harness, men wax thick of hearing. Justice hideth her face when she seeth this to be allowed for a law: he that is the stronger shall oppress and spoil the weaker and no man say he doth evil.

Richard Morrison, 'A Remedy for Sedition Wherin Are Contained Many Things con-cerning the True and Loyal Obeisance That Commons Owe unto Their Lord Prince and Sovereign Lord the King', in *Humanist Scholarship and Public Order: Two Tracts against the Pilgrimage of Grace by Sir Richard Morrison*, ed. David Berkowitz (Washing-ton, 1984), pp. 109–46., STC 18113.5, pp. 109–10.

[59] It is interesting to note the extent to which Halle's construction of the events of the Amicable Grant reflects the kind of negotiations that John Walter and Keith Wrightson have argued were fundamental to social order in the early modern period. See John Walter and Keith Wrightson, 'Dearth and social order in early modern England', *P & P*, 71 (1976), pp. 22–42.

[60] Halle, *Chronicle*, p. 701.

remitting the grant. In Halle's history an event that potentially threat-
ened to expose a serious rift between the needs of royal policy and the
perceived legitimacy of this policy by the people is turned into an
illustration of Henry's status as a king who rules in the interest of the
whole commonwealth.

In this text all sides of the conflict over the Amicable Grant draw on
the discourse of publicness to mediate their behaviour: the city councillors to avoid being constructed by Wolsey as disloyal, the commons in
order to avoid looking like rebels and the king to give in to their
demands in a way that appears to confirm his status as a perfect, early
modern monarch. Halle's history of this rebellion draws on the language of the public sphere to produce an account of the resistance to
and defeat of the Amicable Grant in which everyone wins and there are
no defeated. The grant is the result of a corrupt situation which leads to
the emergence of the non-public, the commons, symbolized in allegorical figures of Poverty and Necessity, into the public sphere. This in turn
produces the motivation for the public to become strong, for the monarch to respond, Poverty is banished, the commons return home and the
public can return to its normal, natural, weak state. This structure
mediates between Halle's commitment to the existing social order and
his account of the Amicable Grant. If his history of these events had left
the reader with the image of a defeated or even humbled Henry it would
have failed in its stated intention of validating the status quo. If history
is that which protects the relation between king and beggar from dissolution by the malign forces of oblivion then it had better not show a
monarch being forced to change, indeed abandon, royal policy at the
behest of an individual city councillor and John Grene.

Publicness and reformation

In his history of the Henrician Reformation Halle again uses images of
publicness to make sense of a potentially difficult set of historical
events. Halle's use of the discourse of publicness in this case, however,
produces history that ends up criticizing royal power precisely for its
lack of publicness. The Henrician Reformation in Halle's historiography
produced a crisis similar to that which it caused within Tudor political
praxis as a whole – one that was primarily the result of the irreconcilable tension between its expressed causes and its actual results. The
Henrician Reformation posed a number of serious, if not irreconcilable,
questions to those trying to make sense of it: what was the relationship
between the royal divorce and the Royal Supremacy? Whose authority
(God's? Henry's? Parliament's?) made the Royal Supremacy? In its

markedly different accounts of the royal divorce and the affair between
Henry and Anne Boleyn, Halle's text reflects these tensions. In particular, the status of Henry's relationship with Anne Boleyn was extremely
problematic; how could one can make the king's carnal lusts public?

The first mention in the *Chronicles* of possible doubt over the status
of Henry's marriage to Catherine of Aragon comes at the moment of
their wedding when Halle writes:

> This mariage of the brothers wife, was muche murmured against in
> the beginnyng and euer more and more, searched out by learning
> and Scripture, so that at the laste by the determinacion, of the best
> vniuersities of Cristendo[n] it was adiuged detestable, and plain
> contrary to Goddes lawe, as you shall here, after. xx. yeres.[61]

As Halle points out, however, despite the people's knowledge of the
sinful nature of their monarch's marriage, it is not for another twenty
years that these doubts are given public expression. He comments:

> Now let vs returne to the kyng of England which was in a great
> scruple of his conscience [and] not quiet in his mynde, because that
> divers diuines well learned secretely enformed him that he lived in
> adultry [with] his brothers wife to the great peril of his soule, and
> told him farther [that] the court of Rome cold not dispence [with]
> Gods co[n]mau[n]dement [and] precept. These thinges were talked
> among the co[m]mon people sith the fyrst day of his mariage as
> you haue heard before, insomuch that now the kynges counsailors
> advised him to know the trueth.[62]

The only person depicted as unknowing in this passage is the king and
it is his private life, his conscience, that must be exposed to the truth of
the public in order to rescue him from sin. This passage also implicitly
undermines one of the central polemical purposes of *A Glasse* which
was to open up the truth of the king's cause to the public. Why would
this be necessary if, as Halle argues, the public already knew that
Henry's marriage to Catherine was adulterous?

From this moment Halle's history undergoes a subtle but fundamental change. Its narrative motivation shifts from being the celebration of
Tudor rule to becoming a celebration of this rule as a process of reformation. Halle's history sought to create an image of the Henrician
Reformation as an example of a perfectly functioning commonwealth in
which the monarch listens to the complaints of the people and acts on
them. In the process Halle is keen to point out that this strengthens
rather then undermines royal authority.

---

[61] Ibid., p. 597.
[62] Ibid., p. 753.

> The kyng whiche all the twentie yere paste, had been ruled by other, and in especial by the Cardinal of Yorke, began now to be a ruler [and] a King, yea, a Kyng of suche witte, wisedome, and pollicie, that the like hath not reigned ouer this Realme, as you shall playnly perceiue here after: aswell for the setting furth of true Doctryne, as also for the augmentacion of his Croune.[63]

Halle represents the Henrician Reformation as the restoration of royal power, or perhaps more accurately as the reform of the public sphere so that, as in Tyndale's text, the public representation of power is defined by singularity and is focused entirely on the king. For Halle, reformation, at this point in his history, produces a purged public sphere focused entirely, and properly, upon the monarch. At the same time the introduction of the topic of religious reform into Halle's text allows him to give historical agency to a new class of people or events. For example, the story of Tyndale's translation of the *New Testament* introduces a relatively new note into Halle's text, one that relates not to royal power or prestige but to the spirit of God. However, as with the account of the Amicable Grant, in Halle's text it is acceptable for the people, or their representatives, to step on to the historical stage provided that such a move takes place within the discourse of publicness.

The status of Anne Boleyn, however, is deeply problematic for Halle throughout his account of the Henrician Reformation. She becomes a denied cause which cannot be spoken but which lurks in the wings implicitly undermining the writer's construction of the royal divorce and attack on the Church. While the people knew the truth of the king's first marriage, the process by which he achieved his second was not open to their view. They become, in Halle's text, representative of those whose ignorance and foolishness made them suspect that Henry's desire for a divorce was motivated by anything other then his unquiet conscience. After Henry and Catherine separated for the last time Halle writes:

> Wherfore the Commen people dailye murmured and spake their folysh fantasies. But the affayres of Princes be not ordered by the commen people, nor it were not conuenient that all thynges were opened to theim.[64]

This comment seems to fly in the face of Halle's earlier construction of the people as having always known the truth about the Henry's sinful marriage to Catherine. This apparent contradiction, however, relates to the status of the people as passive and voiceless within the public sphere. It is the act of speaking in public against Henry's love life that

---

[63] Ibid., p. 759.
[64] Ibid., p. 781–2.

makes the people now sound like *A litel treatise*'s papists, muttering and fantasizing against the government.

Later Halle again refers to the reaction of the people to the royal divorce.

> In the beginnyng of this. xxxiii. yere, the Lady Anne Bulleyn was so moche in the Kynges favour, that the commen people which knew not the Kynges trew entent, sayd and thought that the absence of the Quene was onely for her sake, which was not trew: for the king was openly rebuked of Preachers for kepyng company with his brothers wife, which was thoccasyon that he eschued her companye, tyll the truth wer tryed.[65]

But the process by which Anne Boleyn goes from being royal favourite to secret wife to open consort is so convoluted and obscure in Halle's account of Henry's second marriage that it undermines his criticism of the reactions of the people to these events.

> The kyng after his returne, maried privily the lady Anne Bulleyn ... which marriage was kept so secrete, that very fewe knewe it, til she was greate with child, at Easter after.[66]

No one knows of the king's marriage until the body of his mistress/wife announces it to the world. Given the status of bodily eruptions in early modern political discourse as signs of corruption the fact that the royal marriage is made public by Anne's pregnant body reflects the polemical problems that the relationship between Henry's second marriage and the Henrician Reformation caused Halle.[67] The lengthy and detailed account of Anne Boleyn's coronation that follows cannot entirely remove the impression previously created by the text, that the public repudiation of the Aragon marriage was undermined by the private nature of the Boleyn one.

The implications of these issues become clear when Halle, and at this stage Grafton, turn to tell the story of Anne Boleyn's fall and Henry's third marriage. Halle does not mention the charges brought against the king's second wife and implies that if the reader wishes to find out more they can read the act of Parliament that declared the Aragon and Boleyn marriages unlawful.[68] A similar textual manoeuvre is repeated when

---

[65] Ibid., p. 788.

[66] Ibid., p. 794.

[67] Indeed John Foxe claimed that the obscurity of the relation between Henry's matrimonial affairs and the process of Reformation itself proved the latter's status as God-given. See John Foxe, *The Ecclesiastical History, Contaynyng the Actes and Monumentes of Thynges passed in euery Kynges tyme in this realme especially in the Church of England principally to be noted* (London, 1570), STC 11223, p. 1195.

[68] This is a clear example of the inaccuracy of the claim that the principle of selection

dealing with the execution of Cromwell.[69] In the case of Robert Barnes and his fellow reformers, Halle is even more circumspect.[70] He writes that 'wherfore they [Barnes and his fellow martyrs] were now cruelly executed, I knowe not, although I have searched to knowe the truth. But this I finde in their attainder ... '.[71] In this passage the truth and what was said in the act of attainder are constructed as different, if not incompatible. The historian tells how he has searched the records, read the attainder and knows that Barnes was accused of preaching heresies but he cannot find the detail of what these detestable and horrible heresies actually were. A note of irony enters Halle's text at this point as he compares the truth with the official documents and comments that Barnes was sent to the school-house, the Tower, and then felt the rod, the fires at Smithfield, without ever being told what the accusations against him were.

Halle's account of Barnes's execution effectively privileges a truth that endangers the very principle on which his historiography is predicated. At the beginning of the *Chronicles* Halle constructed two potentially conflicting roles for himself, that of flawed historian and that of defeater of Oblivion. Now at the end of his work these two roles come into sharp focus as a third one starts to take shape, that of the writer of a truth that is itself ahistorical and asocial, the truth of the gospel. To remain true to this truth Halle has to reverse the relationship between his other two roles; he now has to play the role of Oblivion, writing around or through the official records of the past in order to produce the truth. Halle's account of the execution of Barnes exemplifies the potentially subversive nature of the Henrician Reformation on the discourse of publicness. No longer is it being used to support and buttress the traditional social order. In his account of these martyrdoms Halle juxtaposes the truth for which Barnes died, his reformed preaching, with that of the royal attainders in order to emphasize the more open and public nature of the former. Now it is the truth of Barnes and his fellow martyrs that is public, that is anti-Oblivion, while the truth of royal justice has become that of Oblivion, a non-truth. Implicit in Halle's account of Barnes's execution is a representation of Henry him-

---

in such texts as Halle's was primarily one of accretion. Halle states that he had access to the facts of Anne Boleyn's attainder and chose not to repeat them. Halle, *Chronicle*, p. 819.

[69] Ibid., pp. 838–9. Halle implies that while Cromwell was convicted of treason it was the enmity of some prelates that ultimately shortened his life.

[70] Halle was not alone in claiming not to know or understand why Robert Barnes, Thomas Garrett and William Jerome were executed, as Susan Brigden points out. See Susan Brigden, *London and the Reformation* (Oxford, 1994), p. 316.

[71] Halle, *Chronicle*, p. 840.

self as the source of Oblivion, as that which attempts to corrupt, hide and destroy the truth.[72]

Although Halle's *Chronicle* goes on to heap more praises on Henry's shoulders this cannot undo the implications of the text's radical representation of Barnes' martyrdom, when, within the work of a notorious supporter of the Tudors, publicness and truth are constructed as antithetical to royal power. In its construction of Barnes's execution Halle's text performs the supplantation of an old truth with a new one; the truth of royal power is shown to be hollow and corrupting in comparison with that of the martyr, the witness bearer to God.

John Bale's *King Johan*, the public sphere and godliness

John Bale's *King Johan*[73] dramatizes the events of the reign of King John and relates them directly to those of Henry VIII and Elizabeth. It begins as a dramatic history of John's reign and concludes with a polemical account of the Henrician Reformation. The model of history that Bale's play contains is clearly influenced by the work of Tyndale and by the author's own apocalyptic studies.[74] At the same time history in *King Johan* has a similar status to that given it by Halle. However, while for Halle it is the socially disruptive Oblivion that history exposes and defeats, in Bale's play history is the process of bringing to light, and therefore disempowering, the private actions of the papist clergy.[75] In-

---

[72] This representation of Henry as oppressive and in league with the papist corrupters of the public sphere is reproduced in the 1563 edition of Foxe's *Acts and Monuments*. The account of the trial of John Lambert in this edition of Foxe's work contains an image that relates Henry directly to the exemplary image of tyranny in mid-Tudor political discourse, Herod. See John Foxe, *Actes and Monuments of these latter and perilous dayes, touching matters of the Church, wherein ar comprehended and described the great persecutions and horrible troubles ... Gathered and collected according to true copies and wrytinges certificatorie, as wel of the parties them selues that suffered, as also out of the Bishops Registers, which wer the doers therof* (London, 1563), STC 11222, p. 530.

[73] All quotations from John Bale's *King Johan* come from *The Complete Plays of John Bale*, ed. Peter Happé, 2 vols (Cambridge, 1985), vol. I.

[74] There have been a number of studies of Bale's writings, historiography and apocalyptic ideas. See John N. King, *English Reformation Literature: The Tudor Origins of the Protestant Tradition* (Princeton, 1982); Richard Bauckham, *Tudor Apocalypse* (Oxford, 1978); Leslie P. Fairfield, *John Bale: Mythmaker of the English Reformation* (Indiana, 1976); Katherine R. Firth, *The Apocalyptic Tradition in Reformation Britain: 1530–1645* (Oxford, 1979); Avihu Zakai, 'Reformation, History, and Eschatology in English Protestantism', *History and Theory*, 26 (1987), pp. 300–318.

[75] D. Kendall has suggested that one of the main motivations of Bale's thought is the

deed Bale's far more religious agenda crucially changes the nature of this process; for him clergy/oblivion is not primarily a socially disruptive force but a religious one. As befits a sympathetic reader of Tyndale,[76] Bale extends the scope of the clergy's corruption far beyond that of Oblivion to encompass the status of language and truth. His papists are identical to those of *A litel treatise*. In *King Johan* the clergy subvert the social order, obscure the truth of Scripture and undermine the meaning of words, while it is the role of the historian/playwright to penetrate their muttering machinations, to expose their smoky reasons and drive them from the public sphere.

King Johan opens with John alone on stage promising to reform the English commonwealth.

> K.Johan. I have worne the crown / and wrowght vyctoryouslye,
> And nowe do purpose / by practyse and by stodye
> To reforme the lawes / and sett men in good order,
> That trew justyce may / be had in every border.[77]

At this point Englande enters to complain of her treatment by the clergy. The appearance of this female figure,[78] the embodiment of the nation's voice of complaint and supplication, is a clear and unmistakable sign of the need for the public to become strong and purge the corrupters, in this case the clergy, from the public sphere.[79]

The debate between Englande and John is, however, interrupted by the vice Sedicyon who immediately reveals his obsession with lewdness and sexual puns.

> Sedicyon. What, yow two alone? / I wyll tell tales, by Jesus!
> And saye that I se yow / fall here to bycherye.[80]

Such sexual punning remains a constant element in the speeches of the vices and serves to relate them directly to the construction of grotesque

---

exposing of sin, on a personal, institutional, national and historical level. D. Kendall, *The Drama of Dissent: The Radical Poetics of Nonconformity, 1380–1590* (Chapel Hill, 1986), pp. 92–101.

[76] See Rainer Pineas, 'William Tyndale's influence on John Bale's polemical use of history', *Archiv für Reformationsgeschichte*, 53 (1962), pp. 79–96.

[77] Bale, *King Johan*, p. 30.

[78] For an examination of the gender-specific issues involved in Bale's feminine Englande see Jacqueline A. Vanhoutte, 'Engendering England: the Restructuring of Allegiance in the Writings of Richard Morison and John Bale', *Renaissance and Reformation/Renaissance et Réforme*, 20 (1996), pp. 49–77.

[79] For a discussion of the discourse of nationhood in *King Johan* see Peter Womack, 'Imagining communities: Theatre and the English nation in the sixteenth century', in David Aers (ed.), *Culture and History 1350–1600: Essays on English Communities, Identities and Writing* (New York, 1992), pp. 91–145.

[80] Bale, *King Johan*, p. 31.

bodily privateness found in the work of Tyndale and Skelton.[81] Sedicyon goes on to make explicit his papist credentials in an image that illustrates Bale's notorious depiction of the papist clergy as sodomites.

> K.Johan.   What arte thow, felow, / that seme so braggyng bolde?
> Sedicyon.   I am Sedycyon, / that with the Pope wyll hold
>   So long as I have / a hole in my breche.[82]

Having established the play's dynamic, the conflict between a reforming king and the vice Sedicyon, Bale goes on to represent the process by which the vices in the form of historical characters – Usurpid Powre becomes Pope Innocent the Third and Sedicyon, Stephen Langton – frustrate John's reforms and finally kill him. Ultimately what prevents John from achieving reformation is the use of confession by the clergy to undermine the allegiance of Nobylyte, Cyvyle Order and Commynnalte. As in Elyot's work *Pasquil the Playne*,[83] the aberration of counsel being given in the secrecy of the confessional illustrates the absolutely corrupt nature of the clergy's effect on the English polity.[84]

Without the help of Noblylyte and Cyvyle Order John finds it impossible to reform his kingdom. As Peter Womack suggests, in this play 'the king is shown as *willing* but *unable* to right her [Englande's] wrongs'.[85] Even when he turns to Commynnalte John finds that the support he needs is lacking. The people have been blinded by the false teaching of the clergy and are as likely to turn to them as to help their king.

> K.Johan.   How cummyst thow so blynd? / I pray the, good
>   fellow, tell me.
> Commynnalte.   For want of knowlage / in Christes lyvely veryte.
> Englande.   This spirituall blyndness / bryngeth men owt of
>   the waye,

---

[81] For the role of sexual puns in Bale's polemics and, in particular, his constant accusation that papists were sodomites see Alan Stewart, *Close Readers: Humanism and Sodomy in Early Modern England* (New Jersey, 1997), pp. 38–83.

[82] Bale, *King Johan*, p. 32.

[83] It seems possible that Bale may have known of Elyot's work given the explicit reference to it in the play.

> Sedicyon.   I coulde playe Pasquyll / but I feare to have rebuke.

Ibid., p. 94.

[84] Edwin Shepard Miller comments that:

> The treason of Nobility, Clergy, Civil Order, and Commonalty is embodied in parodies of confession.

Edwin S.Miller, 'The Roman Rite in Bale's *King John*', *PMLA*, 64 (1949), pp. 802–22, p. 804.

[85] Womack, 'Imagining communities: Theatre and the English nation in the sixteenth century', p. 118.

>And cause them oft tymes / ther kynges to
>dyssobaye.[86]

Finally abandoned by all save Englande, John is poisoned by the vice Dissymulacyon disguised as a monk.

In terms of political theory Bale's play draws directly on the discourse of publicness and the debate over counsel. What finally prevents John's attempts at reform is the breakdown of the public sphere under the malign influence of the clergy. This point can be illustrated by returning briefly to Halle's account of the Amicable Grant. Here Halle constructs a functioning relationship between on the one hand the monarch and on the other the nobility and the people, in which the latter bring their justified complaints to their betters, the nobility, who pass them on to the king, who then acts on them. It is this structure that has completely broken down in *King Johan* and it is effectively impossible for John to rule without it; he cannot talk directly to his people in a way that produces action. In effect the clergy prevent the move from a weak to a strong public that would enable and enact their purgation from the public sphere. Only with the appearance of the character Veritas is order restored to the public sphere and only then can Imperyall Majestye instigate reform.

Bale's play presents a model of a public sphere in which stability is produced by the intervention of a character, Veritas, from outside the estates of the realm. There is a direct relationship between Veritas, the bringer of truth, and The Interpretour, a character who appears at the end of Act I to explain the historiographical significance of the events of the play. There is also a textual relation between this character and the role of Bale as historian and playwright. Indeed Veritas/The Interpretour can, at one level, be seen as models for the role of reforming historian/ writer, as dramatic enactments of a role that Bale himself wished to play.

In this context it is important to note that the reforming process in *King Johan* is a continuous one.[87] Even after the appearance of Veritas

---

[86] Bale, *King Johan*, pp. 69–70.

[87] It is in this context that debates over the dating of the various sections of the text of *King Johan* become important. In simple terms the play can be divided into three very uneven sections, part I making up the majority of the play, part II which is a rewrite of the final section of the text as well as a number of other additions and part III comprising of a small number of lines at the very end of the play relating it to the events of Edward's and Elizabeth's reigns. There have been a number of attempts to date these various sections of *King Johan*. By far the most authoritative work on this matter is Greg Walker, *Plays of Persuasion: Drama and Politics at the Court of Henry VIII* (Cambridge, 1991). Walker dates the first two sections of the play in the period 1538–40 before Bale's exile and the final addition of a small number of lines, part III, after the succession of Elizabeth. I have nothing to add to Walker's excellent work in this area.

and Imperyall Majestye the functioning of the public sphere is still open
to abuse. When Imperyall Majestye catches Sedicyon, after Veritas has
left the stage to preach to the people, the vice tells him:

> Sedicyon.   In your parlement / commaunde yow what ye wyll,
> The Popes ceremonyes / shall drowne the Gospell styll.
> Some of the byshoppes / at your injunctyons slepe,
> Some laugh and go bye / and some can playe boo pepe;[88]

When Imperyall Majestye questions the truth of Sedicyon's boasts, the
vice sharply upbraids him.

> Sedicyon.   What can in the worlde / more evydent wytnesse bere?
> First of all consydre / the prelates do not preache
> But persecute those / that the Holy Scriptures teache;[89]

Clearly there is a textual relation between the role of Sedicyon and that
of Veritas, if only because Imperyall Majestye appears to depend on one
or the other of them to tell him what is happening in the country. It is as
though Bale finds it impossible to construct an image of a commonwealth in which the process of reform is complete. Even after the
appearance of Imperyall Majestye it is still possible for the clergy to
behave in an unreformed fashion and for the monarch to need a mediator, even one that is a vice, to tell him what is happening in his own
realm. Bale's text constructs reform as a continuous process but one
which should have, and indeed has had, a historically specific conclusion. As in Elyot's text, *Of the Knowledge which Maketh a Wise Man,*
in which the constitution of an ordered counselled public man is constructed as simultaneously static and dynamic, in Bale's play a truly
reformed state can only be produced by continuous ongoing reformation.

   This structure, however, while implicitly undermining the closure that,
on one level, Bale's texts demand, allows *King Johan* to construct the
historically specific moment of reformation as dynamic and continuous.
The temporary moment of crisis at which the public becomes strong, the
moment of reformation, is kept permanently open, embodied in the
person of Veritas. Indeed, Bale's construction of the role of historian as
purger of the public sphere makes the *gestic* moment at which a strong
public emerges into an aspect of this subject position.[90] Veritas, not the
monarch, is the beneficiary of the authority embodied in Englande's right
to be heard and the transitory crisis-produced moment of the strong
public becomes the permanent site of the veritas-producing historian.

---

[88] Bale, *King Johan*, p. 94.
[89] Ibid., p. 95.
[90] 'Gestic' is a Brechtian term referring to a pivotal moment in a play when ideological
conflicts coalesce and become apparent.

In his latter text, *The first two partes of the Actes or unchaste examples of Englyshe Votaryes, gathered out of theyr owne legendes and Chronicles*,[91] Bale enacts this role of reforming historian scouring the chronicles in order to make public the papists' vices. Bale's version of the private in this text is consistently sexualized. For example, he tells the story of a monk who became fixated with the 'privy parte' of a giant fish that was washed up on a beach. Bale reports that:

> At the laste without modestye, shame, and all bashefulnesse, he [the monk] approched so nyghe [to the fish's privy parte], that by the slyme and fatnesse therof, whych than laye upon the sande, his fotynge fayled him, and he fell flat into the fowle hole, so beynge swalowed up of that whych hys lecherouse harte most desired.[92]

Despite such scurrilous moments, however, Bale's historiographical endeavour in *The Actes of Englyshe Votaryes* is more ambitious than the simple reproduction of anti-clerical stories. For example, he rewrites the famous story told in Bede's *A History of the English Church and People* in which Pope Gregory sees some English slave boys and on the basis of their angelic countenances decides to send Augustine to England to convert their compatriots in order to imply that Gregory's initial interest in the boys was the result of his homoerotic desire for them.

> Gregory the first of that name nowe called S. Gregory beheld in the open market at Rome, En[g]lish boyes to be sold. Marke thys ghostly mistery, for the Prelates had than no wyues. And women in those dayes might sore haue distained their newly risen opinion of holines, if thei had chaunsed to haue bene with child by them, and therfore other spirituall remedies were sought out for the[m] by theyr good prouiders and proctors, ye may if ye wil call them apple squires. And at thys Gregorye behelde them fayre skinned and beautifullye faced, with heare vpon theyr heades mooste comely, anon he a[sk]ed, of what regyon they were.[93]

Bale does not explicitly change the facts of the story but instead glosses it so that it fits into the argument of his text that the untruth of papistry produces a situation in which the public meaning of words and acts is subverted and undermined. This structure is, according to Bale, exemplified by the papist vows of chastity which have the paradoxical effect of turning honest women into whores and producing bastards. He claims that:

---

[91] John Bale, *The first two partes of the Actes or unchaste examples of Englyshe Votaryes, gathered out of theyr owne legendes and Chronicles* (London, 1560), STC 1274.

[92] Ibid., *Part II*, S.i.

[93] Ibid., *Part I*, D.iii (v).

> Christ chaunced in those daies to haue many brethre[n]. For many
> virgins had the[n] childre[n] without fathers, at least the fathers of
> them were neuer knowen.[94]

Bale's historiography in this text is designed to produce a historical
narrative of the truth of the papist's untruthfulness through the process
of unearthing and rewriting the acts of the Roman Church so that:

> In thys boke of myne, is one face of Antichrist chiefly disclosed ...
> wherwith he hath of long time painted oute his whore, the Rome
> Church that she might to [the] worlde appeare a glorious mad-
> ame.[95]

The scurrility and concern with sexual deviancy is not, therefore, an
incidental part of Bale's agenda, simply to be dismissed as polemical
bile. It formed the essential backdrop to the instigation of Protestant
reform. Indeed the production of narratives of papist corruption was
itself a part of this reform process, making the sins of the past resonant
in the present to produce reformation.

This understanding of *The Actes of Englyshe Votaryes* as a moment
of reformation relates directly to Bale's claim, in this text, that the
proper place for the veritas-producing historian is as a privileged speaker
within the public sphere. In the 'Dedication to Edward VI' Bale claims
that the greatest traitors to God and to their prince have throughout
history been the papist clergy. In the conclusion he repeats the message
of the 'Dedication' and produces an image of a functioning polity in
which godly preachers have a vital role.

> [The papists] perceiued that God of his infinite wisedome had
> placed ii. highe administracions in the christianity for the
> conseruacion therof, and that they wer, the publique authority of
> noble princes, and the gratious office of godly preachers. The one
> was for the outwarde wealth of the body, the other for the inwarde
> wealthe of the soule. They thoughte, if these ii. were not peruerted
> and poysened, they shoulde neuer come to theyr ful purpose.[96]

Although this is at one level a conventional image of the respective roles
of prince and preacher, it comes at the conclusion of a text that is
written from the subject position of the latter and that has the intention
of impacting on the realm of the former. Indeed Bale the historian
represents the scale and scope of his authority as far greater than that of
a simple preacher. His status as the person who exposes the papists'
corruption of all aspects of the public sphere means his text must cover
the same ground. To reveal the papists' subversion and corruption of

---

[94] Ibid., *Part I*, C.iii (1).
[95] Ibid., *Part I*, A.iiii (3v).
[96] Ibid., *Part II*, T.ii (6).

the office of the prince is to pass comment on this office oneself, and to claim a subject position that allows one to do so. The veritas-producing historian has a role in the purgation of the public sphere that unites the process of exposing the papists' corruption and insisting upon its reform.

In this role Bale represents himself as essential to the proper ordering of the commonwealth: only through the figure of Veritas/interpreter/historian/Bale can the public sphere be protected from the plots and corruptions of the vices. Bale the historian can, in the public act of writing the history of the past, by producing texts like *The Actes of Englyshe Votaryes* or *King Johan*, produce reform and restore order to the commonwealth. This order is explicitly related to the historian's control of the past and his ability to clear it from the present to make room for the truth to speak. If history is the writing out, the exposing, of the papists' lies, then the end result of history should be the construction of a public sphere in which the truth of the Scripture can be heard without the hindrances of the papists or the distractions of the past.

In *King Johan* this dynamic is portrayed through Bale's use of the allegorical language associated with the morality play genre.[97] While King John, as Rainer Pineas has pointed out, is 'quite incapable of speaking without citing Scripture',[98] the vices are equally incapable of speaking without producing linguistic play and disorder. This creates a situation in which when two of the most playful vices are on stage the dialogue becomes so dominated by puns, jokes and misunderstandings that it comes close to being nonsense.

> *Dissymulacyon.*   I owght to conseder / yowre Holy Fatherhode,
> From my fyrst infancy / ye have ben to me so
>   good.
> For Godes sake wytsave / to geve me yowre
>   blyssyng here,
>   (Knele.)
> *A pena et culpa* / that I may stand this day clere.

---

[97] The status of Bale's play as a conscious Protestant rewriting of the medieval morality genre has recently been subject to a great deal of criticism not least because there is considerable debate over whether there is anything particularly medieval or even Catholic about morality plays (if such a genre really exists at all). See J.P. Debax, 'The diversity of morality plays', *Cahiers Elizabethains*, 28 (1985), pp. 3–15; Robert Potter, 'Afterword', in Donald Gilman (ed.), *Everyman & Company: Essays on the Theme and Structure of the European Moral Play* (New York, 1989), pp. 329–34; John Wasson, 'The morality play: ancestor of Elizabethan drama', in Clifford Davidson, C.J. Gianakaris and John H. Stroupe (eds), *The Drama of the Middle Ages: Comparative and Critical Essays* (New York, 1982), pp. 316–27.

[98] Rainer Pineas, 'William Tyndale's influence on John Bale's polemical use of history', p. 88.

Sedicyon.	From makyng cuckoldes? / Mary, that wer no mery chere.
Dissymulacyon.	*A pena et culpa:* / I trow thow canst not here.
Sedicyon.	Yea, with a cuckoldes wyff / ye have dronke dobyll bere.[99]

The polemical point that Bale is making here is that the language of papistry is inherently antithetical to the production of coherent, stable meaning.[100]

In *King Johan* the language of the vices is marked as inherently untruthful and incoherent. Indeed the vices at times lose all control of their speech so that, for example, Usurpid Powre, as the Pope, has to upbraid Dissymulacyon for telling the audience what tricks, or religious practices, the clergy/vices will use to maintain their power once John is defeated.

Dissymulacyon.	The Popys powre shall / be abowe the powrs all, And eare confessyon / a matere nessessary. Ceremonys wyll / be the ryghtes ecclesyastycall. He shall sett up ther / both pardowns and purgatory; The Gospell prechyng / wyll be an heresy. Be this provyssyon, / and be soch other kyndes We shall be full suere / all waye to have owre myndes. [Usurped Power returns as the Pope, ...]
The Pope.	Ah, ye are a blabbe! / I perseyve ye wyll tell all. I lefte ye not here / to be so lyberall.[101]

If the language of the vices, however, is marked as inherently untruthful, the words of such characters as John need to embody the truth; one that could within the terms of Bale's Protestantism only finally be located in Scripture. The audience is confronted in this play with the two quite different languages, that of the vices, a comic, carnivalesque one, and that of John, a scriptural language, made up of quotations from the Bible. Implicitly the play constructs a model of a reformed

---

[99] Bale, *King Johan*, p. 51.

[100] John Skelton makes an identical polemical point in his poem, *A Replycacion Agaynst Certayne Yong Scolers Adjured of Late*, describing the language of heretics as inherently disordered and disjointed. He writes that heretics have:

A lytell ragge of rethorike,
A lesse lumpe of logyke,
A pece or a patche of philosophy,

John Skelton, 'A Replycacion Agaynst Certayne Yong Scolers Adjured of Late', in *The Complete English Poems*, ed. John Scattergood (New Haven, 1983), pp. 373–86, p. 374.

[101] Bale, *King Johan*, p. 55.

polity in which the only words are scriptural. The end of history, the completion of reform and the institution of a Christian commonwealth will be marked by the disappearance of all untruthful language, of all words that are not scriptural.[102]

At its centre *King Johan* dramatizes an event that brings together these issues of truth and history: the act of martyrdom. In Bale's text John is not only the prototype reforming monarch; he also performs the role of exemplary Protestant martyr, killed by the papists because of his religious convictions. It is noticeable in this context that even Bale's text suggests failings in John as a king. Englande momentarily loses faith in him when he agrees, in order to save the realm from invasion, to surrender his crown to the Pope's legate.

> *Englande.*   Alacke for pyte / that ever ye [John] grantyd this.
>   For me pore Ynglond / ye have done sore amys;
>   Of a fre woman / ye have now mad a bonde mayd.
>   Yowre selfe and heyres / ye have for ever decayed.
>   Alas, I had rether / be underneth the Turke
>   Then under the wynges / of soch a thefe [the Pope] to
>   lurke.[103]

As a king, John clearly has faults but as a martyr he is exemplary. Again it is Englande who provides the gloss to John's actions, in this case his death.

> *Englande.*   Alas, swete maistre, / ye waye so heavy as leade.
>   Oh horryble case / that ever so noble a kynge
>   Shoulde thus be destroyed / and lost for ryghteouse
>   doynge
>   By a cruell sort / of disguysed bloud souppers,
>   Unmercyfull murtherers / all dronke in the bloude of
>   marters.
>   Report what they wyll / in their most furyouse
>   madnesse,
>   Of thys noble kynge / much was the godlynesse.[104]

---

[102] David Scott Kastan has suggested that Bale's whole theatrical/historical endeavour is fractured by the conflict between the status of the language of the play and that of the truth. He writes:

> the singular truth of John's proto-Protestantism can be maintained only by impossibly asserting it as something plain and immediate, as something unfeigned; that is, it can be maintained only by repressing the fact of the play itself.

David Scott Kastan, '"Holy Wordes" and "Slypper Wit": John Bale's *King Johan* and the poetics of propaganda', in Peter C. Herman (ed.), *Rethinking the Henrician Era: Essays on Early Tudor Texts and Contexts* (Urbanna, 1994), pp. 267–82, p. 272.

[103] Bale, *King Johan*, p. 75.

[104] Ibid., p. 86.

Ultimately it is John's godliness, and not his kingship, that determines his true place in the record of the past, one that Englande, the voice of the nation, validates.[105] The moment of John's martyrdom is pivotal in the play as it is immediately following his death that Veritas appears and the play's terms of reference suddenly become contemporary. The king's murder, bearing ultimate witness to the truth of Scripture in death, motivates the appearance of the figure of truth on stage, the collapse of historical time and the instigation of reformation.

At this *gestic* moment Bale's text enacts a moment of polemical slippage in which the status of John as head of the hierarchical social order, as king, is subverted. Englande's celebration of John's status as godly is based on a correspondence of truth, godliness and the collapse of history that has no place for the traditional social hierarchy. Indeed Englande's, and Bale's, representation of John's death reproduces in an implicitly radical form the role of Oblivion in Halle's work. In Englande's discourse the distance between the beggar and the king can be collapsed and written over within the discourse of godliness. Englande's role, however, in Bale's representation of the process of Reformation is simply to authorize the role of Veritas: to give, or allow this figure to appropriate, the authority embodied in her status as the simple voice of truth. For Englande to need to speak after the advent of Veritas would be a sign of the failure of Reformation. It would also undermine the role of the veritas-producing historian as purger of the public sphere. If the people can, or have to, speak directly to the monarch then what need is there for a mediator or interpreter? Indeed, what need is there for a Bale?

John Foxe in 1578 preached a sermon entitled, *A Sermon preached at the Christening of a certaine Jew*,[106] in which he discussed the relation between time, history and the promises of God. Foxe argued that:

> As concerning the promises of God therefore, this is undoubtedly to be holden, that the promises be in their owne nature simply true: yet in such wise true notwithstanding, as God hath not always chained them to time, place or persons of men ...[107]

---

[105] Rainer Pineas comments that: '[John] is a saint, ... , sometimes almost a Christ-figure, married to his Bride, England, as the Church is the Bride of Christ.' In 'The polemical drama of John Bale', in W.R. Elton and William B. Lang (eds), *Shakespeare and Dramatic Tradition: Essays in Honour of S.F. Johnson* (Newark, 1989), pp. 194–210, p. 200. Greg Walker also suggests that John's combination of the two roles of prince and martyr is vital to the narrative motivation of Bale's play. See Walker, *Plays of Persuasion*, p. 183.

[106] John Foxe, 'A Sermon preached at the Christening of a certaine Jew', in *The English Sermons of John Foxe*, ed. Warren Wooden (New York, 1978), STC 11248.

[107] Ibid., C.iii (v).

The promises of God are not chained to history, they are simply true, before time, place and persons. King John's martyrdom is simply true. Englande's speech over the murdered king's body affirms his status as a martyr. It places the death of the monarch beyond time, persons and places. Veritas, however, performs the opposite act; he makes the meaning of John's martyrdom the reason for reformation, for the purgation and reform of the public sphere. It is this moment of appropriation, of re-chaining the simple truth of God to persons and places, that Bale, playing the role of the veritas-producing historian, attempts to perform with the late Henrician martyr Anne Askewe.

The next chapter will examine Bale's attempt to appropriate Askewe's testimony to his magisterial Protestant endeavour. Marian historiography, as discussed in Chapter 3, is also confronted with the problem of making the meaning of an event, Mary's miraculous succession, simultaneously beyond history in the realm of God's promise and tied to the world of men. The agenda of such early Elizabethan historians as Foxe and Brice, the subject of the final chapter, is also dominated by the desire to play the role of the voice of reformation by placing the record of the martyrs at the heart of the public sphere.

Mid-Tudor historians of the English Reformations needed to bring together the ultimately contradictory meanings of John's martyrdom: to make history, the purgation of the public sphere and fulfilment of God's promises one in the moment of reformation. At the same time mid-Tudor history writers invariably claimed the role of Veritas and sought, in their texts, to represent the role of the veritas-producing historian as essential to the process of reform. These potentially conflicting agendas made the relationship of history, the historian, the public sphere and the truth of Scripture problematic for Edwardian, Marian and Elizabethan historians. It is the results of this tension that the rest of this study will address.

CHAPTER TWO

Anne Askewe, John Bale and the 'Unwritten Verities' of History

'Go, read the Scriptures'.
Joan of Kent's words at Smithfield as she was
being burnt to death as a heretic in 1550[1]

The final text of *The First Examination of Anne Askewe*[2] is a translation of Psalm 54 entitled, 'The voyce of Anne Askewe out of the 54
Psalme of David'.[3] What is the status of this voyce that the reader is
encouraged to hear speaking out of the psalm? Is it the reader's voice
that, in reading the words of the psalm, becomes that of Askewe? Is it
the martyr's voice embodied literally in the text? Is it the voice of
Scripture speaking through that of Askewe and therefore illustrating
her status as witness bearer to its truth? Perhaps in the words of the
psalm, the voice of Scripture, Askewe and the reader become one; in
one's own reading one hears the martyr's voice speaking the words of
God. Within this construction of the relationship of reader, martyr and
Scripture there is no need for a mediator, for any authority beyond this
multiple but unified utterance: reader, martyr and Scripture are one,
and speak with one voice. It is therefore ironic that the structure of the
text which is concluded with this psalm, fundamentally undermines this
dynamic by consistently, almost obsessively, inserting the role of interpreter as central to the process of making Askewe's words meaningful.
Across the unity of reader, martyr and Scripture falls the shadow of
John Bale, the explicator of Askewe's words. The multiple voices are
made many and are unified by Bale's editorial voice, speaking from a
position beyond, and enclosing, the other voices of the text.

When Bale published Askewe's first-person accounts of her examinations he 'cut up' her texts and framed each of the subsequent fragments
with copious glosses, notes, prefaces and conclusions that made her
words dependent on his to be meaningful. Bale constructs these texts so

---

[1] John Strype, *Ecclesiastical Memorials*, 3 vols (Oxford, 1822), vol. Iii, p. 335.
[2] John Bale, *The First examinacyon of Anne Askewe* (Marpurg in the Lande of Hessen,
i.e. Wesel, 1546), STC 848, and John Bale, *The Lattre examinacyon of Anne Askewe*
(Marpurg in the Lande of Hessen, i.e. Wesel, 1547), STC 850. To avoid unnecessary
footnotes page numbers to these two texts will be given in the body of the text.
[3] *First*, p. 46(1v)–p. 46(2).

that their structure, despite their contemporary status, resembles that of magisterial Protestant editions of Lollard texts with Askewe's testimony playing the role of the authenticating fragment of the past. He assumes the role of public mediator and translator of Askewe's words, veritas to her Widow Englande, ordering and certifying the martyr's words within the public sphere. This chapter will examine what motivated Bale to turn Askewe's testimony into the raw material of his history, why he needed to make her silences speak. In the process it will reflect on the nature of the engagement of magisterial Protestantism with history and the principle of *scriptura sola*.

The magisterial Protestant historian and the Lollard text

The relationship between Lollardy[4] and English Protestantism has been the source of considerable historical debate.[5] Alec Ryrie comments that:

> Lollards read Tyndale's New Testament, and some of them adopted Lutheran ideas of justification by faith; Protestants adopted the Lollard tradition and made it a part of their own history.[6]

One should note, however, that an important aspect of the motivation for making Lollardy part of the history of English Protestantism was magisterial. Protestantism as a religious movement did not need a history and there are Protestant texts in which the Catholic Church's 'history' is a sign of its worldly corruption.[7] The radical Reformation, with its lack of concern with Church organization and dismissive attitude to existing social hierarchies, did not require history to authorize its teaching since it was based on an immediate and direct experience of the Spirit.[8] Early English Protestants who turned to Lollardy to provide

---

[4] For Lollards see Anne Hudson, *The Premature Reformation: Wycliffite Texts and Lollard History* (Oxford, 1988).

[5] For the relation between the English Reformation and Lollardy see Margaret Aston, "Lollardy and the Reformation: survival or revival?', *History*, 49 (1964), pp. 149–70; J.F. Davis, 'Lollardy and the Reformation in England', *Archiv für Reformationsgeschicte*, 73 (1982), pp. 217–36. For an alternative view see Christopher Haigh, *English Reformations: Religion, Politics, and Society under the Tudors* (Oxford, 1993), pp. 51–5.

[6] Alec Ryrie, 'The problems of legitimacy and precedent in English Protestantism, 1539–47', in Bruce Gordon (ed.), *Protestant History and Identity in Sixteenth-Century Europe: The Medieval Inheritance*, 2 vols (Aldershot, 1996), vol. I, pp. 78–92, p. 80.

[7] See Laurence Saunders, *A trewe mirrour or glasse wherin we maye beholde the wofull state of thys our Realme of England, set forth in a Dialogue or communication betwene Eusebius and Theophilius* (1556), STC 21777.

[8] For the radical Reformation see George Huntston Williams, *The Radical Reformation*, (London, 1962). Michael G. Baylor has recently commented that: 'As a popular

historical provenance for their endeavour did so because they were committed to the existing structures of social and ecclesiastical author-ity.[9] This led them to construct fifteenth-century works as requiring sixteenth-century commentary before their true Protestant, and also magisterial, meaning could be appreciated. The Lollard text could not speak for itself; like the commons during the revolt over the Amicable Grant, it required a mediator to translate its obscure language and make its truth meaningful within the public sphere.

This process of mediation is enacted in the commentaries and pref-aces that sixteenth-century editors invariably place around Lollard texts. At the end of *A Proper Dyalogue Betweene a Gentillman and a Husbandman*, for example, is a piece entitled 'A compe[n]dious olde treatyse shewynge howe that we ought to haue the Scripture in Englyshe'. The preamble to this piece is provided by a poem entitled 'The reusacyon of [the] treatyse'[10] in which the text itself speaks.

> Though I am olde clothed i[n] barbarous mede
> Nothynge garncyhed with gaye eloquency
> Yet I tell the truth yf ye lyst to take hede
> Agaynst theyr forwarde furious frenezy
> Which reken it for a great heresy
> And unto laye people greuous outrage
> To haue goddes worde in their natyfe lang[u]age.
>
> Enemyes I shall haue many a shoven crowne
> With forted cappes and gaye croosfys of golde
> Which to maynteyne ther ambicious renowe
> Are glad laye people in ignoraunce to holde
> Yet to sheweth verite one may be bolde
> Ass though it be a prouerbe dalye spoken
> Who that tellyth trouth his head shalbe broke[n].

Immediately following this verse the treatise itself is printed. There is, however, a problematic relation between the speaker of the poem and the resurrected Lollard text. The 'I' of the poem constructs itself as being of the Lollard treatise through its claim to be 'clothed in a barbarous language', while, in its performance of the verse, implicitly

---

movement, radicals stood at the centre, not at the periphery of the Reformation.' In 'Introduction' to his *The Radical Reformation* (Cambridge, 1991), pp. xi–xxvi, p. xii.

[9] On the importance of order as a concept during the Reformation, for both Protes-tants and Catholics, see Gerald Strauss, 'The idea of order in the German Reformation', in *Enacting the Reformation in Germany: Essays on Institution and Reception* (Alder-shot, 1993), pp. 1–16.

[10] *A proper dyaloge betwene a gentillman and a husbandma[n], eche complaynenge [about] the ambicion of the clergye* (Marborow in the Lande of Hessen, i.e. Antwerp, 1530), STC 1462.5, C.ii(6).

undermining this very claim. In practice it refers simultaneously to the writer of the poem and the treatise itself. It is also a reference to the 'I' who performed the text's resurrection; the person who played the role of historian by rescuing this Lollard work from the obscurity of the past. This multiple subject position bases its authority on the Lollard text for which it claims to speak while asserting a privileged cultural position as this text's rescuer and as its protector from attacks by papists. The 'I' of the poem collapses into one subject position, the authorizing antique Lollard fragment, the role of historian and that of polemical opponent of the papists. In effect the 'I' of this poem occupies a similar position as that claimed by Bale in *King Johan*; the person who makes public and meaningful a truth of the past in the present; the veritas-producing historian.

This subject position was invariably claimed by magisterial reformers to motivate the making of fragments and texts from the past part of the Protestant truth of the present. A very simple example is provided by *The Testament of master Wylliam Tracie esquier expounded both by William Tindall and Joh[n] Frith*,[11] in which the few words of Tracy's will become the reason for these two writers to expound the principles of their faith. The texts of Frith and Tyndale are far longer than the text that is their ostensible reason for existing. A more complex example is provided by the sixteenth-century edition of *The examination of Master William Thorpe preste accused of heresye before Thomas Arundell*.[12] The sixteenth-century publishers of this text did not fundamentally change Thorpe's testimony.[13] What they did add was an address 'Vnto The Christian Reader' and a text that claimed to be 'The Testamente of William Thorpe'.[14] This testament serves the textual function of affirming and summing up the beliefs articulated during the course of the examinations. It effects a fixing down of Thorpe's beliefs that the dialogic nature of the examination prevented and, in the process, asserts their orthodoxy within a magisterial Protestant endeavour by making them compatible with 1530s English Protestantism. The production of this

---

[11] *The testament of master Wylliam Tracie esquier expounded both by William Tindall and Joh[n] Firth* (Antwerp, 1535), STC 24167.

[12] 'The Testimony of William Thorpe', in *Two Wycliffite Texts*, ed. Anne Hudson (EETS o.s. 301, Oxford, 1993), STC 24045.

[13] Anne Hudson has suggested that the sixteenth-century editions of Lollard texts were remarkably accurate. See Anne Hudson, '"No Newe Thyng": The printing of medieval texts in the early Reformation period', in *Lollards and Their Books* (London, 1985), pp. 227–48.

[14] *The Testamente of William Thorpe*, pp. 146–51. Anne Hudson points out that the views expressed in this text are not ' ... out of line with the views of most Lollards or Lutherans from the 1380s to the 1530s'. p. 145.

contained and concluded version of Thorpe's beliefs relates directly to the status of the narrative voice of the address 'Vnto The Christian Reader' which represents itself as the custodian of Thorpe's testimony. It is this 'I' that places Thorpe's text in public with a gloss that sets out how it should be read, what its meaning is and the significance of the act of placing it in the public domain.

> Reade here with iudgemente goode reader the examinacion of the blessed man of god and there thou shalt easelye perceyue wherfore oure holy chirch ... make all their examinacions in darkness all laye people cleane excluded from their councels.[15]

The writer of this piece goes on to ask:

> Who can tell wherfore that good preaste and holye martyr Syr Thomas hitton was brente now thys yere at maydstone yn Kent. I am sure no man. For this is their caste euer when they haue put to deathe or punyshed any man after their secrete examynacyon to slaunder hym of soche thynges as he neuer thought.[16]

The process of printing Thorpe's examination is motivated by a desire to expose the tyranny of the papists and by a perceived need to protect and set down the truth of Thorpe's beliefs. The Lollard's words need to be made public to prevent the clergy charging him with holding beliefs that the writer of this piece knows he did not; beliefs that were perhaps more radical then those held by magisterial Protestants in the 1530s.[17] The veritas-producing historian finds and makes public the truth of God's word in the testimony of people like Thorpe so that it can permanently operate as a provocation for the emergence of a strong public that will produce godly reform of the commonwealth.

This process could, however, be problematical for the magisterial reformers given the potential radicalism of such texts as Thorpe's. There was no point in rescuing texts and testimonies from the past and making them meaningful in the present if the result would be detrimental to the historians' own agenda. The magisterial historian needed to place the truth his labour had resurrected within a discursive structure that shaped and determined its meaning. This meant positioning the authorizing frag-

---

[15] 'Vnto The Christian Reader', p. 141.

[16] Ibid., p. 142.

[17] Indeed it is ironic that, despite the valorization of Lollards like Thorpe by magisterial Protestants, their response to the potential radicalism of Thorpe's insistence on the authority of an individual's engagement with Scripture was based on a similar understanding of its potentially anarchic effects as that of their, and his, opponents. For a discussion of Thorpe's views on authority see Anne Hudson, 'William Thorpe and the question of authority', in G.R. Evans (ed.), *Christian Authority: Essays in Honour of Henry Chadwick* (Oxford, 1988), pp. 127–37.

ment of the past, for example Thorpe's testimony, within a teleological narrative of the untruth that was itself a product of the historian's work. This had the effect of making the meaning of texts like Thorpe's dependent on their place within a magisterial Protestant narrative of the untruth of the past; a history of the past lies and corrupt practices of the papists.

Bale articulated an identical subject position as that embodied in these Protestant glosses to Lollard texts in his *A Brief Chronicle concerning the Examination and Death of the Blessed Martyr of Christ, Sir John Oldcastle, Lord Cobham.*[18] Bale instructs the reader of this text:

> Now pluck from your eyes the corrupted spectacles of carnal or popish judgements, and do upon them that clear sight which ye have by the Spirit of Christ; and, that faithfully done, tell me which of these two [Cobham or Thomas Beckett] seemeth rather to be the martyr of Christ, and which the pope's martyrs?[19]

Bale tells the reader to clear their sight while simultaneously insisting that they place another filter on their glasses. This filter, however, is based on the clear truth that Bale's Protestant historiography has produced in the process of bringing to light the truth of Cobham's history. The historical status of Cobham's beliefs, and that of Bale's labour in bringing them to light is, however, dependent on the existence of past papist corruption. For Bale, in this text, to be a Protestant is to be able to practise a form of active historical reading in which one penetrates the surface corruptions of the papists in order to find the nugget of truth in the past.

The implications of this form of reading are reflected in a relatively obscure mid-Tudor text, *The beginning and endynge of all popery, or popishe kyngedome.*[20] This work, produced by Walter Lynne, contains a set of images that it claims were drawn during a time of great ignorance and blindness. These figures, *The beginning and endynge of all popery* claims, illustrate a historical knowledge of the papacy's status as a limb of the antichrist.[21] Lynne comments that:

---

[18] John Bale, 'A Brief Chronicle concerning the examination and death of the Blessed Martyr of Christ, Sir John Oldcastle, Lord Cobham', in *Select Works*, ed. Henry Christmas (Cambridge, 1849), pp. 5–59, STC 1278.

[19] Ibid,. pp. 56–57.

[20] Walter Lynne, *The beginning and endynge of all popery, or popishe kyngedome* (1548?), STC 17115. Lynne claims to be simply the translator of this text, which is a collection of disparate elements – allegorical woodcuts, apocalyptic passages that have a distinctly Joachistic flavour and editorial comments. The implication of the introduction, however, is that it is Lynne who has wielded them together into a coherent work. For a brief but informative discussion of this text see John N. King, *English Reformation Literature: The Tudor Origins of the Protestant Tradition* (Princeton, 1982), pp. 196–201.

[21] The use of images in this text as a tool of Protestant polemic because of the hidden

> it is manyfest that the fathers of auncient tyme, sawe in the papacie,
> the thinge that they durst not utter, eyther by wordes or writinge
> but trustynge that the time wolde come when men might be bolde
> to speake it: they dyd in the meane tyme kepe it in painting and
> portrature, that such as could coniecture, might gather knowledge
> therby ...[22]

In a comment that strangely echoes Stephen Gardiner's defence of images, Lynne goes on to justify reproducing these 'paintings' on the basis
that they will provide pleasure and profit for the illiterate.[23] Despite this
claim, however, the main function of the figures in this text is to
provide the textual motivation for Lynne to assume the role of veritas-
producing historian. He comments that:

> The Author therefore of this little boke: hath not onelye added
> unto these figures an exposticion to declare [the] meanynge of
> euery of them: but manifest Scriptures also, to prove the thinges
> that they represente, to be true, so that these figures may appeare
> rather to be the figures of some Apocalipsis or reuelacion, then the
> inuencion of any man.[24]

Lynne's construction of his role here is identical to that of Bale in *A
Brief Chronicle*. He is the interpreter capable of explicating these figures from a dark, blind, past. It is Lynne whose skill can weld history, in
the form of obscure images produced under a strangely Tudor-like
regime of censorship, and Scripture together to produce the truth.

The beginning and endynge of all popery claims to contain 'raw'
history in the form of allegorical figures that by their very nature
require explication. Indeed, as with the claim made by Protestant editors that Lollard texts need explaining because they are 'clothed in a
barbarous language', the status of these figures as allegorical itself
validates Lynne's role as commentator. Lynne's authorial function in
The beginning and endynge of all popery enacts a form of textual
iconoclasm.[25] As with the Old Testament role given to Edward VI by

---

truth they contain illustrates the validity of Patrick Collinson's argument that early
Protestant writers were far less iconophobic then their later descendants. See Patrick
Collinson, *From Iconoclasm to Iconophobia: The Cultural Impact of the Second English
Reformation* (Reading, 1988).

[22] Lynne, *The beginning and endynge of all popery*, A.iii–A.iii(v).

[23] Ibid., C.ii(1v). For Stephen Gardiner's discussion with Protector Somerset over the
status of images and their efficacy within a largely illiterate population see Sydney
Anglo, *Images of Tudor Kingship* (Guildford, 1992), pp. 17–19.

[24] Lynne, *The beginning and endynge of all popery*, A.iii(v).

[25] For importance of iconoclasm within the Reformation see Margaret Aston, *England's Iconoclasts: Laws against images*, 2 vols (Oxford, 1988), vol. I; Margaret Aston,
'Iconoclasm in England: official and clandestine', in Peter Marshall (ed.), *The Impact of
the English Reformation, 1500–1640* (London, 1997), pp. 167–92.

Protestant writers,[26] to be a Protestant historian in terms of *The begin-ning and endynge of all popery* depends upon the image-producing corruption of the papists: without icon makers, without censorship, neither Lynne nor Edward would be able to play the role of explicator or iconoclast.

The beginning and endynge of all popery explicitly claims to enact a moment of reformation. It states that the allegorical images it contains were produced within a temporal frame in which meaning was deferred until a later, non-papist, time. Lynne writes that:

> many olde and faithful fathers perceyued and sawe it [the status of the Papacy as antichrist], yet durst they not clearly sette it forthe, excepte only by figures. Trustyng alwais, that thorow the mercy of god a tyme shulde come when they myght be brought to lyghte. And so clearly sette forth, that it were impossible more sightlye to paint them.[27]

The *gestic* moment in King Johan, when history, godliness and reform are brought together and made active, is located in *The beginning and endynge of all popery* at the moment of explication, in Lynne's bringing the past together with Scripture and making these two sources of au-thority one. There is therefore a similarity between the allegorical images in this work and the place of Lollardy within early English Protestant-ism. Both are constructed by their sixteenth-century editors as requiring translation and explication before the historical truth they contain can be made meaningful. The Lollard text, and the allegorical figure, need a Bale, Tyndale or Lynne before they can be safely allowed to speak in public.

The subject-position of the veritas-producing historian therefore has a number of key components in these texts. It claims an authority that derives from the authorizing, but inherently obscure, fragment of the past that it is bringing to light and asserts its right to be heard in public. Indeed it insists on the need for people to act on the corruption that its labour has exposed. At the same time this subject position has clear echoes to that claimed by magisterial Protestants in relation to the Word of God in such texts as, for example, Tyndale's *The Obedience of a Christian Man*. Both the magisterial historian and Biblical translator are positioned between the reader and the source of truth, or untruth. Indeed it is precisely within an identical role as the veritas-producing mediator

---

[26] For Edward's status as Josiah the model of a kingly iconoclast see Christopher Bradshaw, 'David or Josiah? Old Testament kings as exemplars in Edwardian religious polemic', in Bruce Gordon (ed.), *Protestant History and Identity in Sixteenth-Century Europe: The Medieval Inheritance*, 2 vols (Aldershot, 1996), vol. I, pp. 77–90.

[27] Lynne, *The beginning and endynge of all popery*, C.ii(1v).

that Bale constructs his relation to the Book of Revelation in his text *The Image of Both Churches*.[28] This claim to cultural authority was, however, one that understood itself as being under considerable threat during the 1540s from members of the radical reformation. This anxiety was particularly pronounced around the concept of *scriptura sola* and the radical implications of taking this principle to its logical conclusion.[29] In particular, the attacks by religious radicals upon infant baptism brought these issues to the fore. Euan Cameron has recently argued that:

> it is reasonable to suppose that the reformers rejected believers' baptism not *because* of the sometimes rather specious analogies or arguments which they used, but for the much more fundamental reason that they were not about to found a sect rather than a community Church. They insisted that the promises of the Gospel be preached and applied to everyone; they founded *Churches*, not sects or heresies.[30]

Bale, and fellow magisterial Protestants, advocated an authoritative cultural position for the veritas-producing historian because they wanted to be part of recognized, public Churches not hunted, persecuted sects. Taken to its extreme, Scripture alone made this role redundant, indeed potentially papist. By simultaneously emphasizing the need for someone to play veritas and claiming this role themselves magisterial Protestant writers were responding to the potentially radical implications of the principle of 'by Scripture alone'.

The magisterial reformer and the Word of God

The pressures and conflicts within the mid-Tudor magisterial Protestant endeavour over the concept of *scriptura sola* were exacerbated during

---

[28] John Bale, 'The Image of Both Churches: Being an exposition of the most wonderful book of Revelation of St. John the Evangelist', in *Select Works*, ed. Henry Christmas (Cambridge, 1849), pp. 249–640, STC 1296.5. Andrew Hadfield comments with reference to this text:

> Bale is reading Revelation in order to produce a text that, in Roland Barthes's terms, has been 'already read' because all answers are known in advance; all meaning has become confined to an allegorical code which cannot be challenged.

Andrew Hadfield, *Literature, Politics and National Identity: Reformation to Renaissance* (Cambridge, 1994), p. 68.

[29] Alister McGrath has distinguished the radical Reformation as the 'only wing of the Reformation to apply the *scriptura sola* principle consistently … '. Alister E. McGrath, *Reformation Thought: An Introduction* (Oxford, 1993), p. 144.

[30] Euan Cameron, *The European Reformation* (Oxford, 1991), p. 161.

the 1540s, and in particular during the reign of Edward VI. The problem for magisterial Protestants, and Catholics, was that (as John Bossy suggests) if religious authority resided in the nature of the individual's encounter with the Word of God, how was this to be reconciled with the need for established Churches to have clear authoritative and disciplinary structures? Bossy writes, 'The trouble with the Spirit, from the point of view of organized Christianity, has always been that it bloweth ... where it listeth.'[31] The principle of *scriptura sola*, while being an excellent weapon when used in exchanges between fellow members of the magisterial class, was a figure of straw when it came to protecting the God-given status of the social order from attack by the religious radicals. It is therefore not surprising to find that texts written by magisterial Protestants often contain a tension between the use of the concept of *scriptura sola* to attack papists and a simultaneous retreat from this principle in the face of the doctrinal need not to be seen to be articulating ideas associated with the radical reformation. Bale's *A bryefe and plaine declaracion of certayne sente[n]ces in this litle boke folowing, to satisfie the consciences of them that haue iudged me therby to be a fauourer of the Anabapistes,*[32] expresses, in an exemplary fashion, this tension and the anxiety it produced. Despite the fact that the text to which this declaration is attached amounts to a sustained attack on Anabaptism, Bale still claimed to feel exposed to criticism by fellow magisterial writers as 'a fauourer of the Anabapistes'. Why should this be the case? How could anyone regard a text containing the following passage as being sympathetic to Anabaptists?

> ye any man take upon him and presume to be the promysed Dauyd or a kynge of Syon as John Layden at Mynster hath done, hym do we holde for an antechriste aboue all antichristes, yea boue the Romysh Antechryste. How dredful so ever he hath slaundered god, and exalted hym selfe against the almighty god, and yet it is not com to suche an abhominacion, as to put hym selfe a kynge of Sion, or to take upon hym to be a promysed dauyd.[33]

Bale's confessed anxiety relates to his discussion of the sacrament of baptism and his emphasis on the necessity of belief in order for it to be

---

[31] John Bossy, *Christianity in the West: 1400–1700* (Oxford, 1985), p. 108.

[32] John Bale, *A bryefe and plaine declaracion of certayne sent[n]ces in this litle boke foloing, to satifie the consciences of them that haue iudged me therby to be a fauorer of the Anabapistes* (1547). The term Anabaptism was deployed by magisterial Protestants to describe those heretics who not only denied the necessity of infant baptism but who, as magisterial Protestants saw it, also distorted the true message of Protestantism, and Christianity, in numerous other areas, in particular in terms of the relation of Scripture, authority and the social order.

[33] Bale, *A bryefe and plaine declaracion*, B.iii.

efficacious. The text as a whole, however, articulates an uneasiness, indeed almost a lack of confidence, in the status of the beliefs it seeks to express. One reason for the text's production is given by Bale in the prologue in which he advocates that Protestants should carry around written accounts of their beliefs in order to keep their faith firm and protect them from being accused of being heretics.[34] Bale then goes on to produce just such an account in the main body of the text. The implication is that the belief this text claims to embody is not sufficiently robust to maintain its coherence and integrity unless it is written down. What is perhaps equally significant is that the main source of attack on this faith is constructed as coming not from the papists but from those people who have taken the principle *scriptura sola* to its logical conclusion; people who, according to Bale, believed that the individual Christian's engagement with Scripture was not a purely spiritual matter but that it also related to the world and to the social order.

Bale's text embodies an uneasiness over the status of Protestantism and of written language. Its title, *A bryefe and plaine declaracion of certayne sente[n]ces in this litle boke folowing, to satisfie the consciences of them that haue iudged me therby to be a fauourer of the Anabapistes*, marks this unease. It claims to provide a simple explanation of a few sentences but amounts to little more than an assertion that its author does not favour Anabaptism. Bale writes:

> Notwithstandynge though we do not regarde theyr sclaunder, yet neuerthelesse wyll we (so farre as it is possible) mete them [and] wryte (throgh the grace of God) our fayth: bycause that everye man may reade it, and then may they wyth vnderstanding and with christian charitie iudge.[35]

Bale produces a text to prove his lack of concern at the slander that he is a favourer of Anabaptists. *A bryefe and plaine declaracion* is, at one level, an entirely tautological work: it can only be read and understood properly by those who read with understanding and charity but, in terms of this work, this means those who know already that Bale is not a favourer of Anabaptists. This hiatus in Bale's *A bryefe and plaine declaracion* reflects the problems for magisterial Protestants of following through the radical implications of *scriptura sola*. Again and again in mid-Tudor Protestant texts one finds a repetition of this structure in which the primacy of Scripture is asserted while its correct understanding is predetermined on the basis of the writer's magisterial assumptions.

---

[34] This perhaps explains why so many Protestants were caught during the reign of Mary with incriminating confessions of their beliefs written before they were even arrested.

[35] Bale, *A bryefe and plaine declaracion*, A.ii(v).

In *A bryefe and plaine declaracion* Bale becomes the commentator, veritas, to his own text, mediating its meaning within the public sphere by attempting to assert and fix down the orthodoxy of his own words.

These tensions over the principle of *scriptura sola* remained problematic for magisterial Protestant writers throughout the 1540s and are reflected in a number of mid-Tudor texts, in particular Catherine Parr's *The Lamentation of a Sinner*,[36] Thomas Cranmer's *A confutatio[n] of vnwritte[n] verities*,[37] and *The Labouryouse Journey ... of Johan Leylande .. enlarged by John Bale*.[38]

Catherine Parr's *The Lamentation or Complaint of a Sinner* constructs itself as an account of one person's spiritual journey towards becoming a Protestant. Janel Mueller has argued that as an original composition *The Lamentation* is a unique document 'among the religious works in the literary remains of Tudor royal women'.[39] It stresses the necessity of moving beyond the worldly, outward religion of the papists towards a spiritual, inner faith that in terms of this text is Protestantism. This dynamic is played out over the image of the cross and the doctrine of justification by faith alone. Parr's text constantly emphasizes the need to embrace the spiritual cross of Christ and not a worldly or material one.

> Trulie, it may be most iustlie verified, that to behold Christ crucified, in spirit, is the best meditation that can be. I certeinlie neuer knew mine owne miseries, and wretchednes, so well by booke, admonition, or learning, as I haue done, by looking into the spiritual booke of the crucifix.[40]

Towards the end of the text, however, a new theme is introduced that seems fundamentally to undermine this emphasis on the spiritual. It transpires that there are people, who, according to Parr, claimed to be motivated by a spiritual response to the Scripture while acting in a way that belied this assertion.

> For onlie speaking of the gospell maketh not men good Christians, but good talkers, except their facts and works agree with the same; so then their speech is good, bicause their harts be good.[41]

---

[36] Catherine Parr, 'The Lamentation or Complaint of a Sinner', in *The Harleian Miscellany*, 12 vols (London, 1808), vol. I, pp. 286–313.

[37] Thomas Cranmer, *A confutatio[n] of vnwritte[n] verities, both bi the holye Scriptures and moste auncient autors*, trans. E.P. (Wesel?, 1556?), STC 5996.

[38] John Bale, *The Labouryouse Journey ... of Johan Leylande .. enlarged by John Bale* (1549), STC 15445.

[39] Janel Mueller, 'A Tudor Queen finds voice: Katherine Parr's *Lamentation of a Sinner*', in Heather Dubrow and Richard Strier (eds), *The Historical Renaissance: New Essays on Tudor and Stuart Literature and Culture* (Chicago, 1988), pp. 15–47, p. 16.

[40] Parr, *The Lamentation*, p. 301.

[41] Ibid., p. 308.

These acts that reveal the true nature of a person's engagement with the Word of God and its validity are those that relate to an acceptance of the hierarchical social order.

> The true followers of Christes doctrine haue alwaies a respect and an eie to their vocation. If they be called to the ministerie of Gods word, they preach and teach it sincerelie, ... , If they be married men, hauing children and familie, they nourish and bring them vp, ... If they be seruants, they obeie and serue their maisters with all feare and reuerence, euen for the Lords sake, neither with murmuring nor grudging but with free hart and mind.[42]

As in *The Obedience of a Christian Man*, Parr's text constructs the social order as God-given and as conferring authority on the religious practices of Protestants. To be a Protestant in terms of *The Lamentation* is to articulate the doctrine of *scriptura sola* in the context of the naturalness of the existing hierarchical social order. Within this discourse any form of Protestantism, any understanding of what it meant to be a Protestant, based on the principle of 'by Scripture alone' which did not explicitly reproduce the status of the social order as expressed in Parr's text was in danger of being viewed as at best radical, and at worst heretical.

Thomas Cranmer's *A confutatio[n] of vnwritte[n] verities*, despite its status as a pæan to the principle *scriptura sola,* expresses similar tensions over this principle to those articulated in Parr's piece. *A confutation* works through a number of topics, the writings of the Fathers, miracles, General Councils, in order to prove:

> That the word of god written and contained within the Cannon of the Bible, is a treu, sounde, perfect, and whole doctrine, containinge in it selfe fullye all thynges nedeful for our salucyon.[43]

This principle is applied rigorously, for example, to the relation between the Church and Scripture with the text arguing that the testimony of the Church is of the same order as that of any other public record ' ... as the exchequer, the court of the rolles, the office of a recorder, or a register ... '.[44] Like Bale's *A bryefe and plaine declaracion*, however, *A confutation* reveals its unease over the potential radicalism of this position around the question of infant baptism. Cranmer's text argues that the papists' use of this practice to sustain their argument that not all things necessary for salvation are in the Bible provides Anabaptists with a justification for their attacks on this sacrament's unscriptural nature.

---

[42] Ibid., p. 311.
[43] Cranmer, *A confutatio[n] of vnwritte[n] verities*, D.iii. For an important recent discussion of the authorship of this text see Diarmaid MacCulloch, *Thomas Cranmer: A Life* (New Haven, 1996), pp. 633–6.
[44] Ibid., M.iiii(1v).

> O what a gappe these men open both to the Donatistes and to the Anabaptists, that deny the baptising of infantes. For if it were not writte[n] in the worde of god, no manne ought to belleue it or use it. And so the Donatistes and Anabaptistes doctryne were true, [and] ours false.[45]

According to Cranmer the Anabaptists' use of the principle *scriptura sola* to deny the necessity of infant baptism is supported, indeed validated, by the papists' understanding of it as non-scriptural.[46] In order to defeat the pernicious doctrines of the papists and the Anabaptists, however, *A confutation* has to produce its own 'unwritten' verities. It has to 'fill the gap' created in the truth of Scripture by the papists with itself and in the process places itself between the reader and Scripture. This move is motivated not by confidence in the principle of Scripture alone but by anxiety over it.[47] Cranmer's text proves that unwritten verities cannot add anything to Scripture through the production of more unwritten verities.

This structure becomes even more marked in the final section of the work dealing with miracles.[48] The text states that:

> By the manifest and plaine words of the Scriptures, and the consent of the most ancyente authors before written, it is evydente, that neither the visions of Angels, apparitions of the dead, nor miracles, nor all these together ioyned in one, are able or sufficient to make anye one newe article of our fayth, or stablyshe any thyng in religion, wythout the expresse wordes of god; because all such thyngs (as is before proved) may be, yea, and have been (through gods permission for oure sinnes and unbelefes sake) done by the power of the devill hymselfe, or fayned and counterfeited of his lyveley members, Monkes and Friers, with other such hypocrites.[49]

A confutation then goes on to list a number of recent 'counterfeit' miracles, for example the holy maid of Lymester, Anne Wentworth, and Elizabeth Barton, nun of Kent. In each of these stories a woman is described performing a number of invariably bodily miracles that a friar

---

[45] Ibid., M.iiii(4).

[46] Bale often argued that Anabaptists were simply papists under a different name. For example on the alleged teaching of the Anabaptists that all things should be held in common Bale claims that they had this opinion 'first of ther mo[n]kyshe sectes, whose custome was somtyme for themselues to haue all in co[m]men, but for no manne els'. John Bale, *Yet a course at the Romyshe Foxe* (Zurich, 1543), STC 1309., M.iii.

[47] Julia Houston has suggested that one of the most striking aspects of Cranmer's Edwardian Prayer Books is the way they attempt to control the meaning of the eucharist throughout the service. See Julia Houston, 'Transubstantiation and the sign: Cranmer's drama of the Lord's Supper', *JMRS*, 24 (1994), pp. 113–30.

[48] This section of the text was clearly added after Cranmer's imprisonment, and probably after his martyrdom, as it refers to Cranmer in the third person.

[49] Cranmer, *A confutatio[n] of vnwritte[n] verities*, N.iiii(3)–N.iiii(3v).

or a monk has to interpret. The holy maid of Lymester, according to this text, was claimed to subsist on angels' food, the consecrated host, while enclosed in a barred cell. However:

> when the Lord of Burgavenny ... and diuerse other gentlemen [and] gentleweme[n] came to trye the trueth hereof; thei caused the doore to be opened, and strayghte wayes the dogges fought for bones that wer under her bedde. Wherupon they searching farther, founde a privye doore, whereby the Prior myght resort to her and she to hym, at their pleasures.[50]

Inevitably all the other miracles discussed in the text are shown to be similarly 'feigned'. What is interesting about this part of the text is that while in the preceding ten chapters truth is located exclusively and totally in Scripture, in this section the truth is produced by Lord Burgavenny's inquiry and the meaning given to his discovery by Cranmer's work. In this section of the text *A confutation* produces the truth through combining acts of Protestant iconoclastic investigation with the polemics of *scriptura sola*. It becomes a textual repository and frame placing into the public sphere the truth of the papist's false miracles. Unwritten verities, truths not found in Scripture, are untruthful except when exposing the lies of papists. Cranmer's text articulates an authoritative, magisterial Protestant identity located between Scripture and the world. Facing one way this identity is confronted with the absolute, complete, universal Word of God, facing the other with the contingent, particular, untruthful world of the papists – an untruthful world against which this Protestant identity asserts its status as truthful. This produces a textual dynamic in which the validation of the untruthfulness of the papists' feigned miracles is that which guarantees the truth of the text.[51]

A confutation articulates an image of magisterial Protestantism as caught between the complete, whole truth of the Scripture and the production of texts whose truthfulness depends on their exposure of the

---

[50] Ibid., N.iiii(4v).

[51] Claire McEachern has suggested that a similar tension is typical of Protestant texts and is certainly embodied in Bale's text, *The Image of Both Churches*. McEachern comments that:

> *The Image* is a thoroughly inaugural text, uniquely embedded in the moment of the early Reformation; yet in its exfoliation of the shared lability of religious and textual identities, it displays the persistent dilemma of a Church defined against symbolic practice even as it insists on the primacy of the word.

Claire McEachern, '"A whore at the first blush seemth only a woman": John Bale's *Image of Both Churches* and the terms of religious difference in the early English Reformation', *JMRS*, 25 (1995), pp. 243–69, p. 243.

papist's lies and deceptions. There is no room in *A confutation* for positive, written accounts of one's beliefs that are not simply a reproduction of extracts of Scripture. As such, it is a remorselessly negative text, constantly enacting a process of saying what is not the truth while being unable to say what the truth is except that it is Scripture. This creates a situation in which Cranmer's text claims to be authoritative on the basis of its expression of the principle *scriptura sola* while simultaneously representing all non-scriptural texts as inherently non-authoritative. At the same time, however, *A confutation* uses its articulation of this principle to assert, paradoxically, its own status as authoritative against an untruth, papistry, that it constructs as irredeemably contingent, particular, embodied and private.

The tensions expressed in *A confutation* over the principle of *scriptura sola* have a direct bearing on the status of history in mid-Tudor Protestant writing. In John Bale's *The Labouryouse Journey ... of Johan Leylande .. enlarged by John Bale*, history is advocated as a source of protection against inappropriately radical uses of the principle by Scripture alone. In this text Bale glosses a pamphlet by John Leland in which the latter sets out his grandiose programme for a complete and all-encompassing history of England. During the course of this text Bale argues that as a godly prince Edward VI should support the completion of Leland's project. Bale claims that not only are the English uniquely negligent in the search and production of their own histories but that:

> A much forther plage hath fallen of late yeares (I dolorouslye lamente so great an ouersyghte in the moste lawfull ouerthrow of the sodometrouse Abbeyes [and] Fryeryes, when the most worthy monumentes of this realme, so myserably peryshed in the spoyle. ... Couetousness was at that tyme so busy aboute pryuate commodite, that publyque wealthe in that moste necessarye and godly respecte, was not any where regarded.[52]

Bale goes on at length to bemoan the state of English historiography in comparison with that of the continent and to advocate the need for someone to fulfil the grand plans set out by Leland. In the conclusion to the text, which is not a gloss on Leland's words, Bale gives a number of reasons why antiquities should be saved and brought to light in histories. He claims that while the writers of antiquity and those of the Bible sought to keep a record of things past, contemporary Englishmen have followed the opposite course.

> Their labour was to holde thynges in remembraunce, whych otherwyse had most wretchedly peryshed. Our practyses now are, to do so muche as in us lyeth, to destroye their frutefull

---

[52] Bale, *The Labouryouse Journey ... of Johan Leylande*, A.ii(v).

> fau[n]dacyons. They were not so ready in settynge up for their
> tymes, but we in these dayes are as prompte to plucke downe (I
> meane the monumentes of lernynge) as though the worlde were
> now in hys lattre dottynge age, nygh drawynge to an ende.[53]

One of the main reasons Bale gives for following the example of these
earlier writers is that such records act as a stabilizing authoritative
justification for the existing social order. Bale advances this argument
by pointing out that the enemies of learning have also been the destroy-
ers of the social order.

> Jacke Strawe and Watte Tyler. ii. rebellyouse captaynes of the
> commens in the tyme of Kynge Richarde the seconde, brent all
> the lawers bokes, regesters, and writynges within the cytie of
> London ...[54]

Bale goes on to equate this behaviour with the radical reformation:

> The Anabaptystes in our tyme, an unquyetouse kynde of men,
> arrogaunt without measure, capcyose and unlerned, do leaue non
> olde workes unbre[n]t that they maye easely come by ...[55]

Bale's endorsement of the need to keep the records of the past is based
on their value in keeping the Jacke Strawes and the Joan of Kents of this
world at bay. He advocates the building of libraries as a solution to the
problem of Anabaptism. In terms of the principle *scriptura sola,* however, such a course is theoretically unsustainable. Why should records
of the past, histories, have any authority in terms of people whose
beliefs are based on a direct personal interpretation of the Bible? Indeed, Bale does acknowledge this problem albeit in an oblique fashion.
He writes that since Edward VI had shown he was clearly opposed to
Rome:

> that rable of papystes careth not now what becometh of thys
> realme. They muche reioyce whan the honour therof turneth to
> destruccyon, as in thys decaye of lybraryes. So longe as Antichrist
> reygned, they were both writers and speakers, but sens Christ came
> abroade eyther grace and lernynge hath fayled the[m], or els they
> mynde to bestowe non upon hym. Yet some in corners hath bene
> solebolde, as hath wele apered by that wytlesse monstre whyche
> made the laste wylle of heresye ... wyth suche other dottynge
> dastardes.[56]

Bale accuses the papists of not carrying on writing histories since the
advent of Protestantism, or at least not the kind of histories that he

---

[53] Ibid., E.b.(1v–2).
[54] Ibid., E.b.(3).
[55] Ibid., E.b.(3).
[56] Ibid., F.iii–F.iii(v).

approves of. In a sense, however, Bale's papists in not writing histories are simply taking magisterial Protestants at their word; in a world based entirely on Scripture what place is there for history? Indeed if history, and all other non-scriptural writing, lacks all authority or truthfulness as an unwritten verity what is the point of writing? and without history or other non-scriptural texts how does one validate those authoritative cultural discourses that radicals like Joan of Kent effectively rejected? Bale's text, while mounting an attack on the papist failure to write history, reflects magisterial Protestantism's anxiety over the radical implications of the principle 'by Scripture alone' when taken to its logical conclusions.

These texts all display an unease over the rigorous application of the principle *scriptura sola*. They announce this concept, celebrate it and simultaneously represent it as related in a dependent way on an acceptance of the existing hierarchical social order. On the basis of such works as Bale's *The Labouryouse Journey ... of Johan Leylande* or Parr's *The Lamentation*, 'by Scripture alone' was a essential element of Protestantism provided one was not Joan of Kent or Jacke Strawe. These two figures were not, however, of the same order. While the latter was a historical figure, often used to represent social disorder in Tudor texts, the former was a simple pious woman who based her faith on an immediate, personal engagement with Scripture; and yet she was burnt alive by the men who claimed to share her belief in the principle of *scriptura sola*. Joan of Kent spoke from a position within and beyond mainstream Protestantism. Her use of *scriptura sola* to justify radical beliefs was ultimately completely antithetical to the magisterial Protestantism's commitment to the existing social order.

John Bale's response to the kind of radical threat personified by Joan of Kent was twofold. In *A bryefe and plaine declaracion* he constructs it as the production of written accounts of one's belief in order to fix and stabilize it and, therefore, to provide protection from the charge of being a 'favourer of Anabaptists'. His other response was to turn to history and, as he does in *The Labouryouse Journey ... of Johan Leylande,* to advocate it as a bulwark against social upheaval and religious radicalism. In effect Bale's response to the dangers to the magisterial Protestantism implicit in the rigorous application of the principle *scriptura sola* is to insist on the production of historical, written accounts of the content of the moment at which the Christian approaches God through Scripture. The magisterial Protestant endeavour in terms of this agenda can be understood as the writing and, therefore, fixing of the effects of the individual's engagement with Scripture within texts that embody a traditional understanding of cultural authority and the naturalness of the social order. Bale's production of the two examinations of Anne Askewe is an attempt to make her fit into this paradigm, to make her words the source or basis of a magisterial Protestant identity, an identity that Bale himself wanted, indeed desired, to find and produce out of the martyr's testimony. In order to achieve this act of appropriation and reassurance, however, Bale had to make Askewe 'other', in need of explication. In textual terms he needed to make her the past of his history.

Anne Askewe and God's Word

Confronted with Anne Askewe's words in a weathered edition of John Bale's works it is easy to lose sight of their radicalism. In these texts a Tudor woman is depicted arguing in public with men who possessed authority and power. While other Tudor women wrote texts that were subsequently published under the auspices of sympathetic male editors (for example Elizabeth Tudor's *The Mirrour or Glass of the Sinful Soul,* which John Bale published with the addition of a lengthy 'Epistle Dedicatory' and a 'Conclusion')[57] none of these texts provoked the kind of response accorded to Askewe's words. Bale's immediate sympathetic response to Askewe caused Stephen Gardiner, then bishop of Winchester, to complain to the Lord Protector, Somerset, about the circulation of inaccurate accounts of Askewe's examinations.[58] Miles Hogarde, writing during the reign of Mary Tudor, claimed that:

> The sayde Anne Askewe, was of suche charitie, that when pardon was offered, she defied them all, reuyling the offeres therof, with such opprobrious names that are not worthy rehersall, makyng the lyke sygnes too the preacher at her death, as her pure fellowe [and] syster in Christ, Joane Butcher dyd, at Skorie afore sayde.[59]

---

[57] Elizabeth Tudor, 'The Glass of the Sinful Soul', in *Elizabeth's Glass*, ed. Marc Shell (Lincoln, 1993).

[58] Certainly the two texts published by John Bale as *The first examinacyon of Anne Askewe* and *The Latter examinacyon of Anne Askewe*, were, as Fairfield comments, '... something of an early best-seller'. Leslie P. Fairfield, 'John Bale and the development of Protestant hagiography in England', *JEH*, 24 (1973), pp. 145–60, p. 159. For a copy of Gardiner's letter to Somerset see John Foxe, *Actes and Monuments of these latter and perilous dayes, touching matters of the Church, wherein ar comprehended and described the great persecutions and horrible troubles ... Gathered and collected according to true copies and wrytinges certificatorie, as wel of the parties them selues that suffered, as also out of the Bishops Registers, which wer the doers therof* (London, 1563), STC 11222, p. 733.

[59] Miles Hogarde, *The Displaying of the Protestants* (London, 1556), STC 13557, p. 47(v).

The 'lyke sygnes' referred to here relate to Hogarde's claim that at her execution Joan of Kent made the sign of the gallows at John Scory. Hogarde's depiction of Askewe as a rebellious disordered woman was repeated throughout the sixteenth century by Catholic polemicists.[60] However, while people whom Bale would have regarded as papists sought to build an image of Askewe as a wanton, wayward woman, religious radicals like Joan of Kent were also attempting to appropriate Askewe to their own cause. On being condemned to death by the Protestant establishment during the reign of Edward VI, Joan is reported to have told her judges:

> It is a goodly matter to consider your ignorance. It was not long since you burned Anne Ascue for a piece of bread, and yet came yourselves soon after to believe and profess the same doctrine for which you burned her.[61]

As she was being taken to Smithfield to die, Scory tried to persuade her to recant. Joan's response was to tell him, 'Go, read the Scriptures'.[62] Joan's language is that of the radical Reformation, tarring all clergy with the same brush, rejecting all worldly authority, and basing its authority entirely upon the individual's personal understanding of the Scripture. This is also, however, the language that Askewe herself appears to speak during the course of the dialogues.[63]

The relation between Anne Askewe, the persona articulated in the examinations and the small number of passing references to Anne Askewe, the Lincolnshire gentry woman, in contemporary records, is problematic.[64] Susan Brigden has recently pointed out that, 'Anne Askewe's story was told only by partial witnesses'.[65] Indeed it is interesting to note that the strategies adopted by modern scholars when discussing Askewe reflect in a curious but provocative way aspects of Bale's historiographical endeavour. The Askewe of the examinations enacts absolute confidence

---

[60] For example Robert Parson's representation of Askewe cited her rejection of her husband in order to stress her 'lightnesse and liberty'. See 'Extract from Robert Parson's, "Examen of I. Fox his Calender Saints. The moneth of June". Published in "The Third Part of a Treatise intituled: of Three Conversions of England." By N.D.1604.' in *Narratives of the Days of the Reformation*, ed. John Gough Nichols (Camden Society, o.s. 77, 1859), p. 309.

[61] Strype, *Ecclesiastical Memorials*, II.i, p. 335.

[62] Ibid., p. 335.

[63] For the connections between Anne Askewe and Joan of Kent see John Davis, 'Joan of Kent, Lollardy and the English Reformation', *JEH*, 33 (1982), pp. 225–33.

[64] For a recent account of the relationship between Bale's historiographical endeavour and Askewe's account of her examinations see Leslie P. Fairfield, *John Bale: Mythmaker of the English Reformation* (Indiana, 1976).

[65] Susan Brigden, *London and the Reformation* (Oxford, 1994), p. 370.

in her beliefs and sense of self, while articulating this certainty through silence. Historians from Bale onwards seem to have felt the need to fill in blanks in Askewe's testimony with what they expect or want to find there, to make her silences speak. This need is, perhaps, an explanation for the multiplicity of Askewes that have been produced by historians, ranging from the Bale's initial Godly martyr to Elaine V. Beilin's courageous woman and Derek Wilson's historical 'romance' heroine.[66]

The desire to fill up the empty spaces in *The examinacyon of Anne Askewe* has also led historians to attempt to describe Askewe either in terms of her beliefs or gender. Certainly Askewe's 'Confession of Her Faith', printed at the end of the dialogues, does express a rejection of the Mass and an acceptance of a reformed or Lollard understanding of the Lord's Supper as an act of remembrance. There is, however, a historiographical problem in making the views articulated by Askewe fit tightly into a model of sixteenth-century doctrinal positions. To do so one inevitably has to attempt to suture the textual hiatus between an abstracted and coherent understanding of doctrines of one of the founding patriarchs of Protestantism, Luther, Zwingli or Wycliffe, and their articulation by Askewe. Historians who adopt this approach are in danger of treating Askewe's words in much the same way that Bale did by making them meaningful within an implicitly magisterial understanding of religious change in the sixteenth century.[67] At the same time to privilege Askewe's gender in readings of *The examinacyon of Anne Askewe* can create a similar situation in which meaning is produced through the imposition of a category, in this case 'woman', as a transhistorical site of coherence and recognition.[68] This use of the term

---

[66] Elaine V. Beilin, 'Anne Askewe's self-portrait in the Examinations', in Margaret Patterson (ed.), *Silent but for the Word: Tudor Women as Patrons, Translators and Writers of Religious Works* (Kent, 1985), pp. 77–91, p. 77; Derek Wilson, *A Tudor Tapestry: Men, Women and Society in Reformation England* (London, 1972), pp. 34–6. Wilson writes of Askewe's first experiences of London:

> Anne Ayscough found this surly, troubled but vibrant and lively London an exhilarating place. Anywhere would have been exciting after the isolation of the fen and the cramped atmosphere of Thomas Kyme's household ... At twenty-four years of age this educated, but simple, country girl was prepared to find London the city of her dreams. (p. 180.)

[67] Given the tendency within a Reformation historiography to group people in terms of religious beliefs how does one account for, or even notice, the similarities between Askewe and the Catholic martyr Margaret Clitherow? Like Askewe, Clitherow adopted a principled silence to resist those she regarded as un-Godly. See Claire Cross, 'An Elizabethan Martyrologist and His Martyr: John Mush and Margaret Clitherow', in Diane Wood (ed.), *Martyrs and Martyrologists: Studies in Church History*, 33 vols (Oxford, 1993), vol. 30, pp. 271–81.

[68] For a discussion of the potential problems involved in the use of 'woman' as a trans-

woman, like Lollard or Lutheran, can produce understandings of *The examinacyon of Anne Askewe* that, in the process of making Askewe fit the critic's label, write over the historical tensions and conflicts that are embodied in Askewe's texts.

Anne Askewe's testimony

Anne Askewe's persecution, and her eventual execution, formed part of the ongoing doctrinal and factional struggles of the Henrician court; conflicts that were given added impetus in 1545–46 by the approaching death of Henry VIII. In particular, the position of Catherine Parr was put under considerable pressure by Stephen Gardiner, Thomas Wriothesley and their factional allies. As part of their campaign against the queen these men hoped to use Askewe to link Parr with evangelical and heretical groups in London. Their ultimate aim was to persuade Henry that he was married to a heretic. Askewe's position as a member of a leading Lincolnshire family with connections both in the court and among the shadowy world of London evangelism made her a potentially useful tool in this attempt to blacken Parr's reputation. This was also the period when Henry was allegedly unhappy with his queen's habit of discussing Scripture with him, complaining to Gardiner that it was, 'a thing much to my comfort, to come in mine old days to be taught by my wife'.[69] Perhaps in this context Askewe's appearance before the privy council accused of rejecting her husband without any honest reason and being 'very obstinate and heddye in reasoning of matiers of religion' increased her attractiveness as a potential weapon against the queen.[70] Despite all the attempts of Gardiner and Wriothesley, however, it proved impossible to link Askewe conclusively to the queen. The best that they could achieve was an admission that she had received aid from a number of ladies of the court. Even the illegal racking of Askewe, reported in scandalized terms by one Otwell Johnson,[71] failed to produce the desired information.

---

historical category see Margaret W. Ferguson, 'Moderation and its discontents: recent work on Renaissance women', *Feminist Studies*, 20 (1994), pp. 349–66.

[69] For the factional struggles of the last years of Henry VIII's reign see J.J. Scarisbrick, *Henry VIII* (London, 1988). For a concise account of Askewe's place in these conflicts see Brigden, *London and the Reformation*, pp. 370–77.

[70] See *Acts of the Privy Council*, ed. J.R. Dascent (1890–1907), I, p. 462.

[71] Otwell wrote to his brother John Jonson that, 'yet she [Askewe] hath ben rakked sins her condempnacion (as men say) which is a straunge thing in my understanding. The Lord be merciful to us all.' *Original Letters relative to the English Reformation*, ed. H. Robinson (Cambridge, 1846–47), pp. 177–8.

Wriothesley's failure, and that of his fellow interrogators, to use Askewe to bring down the queen was made worse by the publication of Askewe's account of her examinations. Bale alluded to the process by which these texts reached him claiming that his version of Askewe's testimony was, 'lyke as I receyued it in coppye, by serten duche merchauntes co[m]mynge fro[m] thens [London], whych had bene at their [Askewe and her fellow martyrs] burnynge, and beholden the tyrannouse vyolence there shewed' (*Lattre*, p. 11). Bale implies in this passage that there was a direct relation between the texts that made up *The examinacyon of Anne Askewe* and the act of martyrdom.[72] For Bale the presence of the 'duche merchants' at Askewe's execution validates the 'coppye' of her testimony that they brought him. He collapses the relation of the texts of *The examinacyon of Anne Askewe* and the moment of martyrdom as a way of asserting their authenticity and authority.

The image Anne Askewe creates of herself in her texts is based on her rejection of all non-scriptural authority. Throughout the dialogues Askewe represents herself as the possessor of truth and her interrogators as hopelessly mired in tradition.[73] It is this tradition which prevents them, in Askewe's eyes, from knowing the truth of the Scriptures. This failure and the resulting frustration are for Askewe the reasons why they are so insistent that she speak her truth. Her questioners fear that Askewe knows a truth which is denied them; a truth which all their human knowledge can never give them. For Askewe the truth comes from an individual's personal and immediate engagement with the Word of God, with Scripture, and no amount of human debate can alter this fact.

> Askewe: Therfor it is mete, that in prayers we call unto God, to grafte in our foreheades, the true meanynge of the holye Ghost concernynge thys communyo[n]. (*Lattre*, p. 13.)

Although it would be difficult to argue that Askewe was directly influenced by religious radicals from the continent her attitude towards the truth of God's Word as articulated here is remarkably similar to that expressed by Thomas Munster:

> But where the seed falls on good ground [Mt. 13:5] – that is, in hearts that are full of the fear of God – this is then the paper and

---

[72] *The examinacyon of Anne Askewe* was initially published in two parts and is clearly made up of a number of disparate texts.

[73] One should note that to designate these events as interrogations is to reflect Askewe's and Bale's view back upon them. Certainly it would be equally accurate to describe Bonner's first encounter with Askewe as an act of pastoral care by a man of the Church seeking to bring a straying member back into the flock.

parchment on which God does not write with ink, but rather writes the true holy Scripture with his living finger, about which the external Bible truly testifies.[74]

Munster and Askewe construct a relation between believer and God based on passivity and blankness. Implicit in these versions of the engagement of God with the true Christian is an image of the later as passive, silent and, therefore, non-magisterial.

Indeed for Askewe silence and truth are synonymous while talk and debate are inherently untruthful. The more her tormentors wish her to speak, to declare the secrets of her heart, the more she defies them. Throughout her examinations Askewe refuses to engage in debate with her questioners and adopts a number of strategies to facilitate this refusal. The end result, however, is always to avoid her speaking her tormentors' language, to avoid expressing her truth in a manner they would, or could, understand. So, for example, when Christopher Dare first questions her over the Mass Askewe turns the tables on him.

> Askewe: First Christofer dare examyned me at Sadlers hall ... and asked yf I ded not beleue that the sacrament hangynge ouer the aultre was the verye bodye of Christ realye. Then I demanded thys questyon of hym, wherefore St Steuen was stoned to deathe? And he said he could not tell. Then I answered that no more wolde I assoyle his vayne questyon. (*First*, p. 1(v)–p. 2.)

When Bishop Bonner puts a similitude to her Askewe subverts it by reading it literally:

> Askewe: Then brought he fourth this unsauerye symltude, that if a man had a wounde, no wyse surgeon wolde mynstre helpe unto it, before he had seane it uncouered. In lyke case, (sayth he) can I geue you no good counsel, unless I knowe wherwith your conscyence is burdened. I answered, that my conscience was clere in all thynges And for to laye a plaistre unto the whole skynne, it might apere muche folye. (*First*, p. 23(v)–p. 24.)

Askewe is equally dismissive of attempts to make her debate in a 'proper' fashion.

> Askewe: And he sayd it was agaynst / the order of scholes, that he whych asked the questyon should answere it. I tolde him I was but a woman, and knew not the course of scholes. (*First*, p. 13(v)–p. 14.)

It should be noted that this last answer is perhaps rather disingenuous given the evidence that Askewe's education was influenced by humanist

---

[74] Thomas Munster, 'The Prague Protest', trans. Micheal Baylor in *The Radical Reformation* (Cambridge, 1991), p. 4.

ideas. Above all Askewe rejects any attempt to reduce her truth, her faith in the Scriptures, to human understanding.

> Askewe: Then sayd I, that it was an abomynable shame unto hym to make no better of the eternal worde of God, than of hys slenderlye conceyued fantasy. A farre other meanyng requyreth God therein, than mannys ydell wytte can deuyse, whose doctryne is but lyes without hys heauenlye veryte. (*Lattre*, p. 22(v).)

Clearly there were good reasons for Askewe to attempt to avoid answering these questions directly. There is, however, more to her refusal to speak the language of her tormentors than a desire to avoid incriminating herself. As she tells Bishop Gardiner, she will not sing a new song in a strange land;[75] she will not make her beliefs fit the tune of the questioner's song, a song of categories, labels and schools. Throughout both dialogues Askewe represents her truth as one that transcends the categories and structures of her opponents. It is not the case, however, that she simply refuses to answer their questions, rather that she views her truth as beyond their competency. Askewe performs absolutely, and indeed even more rigorously, the dynamic of Cranmer's *A confutation*; she does not need to speak her truth except to refer to the place in the Bible where it has already been said. As such this structure inherently undermines the need for anyone to mediate between the believer and Scripture. It embodies a potentially radical understanding of the relationship of Scripture, believer and authority. Where in this schema is there a place for the Church?

The structure of Askewe's texts also embodies a radical emphasis on the principle of *scriptura sola*. Their narrative motivation is constructed as external to or outside the range of the martyr's beliefs. If the truth had already been definitely said in Scripture for all to read, why write any more texts given their inherently untruthful nature? Askewe's text, however, solves this problem by constructing its moment of articulation as dependent on the need to enact and display the confrontation between the martyr and her persecutors, between the world and the Word. The narrative motivation for Askewe's text is provided by the discourse of interrogation which forces Askewe to produce her texts. This discourse, perhaps one could call it the Catholic narrative, albeit in a distorted and maligned form, is therefore one of the narratives that constitute Askewe's texts. Another narrative, Askewe's own, makes up those texts that consist of the writer's responses to the questions and her attempts to articulate her beliefs while protecting herself from condemnation. The final narrative level is that of Scripture which is at the heart of Askewe's narrative

---

[75] *Lattre*, p. 16.

but which is constructed as incompatible with the Catholic one. While each question moves the text on, it does so in a purely circular fashion because there is no relationship among the various narrative levels of the text apart from the need to keep them separate.

> Askewe: Then he asked me whye I had so fewe wordes. And I answered, God hath geuen me the gyfte of knowlege, but not of utteraunce. And Salomon sayth that a woman of fewe wordes is a gyfte of God. Prov. xix. (*First*, p. 28(v)–p. 29.)

Askewe's narrative fills the gap between the question and Scripture; it is the text and, at the same time announces itself as a non-text, as a negative piece of writing motivated on the one side by questions it does not construct as valid and on the other by a truth that has already, and definitively, been said. Indeed, Askewe represents herself as the unwilling writer of a narrative that is authored by the questioners. Her texts are dragged out of her. Without the questions, and the discourses from which they come, there would be no need for Askewe's narrative. Instead there would be silence, a silence broken only by the turning of the pages of the Bible and the voice of the humble believer reading the Words of God.

> Askewe: And as I was in the mynster, readynge upon the Bible, they [the priests] resorted vnto to me, by .ii. and by .ii. by .v. [and] by .vi. myndynge to haue spoke[n] to me; yet went they theyr wayes agayne, with out wordes speakynge. (*First*, p. 33.)

In the silence of the Word the simple handmaiden of God performs her faith in the face of the hostile agents of the world.

The authority, but also the radicalism, implicit in Askewe's perform-ance is reflected in the John Champneys' text *The harvest is at hand, wherin the tares shal be bound, and cast into the fyre and burnt,* 1548.[76] Champneys volunteers in this work to place himself in an identical position to that Askewe claimed in her texts in order to prove the truth of his teaching. In *The harvest* he attacks all clergymen, Protestant and Catholic, because they 'marke out' the Scriptures and prevented people from receiving the complete Word of God.[77] Champneys

---

[76] John Champneys, *The harvest is at hand, wherin the tares shal be bound, and cast into the fyre and burnt* (London, 1548), STC 4956. For a brief discussion of Champneys see J.W. Martin, *Religious Radicals in Tudor England* (London, 1989).

[77] Champneys supported this description:

> not onely because they [priests] are marched in their bodies [and] some-times weare disguysed mo[n]strus garme[n]tes, but because their doctrine is marched also, for ... they wolde haue the people to beleue it [the holy Scripture] [and] receive it; only as they do marche it [and] appoynt it out unto the[m] ...

The harvest, B.ii(v).

offers to prove his arguments by debating with all these marked men before Edward VI so that the monarch can see how the clergy had corrupted God's word. Champneys' text imagines the staging of an examination similar to that which Askewe was subjected: it seeks to incite an interrogation precisely so that Champneys can play the role of simple believer faced by the mass ranks of the clergy. The truth demanded of the accused in heresy trials is represented by Champneys as the truth of Scripture that can only be produced through the performance of the role that Askewe played during her examinations.[78]

Champneys' text reflects the radicalism of Askewe's self-fashioning in the dialogues. In *The harvest* Champneys accepts his status as of the non-public in order to validate the authority of his voice: to be Tyndale-like prophet. Askewe, however, does not make this culturally validated move. Indeed she resists attempts to use her gender to define her place within the public sphere. As has been suggested, in times of corruption or disorder the voice of one of the non-public, the poor or the feminine, could be allowed, and indeed valorized, as that which speaking from beyond the public sphere motivated its reform. Askewe, however, does not or is not prepared to play this role. Her subjectivity, her status as a simple woman of God,[79] is based entirely on her relation to the Word of God which is itself represented as radically ahistorical and asocial.[80] Within such an understanding of Scripture there can be no public sphere given the latter's embodiment of cultural and material conflicts. Askewe's testimony has no place for the social, it has room only for the spiritual.

> Askewe: Secondly, he [Christopher Dare] sayd, that there was a woman whych ded testyfey, that I shuld reade, how that God was not in temples made with handes. Then I shewed hym the .vii. and the .xvii. chaptre of the Apostles actes, what Steuen [and] Paule had sayd therein. Whereupon he asked me, how I toke those sente[n]ces? I answered, that I wolde not throwe pearles among swyne, for acornes were good ynough. (*First*, p. 2(v).)

---

[78] When Champneys achieved his aim, however, and was examined by Edwardian clergymen he failed to live up to the claims made in *The harvest*. See A.G. Dickens, *The English Reformation* (London, 1989), pp. 263–4.

[79] However one should note that, as Paula McQuade has recently persuasively argued, the Askewe of the dialogues is surprisingly aware of the niceties of English law for someone who consistently insists on her innocence of the ways of the world. See Paula McQuade, ' "Except that they had offended the Lawe": Gender and jurisprudence in *The Examinations of Anne Askew*', *Literature and History*, n.s. 3/2 (1994), pp. 1–14.

[80] Clearly the Bible was a part of culture at this time and to posit a conflict between these terms is potentially theoretically naive. However the fact that the Bible was a part of sixteenth-century English culture does not mean that as a source of authority it could not be used to construct self-understandings and views of the world that were outside or beyond the norms of the culture of which nonetheless they were part.

This structure becomes particularly apparent around the question of gender and its meaning. In Askewe's texts the relation between her gender and her status as believer is entirely Biblical. She understands her sex in terms of Scripture and rejects the attempts of her questioners to use conventional sixteenth-century models of appropriate feminine behaviour to attack her. Askewe regards the Bible as the authoritative text, one that writes over or de-legitimates all other discourses, for example those of convention or tradition. So when one of her interrogators reminded her of Paul's injunction forbidding women to ' … speake or to talke of the worde of God. I answered hym that I knewe Paules meanynge so well as he, whych is i. Corinth. xiv. that a woman ought not to speake in the congregacyon by the waye of teachynge' (*First*, p. 10). Later in the text Askewe reports the following exchange:

> Askewe: And then doctor Standish desyered my lorde to byd me saye my mynde concernynge that same text of S Paule. I answered that it was agaynst saynt Paules lernynge that I, beynge a woman, shold interprete the Scriptures, specyallye where so manye wyse lerned men were. (*First*, p. 31(v).)

In this exchange, however, and throughout the dialogues, while it is debatable to what extent Askewe speaks her beliefs in public, she never stops performing them. Askewe consistently depicts herself as a humble, weak but faithful believer in Christ. Her self-dramatization is entirely based on this performance and on its ultimate incompatibility with her other roles as gentry woman, daughter of an important courtier, and wife of a rich Lincolnshire burgher. It is Askewe's performance of the role of the witness bearer to Christ that creates the space for her negotiation and denial of sixteenth-century gender stereotypes. By constructing an absolute difference between the narrative of her questioners and the world, and that of Scripture Askewe implicitly places all social conventions, including the hierarchical social order that magisterial Protestants represented as necessary, and indeed validating in terms of the status of a person's understanding of Scripture, into a de-legitimated non-authoritative space beyond and alien to the truth. Her texts express a doctrine and a sense of identity that implicitly robs these conventions of all their validity.

For Askewe the language her questioners wish her to speak is a strange land, one in which her song, based on her personal faith, has no place. For her this strange land is everything which attempts to make her recant her faith, be it the Church, tradition, the language of her tormentors or her husband. Askewe, however, strengthened with the certainty of election and armed with God's word, defies all these worldly authorities and, with wit and eloquence, wins the right to play the role of the humble faithful servant of God.

> Lyke as the armed knyght
> Appoynted to the fielde
> With thys wyll I fyght
> And fayth shall be my shielde.
>   Faythe is that weapon stronge
> Whych wyll not fayle at nede
> My foes therfor amonge
> Therwith wyll I procede. (*Lattre*, p. 63.)

John Bale's historical Anne Askewe

Askewe's dismissive attitude to all non-scriptural language makes it ironic that the first, and by far most influential, responses to her words were the prefaces, glosses and conclusions that Bale attached to them. In Bale's hands Askewe's texts become the reason for more human words, more worldly language. The role Bale constructs for himself in these texts corresponds to that of confessor and advocate that had to be performed, as Sarah Beckwith suggests, by male spiritual advisers of medieval women who wished to speak with authority on spiritual matters.[81] Bale's, and Askewe's, commitment to the principle of *scriptura sola*, however, effectively made this role redundant. Indeed the role of male confident to a female mystic is mocked in Cranmer's *A confutation*.[82] Clearly Bale and Askewe would have sympathized with Cranmer's attitude to unwritten verities. Askewe tells her examiners:

> Askewe: Yea, and, as St Paul sayth, those Scriptures are suffycent for our lernynge and saluacyon, that Christ hath lefte here with us. So that I beleue we nede no unwritten verytees to rule hys Churche with. Therfor loke what he hath layed unto me with hys owne mouthe in hys holye Gospell, that have I with God's grace, closed up in my heart. (*Lattre*, p. 57(v)–p. 58.)

However, while Bale inevitably glosses this text approvingly, the doctrine it expresses potentially undermines his role as Askewe's commentator. The problem for Bale, and the logic of Askewe's text, is that the truth no longer needs to be validated; that 'verytees written' are simply the words of the Scripture. Indeed to be truthful one should say nothing, but refer constantly to Scripture. This is precisely what Askewe does, her exchanges with the inquisitors remorselessly play out this

---

[81] Sarah Beckwith, 'A very material mysticism: the medieval mysticism of Margery Kempe', in David Aers (ed.), *Medieval Literature: Criticism, Ideology and History* (Brighton, 1986), pp. 34–57, p. 49.

[82] In Cranmer's text there is inevitably much play on the potential impropriety of the relation between these women and their male confessors.

structure. Bale, however, wants to perform the role of the advocate; he wants to protect Askewe from the attacks of such opponents as Miles Hogarde and prevent her from being appropriated by radicals like Joan of Kent. Bale requires Askewe's truth to be spoken so that he can prove that it did not need speaking in the first place.

Bale solves this doctrinal problem, the need to speak Askewe's truth for her, by making Askewe's text into a piece of the past, one that has to be dug up and explained in order to protect, and, perhaps more importantly, to create the truth of its articulation of a magisterial Protestant identity. He uses the textual 'space' created by the martyr's silences to authorize his right to play the role of the veritas-producing historian, to claim the right to be the person who resurrects, orders and certifies the meaning of Askewe's words. In effect Bale's treatment of Askewe's words places him in an identical position as that occupied by her examiners. Both glosser and examiner act, or perhaps more accurately desire to act, as the producer and judge of the martyr's words. However while all trials, and all examinations, attempt to fix and stabilize the beliefs of those under interrogation, Bale's need to make Askewe speak relates directly to the crisis in mainstream Protestantism over the status of the principle *scriptura sola* in the 1540s. Bale requires Askewe's truth to be made public in order that it can be seen to be that of magisterial Protestantism; he needs to make Askewe's truth his own.

The process of historicization that Bale uses to justify his role as interpreter and, by implication, validator of Askewe's words, can be illustrated by the way he draws a comparison, in the preface to the first pamphlet, between the early Christian martyr Blandina and Askewe:

> Bale: Manye were converted by the sufferaunce of Blandina. A farre greatter nombre by the burnynge of Anne Askewe. (*First*, Preface, p. 9.)

By comparing Askewe with Blandina, a figure found in the historical writings of the Fathers, Bale is effectively turning Askewe into a similar historical figure, a worthy object for a Church historian. He is also constructing the true meaning of the martyr's testimony against a teleological narrative of untruth, like the one produced in *The Actes of Englyshe Votaryes*, that simultaneously stresses the significance of her testimony in terms of this narrative and lessens it as regards its own validity as devotional writing. Askewe's text becomes important because of its place in a history of the untruth. This creates a situation whereby, before the reader reaches any text actually written by the martyr, the context within which he or she should read it is has already been marked out. In his preface to the second pamphlet Bale compares

Askewe with other English martyrs. In the process he again places her within a clear historical context, an ordering of the past.

> In Engla[n]d here, sens the first pla[n]tacyon of the popes Englysh Church, by Augustyne and other Romysh monkes of Benettes supersticyon, ii kyndes of martyrs hath bene: One of monasterye-buylders and chanetrye-founders, whom the temporal prynces and secular magistrates haue dyverslye done to deathe, sumtyme for dysobedyence, and sumtyme for manyfest treason; ... The other sort were preachers of the Gospell, or poore teachers thereof i[n] corners, wha[n] the persecucyon was soche that it myght not be taught abroade. And these poor sowles, ... , were put to deathe by the holye spirytuall fathers, Byshoppes, prestes, monkes, chanons, and fryars, for heresye and lollerye, theye say. (*Lattre*, Preface, p. 3(v)–p. 4.)

This framing of Askewe's testimony has the effect of constructing her as sharing the same basic characteristics as all the other martyrs Bale placed within this tradition and making her testimony, like theirs, in need of explication. It also has the effect of historicizing Askewe's words in terms of their significance and making them important in relation to a polemical understanding of the past. Askewe's words, in Bale's hands, become, like Thorpe's testimony, a motivating and author-izing piece of evidence from the past to further the attack on the papist enemies of the magisterial reformer. However, in the process of explain-ing Askewe's words, Bale's text writes over the martyr's silent truth. At the point where Askewe's text falls silent, Bale's text begins; his glosses claim to provide the words to give her silence meaning.

In a sense Bale needs Askewe to speak almost as much as his ortho-dox opponents do. They need her to speak, to tell the secrets of her heart to condemn her; Bale needs her to speak in order to justify his canonization of her as a mainstream Protestant saint. In her second examination Askewe comments:

> Askewe: Then had I dyuerse rebukes of the counsell bycause I wolde not express my mynde in all thynges they wolde have me. (*Lattre*, p. 16(v).)

Askewe's failure to answer all the council's questions and to implicate powerful court ladies as heretics drove some counsellors, in despera-tion, to racking her illegally. Despite this torture, Askewe refused to satisfy their desires and give them the names of her noble supporters. Bale did not need to resort to such drastic measures to make Askewe speak; he merely had to write her story in a way that constructed her secrets as those in which he believed. Like the Protestant editors of Lollard texts, Bale 'finds' in Askewe's testimony the Protestant identity that his text of *The Examinations* embodies and performs at the moment of its articulation. The veritas-producing historian looks into the past knowing that his history will reflect his own image.

There is, however, an important difference between Bale's desire to make Askewe speak and that of her tormentors. The latter wanted Askewe to tell them her secrets to condemn her and her supporters at court. Bale's need is not, however, simply that Askewe speak so that he can canonize her as a Protestant saint, but also that she does so in a language which he, his fellow magisterial reformers, and, ironically, her questioners accepted as appropriate for matters of faith. By speaking when Askewe remained silent Bale takes up the challenge of her questioners. While Askewe refused to reduce her faith to their vain fantasies, Bale does so on her behalf. He uses her testimony to sustain his rhetorical debate with her questioners. For example, Bale's gloss on the exchange quoted above when Askewe refers to the Acts of the Apostles 7 and 17 relates directly and almost exclusively to the status of the woman who was the alleged source of this accusation.

> An ignora[n]t woman, yea, a beast without faythe, is herin allowed to iudge the holye Scriptures heresye, and, agaynst all good lawes, admitted to accuse thys godlye woman, the serua[n]t of Christ, for an heynous heretyc, for the onlye readinge of them. As peruerse and blasphemous was thys questmonger [Askewe's questioner] as she, [and] as beastlye ignorau[n]t in the doctryne of helthe, yet is neyther of them iudged yll of the worlde, but the one permitted to accuse thys true membre of Christ, and the other to co[n]dempne her. Wherfore her answere, out of the .vii. chapter of Mathew, was most fyt for them For they are no better than swyne, that so condempne the precyouse treasure of the Gospel for the myre of mennys tradycyons. (*First*, p. 2(v)–p. 3.)[83]

In the process of adding this gloss to Askewe's words the centre of the text is moved away from the martyr and is placed on Bale's attacks on her questioners. A very similar structure can be observed in the writings of one of Bale's fellow reformers, George Joye. In his work, *A Present consolation for the sufferers of persecution for ryghtwysenes*,[84] Joye saves all his eloquence for his attack on his papist enemies. His 'consolation' largely consists in quoting from the Bible while his attack on those he terms persecutors is eloquent and powerful. In particular Joye suggests that there is something about the papist religion which means it cannot be written down, as though the disorder, the corruption that is

---

[83] This is the entire gloss that Bale writes on Askewe's text. As one can see it is not uncommon for Bale's gloss to be at least three times the size of the original text, and indeed they are often even longer.

[84] George Joye, *A Present consolacion for the sufferers of persecucion for ryghtwysenes*, (1544), STC 14828.

the religion of the Antichrist is impossible to express in words.[85] Joye, as Bale did, also accuses the papists of wanting, 'to dispute with us [reformers] with fagots fyer and swerde, and even a certayn blody cardinall, offred him selfe to wryte us an answer with our owne blode'.[86] A consolation for those suffering persecution becomes the reason for a polemical attack on Joye's orthodox opponents. In the same way Bale's eloquence, his invective, displaces Askewe's own concerns from the centre of the dialogues towards the periphery. They become a source, a justification for him to argue with, and defeat, his papist enemies. Bale claims, in the conclusion to the first pamphlet, that these papist opponents argue not with words but with acts:

> Bale: They [the papists] recken that with fyre, water, and swerde, they are able to answere all bokes made agaynst their abuses, and so to dyscharge their inuynciyle [invincible] argumentes ... (*First*, p. 42(v).)

The irony of this statement is that while Bale is indeed a writer of books, of histories, the woman he is writing in praise of was not. Askewe bore witness to her faith in the material fire that Bale here appears to be devaluing. Where Askewe's encounters with her persecutors move from their question to her response to the final authority of the Scriptures and her refusal to speak, Bale's glosses move in the opposite direction – from the Scriptures to a specific reading of them to a refutation of the question. Askewe's text inevitably ends in the silence, in an act of faith; Bale's gloss in the language of debate.

Bale's approach to Askewe's testimony is designed to locate her clearly and explicitly within the magisterial Protestant endeavour. He makes Askewe fit the parameters of Protestantism as laid down in his *A bryefe and plaine declaracion* by producing a written account of her beliefs that fixes and stabilizes them in a way that her silences and simple references to the Bible did not. He also makes her fit the other aspect of his magisterial endeavour as articulated in *The Labouryouse Journey ... of Johan Leylande,* by placing her within a historical narrative implicitly designed to validate a traditional understanding of cultural authority and the naturalness of the social order. Bale's agenda is starkly illustrated in terms of the narrative structure of the combined Askewe/Bale text as opposed to that of the martyr's. While the latter's structure implicitly reversed the structures of magisterial Protestant texts, Bale's glosses effectively restore this order. In Askewe's text the questions provide textual motivation, while Askewe's words separate this narra-

---

[85] Ibid., F.v.
[86] Ibid., F.ii(v).

tive from the text's core, the truth of Scripture. In Bale's text textual motivation is effectively provided by Bale's performance of the role of glosser. This fundamentally changes the nature of Askewe's narrative and the status of Scripture. Bale makes Askewe speak in the world of her questioners by explaining her silences because this is the world in which he constructs his own narrative position in these texts. The position of the questioner and the glossator may be fundamentally different but in terms of the narrative structure and the violence they do, or desire to do, to Askewe's texts, and the subjectivity they embody, they are identical. For both questioner and glossator the public narrative, the discourse of examination, is the one that counts.

It is interesting to compare Bale's treatment of Askewe's testimony and the way he tells her story with another early Protestant martyr story, Martin Luther's brief account of *The Burning of Brother Henry*.[87] Obviously there are important differences between this text and *The Examinations*. In particular, while the latter is a complex text made up of a number of different narratives Luther's work is constructed as an entirely homogenous work. This is interesting since Luther claims that he received the details of Henry's martyrdom in a similar fashion to Bale. He writes:

> I did not want the story of the martyrdom of your [Christ's] evangelist, the sainted Brother Henry of Zütphen, to be hidden in darkness and doubt. Since I know part of it from personal experience and have gathered the rest from trustworthy reports of godly people, I have decided that this story should be made known to the praise and honour of God's grace ...[88]

It would clearly have been possible for Bale to make a similar claim regarding his knowledge of Askewe. Instead he emphasizes the authenticity of the copy of her testimony he gathered from the Dutch merchants. Having made this claim Luther goes on to discuss Henry's status as a martyr before moving on to give an extended exposition of the ninth

---

[87] Martin Luther, 'The Burning of Brother Henry', trans. A.T.W. Steinhäuser, in *Luther's Works*, ed. George W. Forell, 55 vols (Philadelphia, 1958), vol. 32, pp. 261–86. For Luther's attitude to martyrdom see Robert Kolb, *For all the Saints: Changing Perceptions of Martyrdom and Sainthood in the Lutheran Reformation* (Macon, GA, 1987); Robert Kolb, 'God's gift of martyrdom: the Early Reformation understanding of dying for the faith', *Church History*, 64 (1995), pp. 399–411. For Luther's influence on the early English Protestants see Carl R. Trueman, *Luther's Legacy: Salvation and the English Reformers, 1525–1556* (Oxford, 1994). It is worth noting that *The Burning of Brother Henry* and *The Examinations* were both to a large degree inaugural texts in national terms. They both preceded the far more detailed and ambitious works produced later in the sixteenth-century by Protestant writers. For a brief discussion of these texts see Cameron, *The European Reformation*, pp. 356–60.

[88] Luther, *The Burning of Brother Henry*, p. 265.

Psalm. Luther, therefore, prefaces his account of Henry's life and martyrdom with similar explanatory material to that Bale uses to frame
Askewe's testimony. It is significant, however, that Luther's text does
not make any real attempt to place Henry's death within a historical
narrative of martyrdom. Instead it suggests that the fact of martyrdom
means that history has been suspended or negated. Luther writes:

> In our day the pattern of the true Christian life has reappeared,
> terrible in the world's eyes, since it means suffering and persecu-
> tion, but precious and priceless in God's sight.[89]

For Luther Henry's martyrdom signals or enacts the return of the true
Christianity: it is a non-, perhaps even an anti-, historical event sweeping aside the years to reproduce an image of true Christian life.[90] Bale's
text expresses a similar understanding of the status of martyrdom;
however, it feels the need to explicitly enact this negation of history.
While Luther's text asserts the ahistorical nature of martyrdom, Bale's
places Askewe's story within a historical context making its meaning
part of a history of English martyrs while at the same time asserting its
essentially transhistorical nature.[91] This difference of approach is reproduced in the way these two writers treat the encounters between their
heroes and the forces of persecution. *The Burning of Brother Henry* is a
much shorter text than *The Examinations* and it is not in the form of a
dialogue. Indeed Luther seems unconcerned with Henry's teachings having asserted that he died a true Christian.

The behaviour of Luther's persecutors is, however, in many respects
identical to that of Bale's. For both authors the papists are represented
as being violent, disordered and devious. Luther constantly relates the
behaviour of Henry's clerical persecutors to that of the drunken peasants they have corrupted and misled. *The Burning of Brother Henry*
deploys carnivalesque images of popular culture as a source of disorder
and violence against the purity and order of its central characters.[92]
Luther writes:

---

[89] Ibid., pp. 266–7.

[90] For Luther's approach to history one of the most recent accounts is Markus Wriedt,
'Luther's concept of history and the formation of an evangelical identity', in Bruce
Gordon (ed.), *Protestant History and Identity in Sixteenth-Century Europe: The Medi-
eval Inheritance* 2 vols (Aldershot, 1996), vol. I, pp. 31–45.

[91] Kolb argues that, 'Lutherans preferred a history of dogma … to a history of martyrs
… '. Kolb, *For all the Saints*, p. 157.

[92] The place and status of carnival in sixteenth-century European culture has received
a great deal of historical attention. For an excellent short discussion of the term carnival
that stresses its often neglected violence see Peter Stallybrass, ' "Drunk with the Cup of
Liberty": Robin Hood, the carnivalesque, and the rhetoric of violence in early modern
England', in Nancy Armstrong and Leonard Tennenhouse (eds), *The Violence of Repre-*

> Suddenly Claus Jungen's wife ... stepped forward and standing
> before the fire offered to go to the whipping post and let them take
> their wrath out on her ... But when the crowd heard these words
> they went stark raving mad with fury and struck the woman to the
> ground and trampled her with their feet. They began beating the
> good martyr of Christ with all their might. One man beat him over
> the skull with his rapier, but John Holm of Neuenkirchen struck
> him with a mace. The rest stabbed him in the sides, the back, the
> arms and wherever they could get at him, not just once, but as
> often as he attempted to speak.[93]

This passage suggests a causal link between Jungen's wife's offer and the
violence inflicted on Henry. This link depends on the crowds desire to
penetrate and destroy Henry's body and their collective embodiment of
the forces of carnivalesque disorder. It also relates directly to the argument advanced by Bale and Joye that the papists wish to argue with the
sword and the fire. Whenever Henry attempts to speak, the peasants in
a state of orgiastic disorder attack his body. The papists, in Luther's
account, incite and encourage this moment of carnivalesque violence.

> Meanwhile Master Günther egged the crowd on and baited them,
> shouting to them, 'Go to it, my fine fellows! This is God's work!'[94]

Luther's representation of the papists in *The Burning of Brother Henry*
as agents of carnivalesque disorder is almost identical to that of Bale,
and indeed most mid-Tudor English Protestant writers.

Bale and Luther construct their authorial roles as being charged with
the duty of making the godly example of true martyrs speak within the
public arena. For both these writers the opponents of true Christianity
are irredeemably disordered, corrupt and bodily. Indeed in symbolic terms
these opponents share the same characteristics as the heretics of Catholic
writers. In *The Burning of Brother Henry* and *The Examinations* the
godly martyr is opposed by the forces of papistry and defeats them. This
victory is, however, only assured by the process of making their example
public. The defeat of disorder by order, lies by truth, body by spirit, is
performed by the martyr but certified by the martyrologist.[95]

One can see such texts as *The Burning of Brother Henry* and *The
Examinations* as being on one level part of a struggle over who has the

---

sentation: *Literature and the History of Violence* (London, 1989), pp. 45–76. For a
European-wide discussion of ritual and carnival in the early modern period see Edward
Muir, *Ritual in Early Modern Europe* (Cambridge, 1997).

[93] Luther, *The Burning of Brother Henry*, pp. 285–6.

[94] Ibid., p. 286.

[95] For the importance of order as a concept for both Protestant and Catholic writers in
Reformation Europe see Strauss, 'The Idea Of Order in the German Reformation', in
Enacting the Reformation in Germany: Essays on Institution and Reception (Aldershot,
1993), pp. 1–16.

right or authority to play the role of certifier: to produce public order from and against (papist or heretic) disorder. At the same time this conflict over the right to certify itself marks an unease over the status of this role and the place within European culture of the *literati* who had traditionally filled it.[96] R.I. Moore has recently discussed the emergence in the period 950–1250 of a persecuting society in Western Europe. He has argued that heresy trials and examinations should be seen as attempts to control popular beliefs and that the classificatory process they enacted embodied a claim to power by the literate examiners over the illiterate, the popular and the alien.[97] One could suggest that the effects of technological changes during the late fifteenth and sixteenth centuries, in particular the advent of printing,[98] inevitably raised similar concerns among the *literati* over their status as those that led to the formation of a persecuting society in the first place. One can read *The Examinations* as a microcosm of the struggle, in sixteenth-century England and Europe, over who will be the questioners, torturers and persecutors; over who should have the authority to judge the beliefs and the silences of the public's others.[99] The conflict for Bale is who has the right to make Askewe speak. For Askewe, however, the conflict is over the examiners', and the explicator's, insistence that she speak with a voice that, unlike that of Psalm 54, has already been certified, judged and sanitized by men's traditions and unwritten verities.[100]

---

[96] One can relate this unease directly to the doctrinal instability and resulting crisis of authority within the Catholic Church in the late fifteenth century that, Alister McGrath has suggested, produced a need for a clarification of Christian faith in the early sixteenth century. See Alister McGrath, *The Intellectual Origins of the European Reformation* (Oxford, 1987), pp. 200–203.

[97] Moore argues that:

> In the early middle ages as in the later, persecution began as a weapon in
> the competition for political influence, and was turned by the victors into
> an instrument for consolidating their power over society at large.

See R.I. Moore, *The Formation of a Persecuting Society; Power and Deviance in Western Europe 950–1250* (Oxford, 1994), p. 146.

[98] See Elizabeth L. Eisenstein, *The Printing Press as an Agent of Change* (Cambridge, 1994).

[99] It is worth noting that Askewe occupies an important place in the short history of torture in England as one of the first people to be tortured because of doctrinal conflict. See James Heath, *Torture and English Law: An Administrative and Legal History from the Plantagenets to the Stuarts* (Westport, Connecticut, 1982); Elizabeth Hanson, 'Torture and truth in Renaissance England', *Representations*, 34 (1991), pp. 53–84.

[100] As a historian or literary critic one is to a degree complicit in this certifying and ordering process. For an insightful discussion of these issues see John Arnold, 'The historian as inquisitor: the ethics of interrogating subaltern voices', unpublished research article; Steven Justice, 'Inquisition, speech, and writing: a case from late-medieval Norwich', *Representations*, 48 (1994), pp. 1–29.

At the end of Askewe's texts is a prophetic poem in which the martyr recounts a vision of a tyrant sitting on the throne of justice.

> Yet wyll I shewe one syght
> That I sawe in my tyme.
>   I sawe a ryall trone
> Where Justyce shuld haue sytt
> But in her stede was one
> Of modye cruell wytt.
>   Absorpt was rygtwysnesse
> As of the ragynge floude
> Sathan in hys excesse
> Sucte up the gyltelesse bloude.
>   Then thought I, Jesus lorde
> Whan thou shalt judge us all
> Harde is it to recorde
> On these men what wyll fall. (*Lattre*, p. 63(v)–p. 64.)[101]

Askewe does not make clear who the tyrant sitting on justice's throne is, but then neither does Bale.[102] Askewe of course is writing in verse, she is describing a visionary experience. Her words do not need explaining. It is noticeable, however, that Bale does not attempt to gloss Askewe's poem.[103] Perhaps the subject matter was too dangerous? perhaps poetry was not a fit subject for Bale's polemic? or perhaps there is something about the poetic nature of Askewe's final words which is ultimately incompatible with Bale's magisterial Protestantism. Askewe's poem exposes the essential difference between the discourse in which she is writing and the one into which Bale is attempting to fit her words. Bale's glosses attempt to contain the meaning of Askewe's words, to fix them into his narrative. Askewe's poem reveals the impossibility of Bale's endeavour. How can one 'fix' the meaning of a poem, a vision? Askewe's poem can be seen as representing those discourses which are

---

[101] These words are a paraphrase of a passage from Ecclesiastics and, as H.A. Mason has suggested, perhaps relate to a translation of this section of the Bible by Henry Howard, Earl of Surrey. See H.A. Mason, *Humanism and Poetry in the Early Tudor Period* (London, 1959), pp. 243–4.

[102] To read the poem as a criticism of Henry VIII would be to ignore other places in the text in which Askewe expresses a strongly Erastian attitude towards monarchical power. For example Askewe offers to tell the king those things she refuses to discuss with her questioners (*Lattre* p. 14(v)). William Tyndale, however, managed to combine a bitterly critical polemical against clerical power in the state with a moral critique of Henry's government. See William Tyndale, 'The Practice of Prelates', in *Expositions and Notes*, ed. Rev. Henry Walter (Cambridge, 1849), pp. 237–344, STC 24465, p. 344.

[103] This appears relatively insignificant until one discovers that Bale was a writer who, in one of his pamphlets, even glossed the address of the printer of the work he was attacking. See John Bale, *A Mysterye of inyquyte* (Geneva, i.e. Antwerp, 1545), STC 1303, M.iii(3).

irreconcilable with Bale's endeavour, the sublime, the heretical and the poetic.[104] At the end of these pamphlets the reader is confronted with two endings, Bale's polemical conclusion or Askewe's verse which precedes it. It is in this choice that the reader experiences the price of closure, of history. Ultimately Bale must ignore or write over the sublime, the transcendental, in order to produce his history from Askewe's own story.

In his text, *The Vocacyon of Johan Bale to the Bishoprick of Ossorie in Irelande*,[105] Bale recounts his experiences in Ireland prior to, during and after Mary Tudor's succession to the English throne in 1553. In this text Bale plays the role of the veritas-producing historian in relation to his own life; he becomes his own glossator. Commenting on the trials and tribulations of his escape from Ireland to the continent Bale writes:

> Thus had I in my troublous journaye from Irelande into Germanye all those chaunces in a manner that S. Paul had in his journaie of no lesse trouble, from Jerusalem to Rome, saving that we lost not our shippe by the waye.[106]

Bale's response to the crisis of Mary Tudor's rule was to turn to exile and wait for better, God-given days to return to England. Despite the claim to worldly authority attached to the role of veritas-producing historian that Bale consistently claimed for himself, he expressed no sympathy for those Protestant writers who sought to use Mary's religious beliefs as a justification for rebellion. Bale told those writers who sought to use the need for spiritual purgation within a worldly arena that:

---

[104] It is noticeable that John Foxe may have had similar problems with the poetic in terms of its relation to history. In the 1563 edition of *Acts and Monuments* he prints a number of poems by Robert Smith. In the 1570 edition these poems have disappeared to be replaced by a horrific description of Smith's death.

> At length he being wel nigh halfe burnt, and all blacke with fyre, clustered together as in a lumpe lyke a blacke cole, all men thinking him for dead, sodenly rose up right before the people, lifting up the stumpes of hys armes, and clapping the same together, declarying a reiocying hart unto them ...

John Foxe, *The Ecclesiastical History, Contaynyng the Actes and Monumentes of Thynges passed in euery Kynges tyme in this realme especially in the Church of England principally to be noted*, (London, 1570), STC 11223, p. 1876.

[105] John Bale, ' The Vocacyon of Johan Bale to the Bishoprick of Ossorie in Irelande, persecucions in the same, and final Delyuerance', in *Harleian Miscellany*, 12 vols (London, 1808), vol. I, pp. 328–64, STC 1307.

[106] Ibid., p. 332.

> They are truly much deceived which thinketh the Christian Churche
> to be a politicall commen welthe, as of Rome and Constantinople,
> mayntayned by humayne polycyes, and not by the only worde of
> God.[107]

For Bale only the Word of God could produce reformation. Only the
Word of God: an ironic comment from a writer whose copious, if not
voluminous, words completely and absolutely undermined this principle. Only the Word of God: provided this word was first mediated,
explained, glossed, cleaned, explicated, interpreted and translated by
the veritas-producing writer within whose texts the Word of God would
be found.

---

[107] Ibid., p. 332.

CHAPTER THREE

'Making New Novelties Old':
Marian Histories of the Reformation

> By helpe of these the byshoppes effeminate,
> Against lady faith did so much preuaile,
> That certain of hir men to them was captiuate,
> And for hir sake was laide fast in gayle,
> Then before hir was drawne such a vaile,
> That she was so hid, fewe men could hir se,
> Tyll God sawe time, that seene she should be.
> > Miles Hogarde, *The assault of the sacrame[n]t of the Altar*[1]

Miles Hogarde's[2] representation of the Edwardian Reformation as a
time when Lady Faith was veiled perfectly illustrates the problems but
also the opportunities that writing histories of the period 1530–53
created for Marian[3] writers. The problem the veil reflects is how to
describe the Henrician and Edwardian Reformations in a way that
acknowledges their destructive effects while simultaneously constructing them as having no long-term impact on the truth of Catholic teaching.
The opportunity that the veil expresses is the possibility of enacting in
writing the purging of the past from the present and the creation of a
radical discontinuity between pre- and post-1553 of the kind that many
in the Marian regime desired. The veil marks a point of crisis in the self-
understanding of the Marian regime in its embodiment of these two
possibilities. It can be read as a metaphor for the paradoxical nature of
the Marian regime's understanding of its relation to the immediate past
as being simultaneously discontinuous from it and as depending on it
for meaning. The lifting of the veil, the repetition of a moment of
restoration and revelation, was a central element in the Marian regime's
construction of itself. Indeed in a sense the lifting of the veil was the
raison d'être of the Marian regime, the banishment of the cloud that
had obscured the face of truth for the preceding twenty years.

---

[1] Miles Hogarde, *The assault of the sacrame[n]t of the Altar* (London, 1554), STC
13556, G.ii(v).

[2] For the only recent work specifically on Hogarde see J.W. Martin, *Religious Radicals
in Tudor England* (London, 1989), pp. 82–105.

[3] This term is used to designate those writers, and the discourses that they produced,
which supported, indeed in a sense were, the regime of Mary Tudor. In this context one
should note that the phrase 'the Marian Reformation' when used in this chapter refers to
the religious policies and practices of Mary Tudor's government and its supporters.

Marian historiography and the privatization of Protestantism

Unfortunately the dominant, and paradoxical, view of Mary Tudor's regime as being simultaneously obsessed by a sorrowful past[4] and as having produced no historical texts of real importance has led to an almost total neglect of the texts that this chapter will discuss.[5] In fact the relationship between the regime of Mary Tudor and its heretical past was fraught with tension, creating a number of problems but also opportunities for Marian historians. Was the Marian regime a return to a purged normality that had existed before Henry VIII's attack on the Church or a radically discontinuous event whose true meaning transcended the norms of Tudor political discourses? Were the Henrician and Edwardian Reformations caused by political or spiritual corruption? Whose authority enabled the purgation of the private from the public sphere embodied in the moment of Mary's succession?[6] The queen's, the people's or Christ's? The way Marian historians addressed these questions inevitably reflected their understandings of the meaning of Mary's succession and the nature of the events of the preceding two reigns.

Robert Parkyn in his 'Narrative of the Reformation' constructed the Henrician and Edwardian Reformations as contingent temporal events caused directly and exclusively by Henry VIII's corrupting carnal lust for Anne Boleyn.[7] Parkyn opened his chronicle history of the English Reformations with the following entry:

---

[4] In his seminal study, *The English Reformation*, A.G. Dickens refers to Mary Tudor, and by implication her regime, as being 'the prisoner of a sorrowful past'. See A.G. Dickens, *The English Reformation* (London, 1989), p. 313.

[5] J.W. Thompson has claimed that 'During the short reigns of Edward VI and Mary there was an almost complete lapse of any kind of historical writing' *A History of Historical Writing* (Gloucester, Mass., 1967), p. 602. More recently, in a study of English Reformation historiography, Rosemary O'Day effectively ignores the history writing of Mary Tudor's reign and moves straight from the historical activities of Cromwell's agents in the 1530s to the work of John Foxe in the 1560s. See Rosemary O'Day, *The Debate on the English Reformation* (London, 1986).

[6] David Loades has pointed out that 'The nature of Mary's victory in July 1553 puzzled and somewhat alarmed foreign observers. They were accustomed to aristocratic factions and to peasant revolt, but this was neither'. Although the succession of Mary Tudor in 1553 was constructed from the first by its supporters as an exemplary instance of a strong public acting to rescue the commonwealth from the forces of disorder it was not only foreign ambassadors who found this moment difficult to understand. See David Loades, *The Reign of Mary Tudor: Politics, Government and Religion in England 1553–1558* (London, 1991), p. 18.

[7] This understanding of the Henrician Reformation also had the advantage of making the 'cause' of the English Reformation similar, if not identical, to that of the Reformation as a whole; all Marian polemicists *knew* that Martin Luther's only real reason for attacking the Church was his desire for an incestuous relationship with a nun.

> Be itt knowne to all men to whome this presentt writtinge schall
> cum, se, heare or reade, thatt in the yeare of our Lorde God 1532
> and in the 24 yeare of the reigne of Kynge Henrie the 8 thes grevus
> matteres ensewynge first began to tayke roote; and after by processe
> of tym was accomplisshide and browghtt to passe in veray deade
> within this relme of Englande, to the grett discomforth of all suche
> as was trew christians.[8]

Parkyn's approach, which was shared by the majority of Marian writers, effectively downgraded the religious aspects of the events of 1530–53
and understood Mary's succession as the moment at which a strong
public emerged to purge the corruption caused by Henry's first divorce.
In this tradition Henry's tyranny produced reformation which in turn
spawned heresy. Another, although not necessarily contradictory, approach was to understand Mary's succession as a spiritual event that,
while it certainly did purge the public sphere of corruption, should
primarily be understood as part of a lineal apocalyptic playing out of
God's divine purpose. The Henrician and Edwardian Reformations, in
this tradition, were understood as symptoms of a corruption, heresy,
that was ultimately caused by Antichrist. Instead of reformation producing heresy, it was now heresy that produced reformation. This
approach understood the events of 1553 as only the start of a process of
spiritual restoration and therefore implied that the state of emergency
that had necessitated the emergence of a strong public should continue
as a new norm of Tudor government. Finally there was a third understanding of the Marian Reformation that implicitly denied the validity
of the discourse of publicness in terms of the significance of Mary's rule
and stressed instead the absolute priority, over all other concerns, of the
spiritual and the individual. This understanding of the Marian experience produced a narrative that took as its motivation not the public
world but that of the individual believer; its battlefield was the soul and
not the public sphere.

Despite these differences, however, all Marian historians used a similar
set of images and tropes to represent Protestantism as of the private.
Protestantism, in these histories, inevitably produces disorder, corruption
and social upheaval. It is associated with inappropriate linguistic productivity, the undermining of royal power and is invariably represented as
leading to eruptions of the grotesque body within the body politic.[9]

---

[8] Robert Parkyn, 'Robert Parkyn's narrative of the Reformation', ed. A.G. Dickens, *EHR*, 62 (1947), pp. 58–83, p. 64.

[9] Indeed, despite their radically different doctrinal agendas, the discourses and images deployed by Marian historians were often identical to those used by their Henrician and Edwardian counterparts; John Bale's papists are symbolically identical to John Proctor's heretics.

This privatization of Protestantism depended on a number of polemical and textual strategies. The most popular was to represent Henry VIII's carnal lust for Anne Boleyn as a metonym for the corrupting effect of heresy on the public sphere that was the Henrician Reformation.[10] This construction of the Henrician Reformation, however, while stressing its contingent, personal causes, raised a potential problem in terms of explaining its relation to Protestantism. If Henry's attack on the Church was launched simply to satisfy his lusts, how did one account for the existence of Protestants who were not the king? One solution to this problem was the to represent all Protestants as miniature Henry VIIIs, only becoming heretics in order to gain free range for their carnal desires. John Gwynnethe in his dialogue between a Catholic and a Heretic has the former ask the latter:

> *Cath.* For what hath all their practices finally tended vnto, but only to [that] lust of the flesh, [and] such other thyngs as maketh for the same.[11]

John Proctor, in his introduction to the text, *The waie home to Christ and truth leadinge from Antichrist and errour*, uses a traditional image of heresy as a wanton, sensual and deceitful woman in order to stress both the private and the spiritually corrupt nature of Protestantism. He writes:

> that false harlot that hath deceaued you, I meane that maligna[n]t and cursed Church. It is she, that by her flatteringe means and deceatefull allurements hath intized you to come from so swete [and] amiable mothers lappe, into her whorishe armes: fro[m] Church to Church, I gra[n]t, but not from like to like. From an heavenly Church, to a malignaunt Church, from a lovinge mother to a slatteryng harlotte. From the condition of grace, to the state of perdition. From the unitie of Christians, to division of Heretikes. Fro[m] the light of pure knowledge, to the darkness of foule ignoraunce. From the truth of antiquitie, to the falshode of novelties. From faythfull beleuing, to carnall reasonynge. From saving Christ, to deceyning Antichrist. Thus they agree together, that in all thinges they be utterlye unlike.[12]

---

[10] This explanation did have polemical force in the sixteenth century as the attempts by Edward Halle, and later John Foxe, to muddy the relation between divorce and Supremacy illustrate. Both writers delay the appearance of Anne Boleyn in their histories, presumably in order to separate reformation from royal divorce. Indeed the changes Foxe makes in the various editions of *Acts and Monuments* are designed, at one level, to provide the Henrician attack on the Church with a motivation that was completely uncontaminated by Henry's matrimonial problems.

[11] John Gwynnethe, *A Declaration of the state, wherin all heretickes dooe leade their lives* (London, 1554), STC 12558, M.iii(v).

[12] John Proctor, 'The Prologue to His Deer brethren and naturall countree men of Englande', *The waie home to Christ and truth leadinge from Antichrist and errour*, Vincent of Lerins, (1556), STC 24754, A.b(1v)–A.b(2).

Marian writers also stressed Protestantism's privatization of the individual's engagement with the Word of God. They claimed that this privileging of the individual believer inevitably resulted in a reduction in the role of the Church and therefore produced social disorder.[13] For James Brooks the idea that there was an invisible Church made up of true believers:

> was the filthie sinke, and swillowe of all these tragedies whiche hathe raged well nighe over all Christendome, oute of the which hath roked of late so many stinkyng filthie contagious heresies, as sins Christes passion hath never the like ben heard of attones. And no merveil. when the hedge is broken, every man lightely goeth ouer. For this gappe ones opened, that [the] Church is invisible, hid, [and] unknowe, [and] when thei fere not the censure, and verdicte of the visible, open, [and] knowen Church thei affirme, decree, and define uncontrouledlie, what ever to eche one semeth best.[14]

Protestantism, for Brooks, led to each person becoming their own Church and made an inherently public institution a matter for each person's private judgement. This in turn, according to Marian writers, produced such a diversity of religious opinions that no one Protestant could agree with another. John Christopherson writes of Protestants that:

> Some would saye, that mens soules do sleape to the day of iudgemente: and some beleued that they were mortall. Some thoughte, that there was no predestinatio[n]. Some sayd, that Christe died as wel for his owne sinnes, as for other mens synnes. Some held, that a man hauinge the spirite of god, myght lawfully lye with another mans wife. Some affirmed, that the inwarde man dyd not synne, when the outwarde man synned.[15]

---

[13] One should note that Protestantism as a private other of the public was claimed to produce in the texts of these Marian writers an identical set of disruptive social effects to those Tyndale argued papists caused. For example, in John Christopherson's *An Exhortation to all Menne to ... Beware of Rebellion*, heresy has the same socially disruptive effects as papistry does in *The Obedience of a Christian Man*. See John Christopherson, *An Exhortation to all Menne to ... Beware of Rebellion* (Amsterdam, 1973), STC 5207, T.b(1v) and T.b(2).

[14] James Brooks, *A sermon very notable, fructefull and godlie* (London, 1553), STC 3838., B.ii(v)–B.ii(1).

[15] Christopherson, *Exhortation to all Menne*, Z.b(1). John Gwynnethe also provides an exemplary example of this polemical strategy when he comments on the Protestants' alleged handling of the communion table:

> for how hath that ben tossed from poste to pillare, now east, now weast, nowe north, now south, now up, now down, this way and that wai, [and] sildome in rest? In so much that in many places, the chauncel could not holde it, but downe it went, into the body of the Church, to drawe somewhat nere the doore: where as men saie, it had gone out and cleane awaie, if thei had be[n] suffered but a little while longer.

Gwynnethe, *A Declaration of the state*, N(v).

Although this list is a mixture of smears and half-truths it is not primarily its accuracy that is important for Christopherson's polemical strategy. Like Bale's catalogue of religious orders in *King Johan*,[16] it is the list's existence and the textual disorder it enacts that is important. Marian polemicists constantly produced images of Protestantism as textually disordering and as leading to the endless production of pointless texts.

For Marian writers Protestants were not people who held a coherent set of beliefs and doctrines, they were simply debased Catholics, heretics, who twisted words and distorted the truth. John Proctor, in a comment that symbolically combined these two aspects of the Marian construction of Protestants, wrote:

> Thus thoughe they [Protestants] woulde not abide to bee papishe, yet were thei stil apishe. Thei haue lost but one letter of the name, but they lacke an hundreth good conditions of them, that be so named.[17]

Proctor argued that the ability of Protestants to deceive was, like that of morality play vices, necessarily based on their partially successful mimicry of the truth.

> Howbeit for asmuch as no untrueth can deceaue, but by colour of truth; no hereticall poyson can beguyle, but when it is geuen in fourme of medicine, therfore thys whorish Churche laboureth by al meanes to resemble in utter shewe and countenaunce thother good Churche ...[18]

In the polemics of Marian writers like Proctor, Protestantism became that which must be purged out of the public sphere for order to be restored.

Indeed the writing of histories of Protestantism was itself part of this process of purgation. Marian historians constructed images of Protestantism as the private in order to enact in their texts its banishment from the historical stage, a process that, in Proctor's words, saw 'good olde orders ... newly restored and so many new erronious novelties antiquated and made olde'.[19] However, despite Proctor's claim, the

---

[16] In Bale's *King Johan* the reciting of the names of all the monastic orders creates a polemical relationship between their inappropriate multiplication and the theatrical performance of the list as an act of linguistic over-productivity. The full list, which Bale added to as he made corrections to the text, extends for almost twenty lines. See John Bale, 'King Johan', *The Complete Plays of John Bale*, ed. Peter Happé, 2 vols (Cambridge, 1985), vol. I, pp. 40–41.

[17] Proctor, *The Prologue to His Deer brethren*, C.ii(v)–C.iii.

[18] Ibid., A.B(2v).

[19] Ibid., A.iii(1).

process of making new novelties old was problematic for Marian historians. In particular the need to stress an absolute difference between pre- and post-1553 created tensions that were exasperated by the use of the discourse of publicness in the texts of these writers. Were the Henrician and Edwardian Reformations political or religious events? Was Mary's succession *the* or *a* purgation of the private from the public sphere? Was the public a historical or a spiritual category?

The Marian writing of the Henrician Reformation

George Cavendish's *Life of Cardinal Wolsey*, Nicholas Harpsfield's *Life of St Thomas More* and the anonymous *Life of John Fisher* are more than histories of the Henrician Reformation.[20] However for all three texts it is the struggle over the divorce and the Royal Supremacy that provides narrative motivation. In his *Life of Cardinal Wolsey* Cavendish attempts to make sense of the Henrician Reformation in a way that protects his old master, Cardinal Wolsey. In order to achieve this aim he needs to account for Wolsey's rise and fall and provide an explanation for the Henrician Reformation: tasks which were separate from, and indeed antithetical, to each other. Cavendish achieves this by using two models of history, a true providential one relating to Wolsey and a false, rumour-based one that symbolizes and embodies the Henrician Reformation.[21]

These alternative models of history are articulated in the opening pages of Cavendish's work in the form of two different statements of authorial intention. Cavendish makes it clear that one reason for writing his *Life of Cardinal Wolsey* is to correct the rumours and light tales told about his old master:

> I have harde and also sene sett forthe in divers printed bookes
> some vntrue imaginations after the death of divers parsons, w[hi]ch
> in there lyffe, were of great estimation, that weare inventyd rather
> to bringe there honest names into infamie and perpetuall slander of
> the common mvltitude then otherwyse ...[22]

---

[20] Indeed I would suggest that all three texts could be regarded as the first steps towards introducing a new form of saints' lives into English devotional practice.

[21] In a sense all Tudor historiography is providential in that it has the didactic aim of teaching such lessons as that pride comes before a fall and that the wheel of fate is always turning. In terms of this chapter the term providential relates specifically to such an attitude and is certainly not intended to imply a dichotomy between medieval providential and modern lineal or apocalyptic history.

[22] George Cavendish, *The Life and Death of Cardinal Wolsey*, ed. Richard S. Sylvester (EETS o.s. 243, London, 1961), p. 3.

In place of this false history Cavendish proposes to tell the true story of Wolsey's rise and fall, and in order to do so he deploys a providential structure, telling his readers:

> I wold wysshe All men in Auctorytie and dignytie to knowe and feare god in all ther tryhumphes and glory consideryng in all ther doynges that Auctorytes be not permanent but may slide And vanysh as prynces pleasures do Alter and chaynge.[23]

These two models of history are, in Cavendish's texts, written as contradictory; while rumour corrupts and distorts the past, a providential history teaches history's true lessons. Describing Wolsey's story in providential terms therefore places him within a true, 'proper' historical discourse. It is the Henrician Reformation that is untruthful and disordered, that is the product of, and produces, the forces of rumour, imagination and false history. While Judith Anderson is absolutely right to suggest that, 'Cavendish's *Life and Death of Cardinal Wolsey* is imbued with moral pattern and purpose ... ' [24] this is only true in terms of Wolsey's life. Cavendish explains the events of the late 1520s and 30s entirely in terms of Henry's desire for Anne Boleyn.

> The kyng fantazed so myche his doughter Anne [Boleyn] that allmost euery thyng began to growe owt of fframe and good order.[25]

The king's desires for Anne Boleyn and her effect on the public sphere act as a subtext to Cavendish's providential history, constantly threatening to break out and disrupt the moral narrative of Wolsey's rise and fall.

In Cavendish's work 'good order' and providential history are synonymous; Anne Boleyn, Henry's desire and its effects on the public sphere are disordered and untruthful.[26] Cavendish constructs a clear relation between Henry's immoderate desires, Anne Boleyn's femininity and the distortion of the truth by whispers and rumours. He writes that

---

[23] Ibid., p. 6.

[24] Judith Anderson, *Biographical Truth: The Representation of Historical Persons in Tudor and Stuart Writing* (New Haven, 1971), p. 27.

[25] Cavendish, *Life of Cardinal Wolsey*, p. 29.

[26] It is important to distinguish here between Henry's desires as corrupt and as acceptable. Clearly there were good politic reasons why Henry should seek to remarry, in particular to provide the country with a male heir to the throne. However, such reasoning is not part of Cavendish's historical agenda. For Marian historians the effects of Henry's divorce and marriage to Anne Boleyn were so obviously morally corrupt that the king's motivations for pursing this course must also have been equally corrupt. For an extreme Elizabethan version of this argument see Nicolas Sanders, *Rise and Growth of the Anglian Schism*, trans. David Lewis (London, 1877), p. 101.

as the love between Henry and Anne became common knowledge 'Imagynacions ware Imagyned'.[27] Cavendish later goes on to extend this imagery in a way that relates the secrecy of Henry's affair with Anne to the corruption of the public sphere. He achieves this by representing the effects of Henry's behaviour as resulting in the public sphere itself behaving like a grotesque body.

> Than began other matters to brewe and take place that occupied all mens hedes w[ith] dyuers Imagynacions whos stomakes ware therw[ith] fulfilled w[ith]out any perfect disgestion. The long hyd and secrett love bytwen the kyng and mrs Anne Boloyn began to breke owt in to euery mans eares the matter was than by the kyng disclosed to my lord Cardenall whos perswasion to the contrarie made to the kyng vppon his knees cowld not effect the kyng was so amorously affeccionate ...[28]

This is a complex piece of writing drawing on early modern political discourse in its use of the image of the body politic as literally a body, in which the private love and machinations of the king have produced indigestion in the form of 'imaginations' and rumours. Indeed it is clear that Henry's love for Anne Boleyn has turned him into a 'feminine' king, a slave to his demanding body, one who, in Tyndale's words, has become such a victim to his lusts that, like a woman 'he cannot resist them'.[29] Cavendish is quite certain that the cause of the Henrician Reformation was Henry's weakness in the face of his bodily desires.

> ther is no oon thyng that causithe theme [princes] to be more wylfull than Carnall desier and voluptious affeccion of folyshe love ... ffor what surmysed Invencions hathe byn Invented, what lawes hathe byn enacted, what noble and auncyent monastorys ouerthrowen & defaced ... And what alteracions of good and holsome auncyent lawes and customes hathe byn tossed by wyll and wyllfull desier of the prynce? almost to the subuercyon and desolacion of this noble Realme and all men may understand what hathe chaunced to this reegion.[30]

It is after Wolsey's fall that the polemical skill of Cavendish's text becomes clear. By associating Wolsey's story with an ordered, truthful and providential history, and the Henrician Reformation with its opposite, it was possible for Cavendish to represent his old master as the

---

[27] Cavendish, *Life of Cardinal Wolsey*, p. 36.

[28] Ibid., pp. 74–5.

[29] William Tyndale, 'The Obedience of a Christian Man', in *Doctrinal Treatises and Introductions to Different Portions of the Holy Scriptures*, ed. Henry Walter (Cambridge, 1848), pp. 127–344, STC 24446, p. 180.

[30] Cavendish, *Life of Cardinal Wolsey*, p. 78.

voice of the former against the false claims of the latter. Anderson points out that at the moment when 'Wolsey's fall becomes irreversible and he conveys the Great Seal to the king, his statements begin to echo the Bible ... '.[31] Once Wolsey has fallen and has experienced the lesson of history he becomes a voice of prophecy. His pronouncements speak the truth of the course that the king was embarking on, one that would lead to social disorder and anarchy. This creates a structure in which the meaning of Henry's divorce can only be expressed after Wolsey has been through or round the circle of history. Wolsey tells one of those sent to bring him before Henry that, if the king puts his trust in heretics and dismisses all his prudent counsellors:

> than wyll ensewe myschefe vppon myschefe Inconvenyence vppon Inconvenyence barynes and skarcyte of all thynges for lack of good order in the comen welthe to the vtter distruccion and desolacion of this noble Realme ...[32]

The providential rise and fall that Wolsey suffers allows him to speak with authority about Henry's divorce and his attack on the Church. In experiencing the full force of history in his rise and fall Wolsey earns the right to speak from a position of authority beyond the bounds of history, and with a prophetic voice to relate the past, the present and the future in a message of warning to the king. Indeed, this role was one that Cavendish was effectively claiming for himself in this text as a producer of historical truth from a mass of false rumours and imaginations. Wolsey the historian, the victim but also the child of history, in his final words instructs Henry in the lessons of the past.[33] He gives the king a history lesson.

> Ther is no trust in rowttes or onlawfull Assembles of the comen pepolle ffor whan the ryotouse multytud be assembled there is among theme no mercy or consideracion of ther bounden dewtie As in the history of kyng Rycherd the second oon of hys [Henry's] noble progenytours w[hic]he in that same tyme of wykclyffes sedicious oppynyons dyd not the Comens I pray you rise ayenst the kyng and nobles of the Realme of Englond ...[34]

...

---

[31] Anderson, *Biographical Truth*, p. 32.

[32] Cavendish, *Life of Cardinal Wolsey*, p. 181.

[33] R.H. Britnell has recently pointed out that 'By the time Cavendish was writing he knew that Wolsey's prophecies were true ones'. R.H. Britnell, 'Penitence and prophecy: George Cavendish on the late state of Cardinal Wolsey', *JEH*, 48 (1997), pp. 263–81, p. 274.

[34] Cavendish, *Life of Cardinal Wolsey*, p. 180.

> Dyd not also that trayterouse herityke sir Iohn OldCastle pytche a
> feld ayenst kyng herry the .vth. ayenst whome the kyng was
> constrayned to encontre in his Royall person ...[35]

In Cavendish's work the Henrician Reformation is purely and simply the
result of Henry giving in to his lusts, of becoming a feminine monarch, a
tyrant. This construction of the Reformation, however, reveals the extent
to which the *Life of Wolsey* is a profoundly post-Reformation text.
Although Cavendish was writing within a doctrinal position which completely rejected the Royal Supremacy he makes sense of it by using a
symbolic structure that replicates, in a mirror image, the supremacy itself.
In this work it is the body of the monarch that literally expresses the
meaning of the Reformation; the state of the Henrician Church is represented as relating symbolically and historically to Henry's royal, but
carnal, disordered, grotesque body. The Royal Supremacy over the Church
is re-enacted in this symbolic structure; in Cavendish's work it is the state
or behaviour of the monarch that gives meaning to the Church.

Nicholas Harpsfield's *Life of More* is a similar text to Cavendish's in
the sense that it is at one level an attempt to explain the events of the
early Henrician Reformation in the form of a life story, that of Thomas
More. However it departs fundamentally from Cavendish's work by
placing the genesis of the Reformation in Wolsey's ambition and desire
for revenge.

> Which thinges, though he [Wolsey] never intended, or once, I sup-
> pose, thought should so chaunce, yet did all these and other many
> [and mayne] mischiefes rise and springe originally, as it were certaine
> detestable braunches out of the roote of his cursed and wicked
> ambition and reuenging nature.[36]

The *Life of More* is, at one level, a piece of political theorizing in which
More represents the proper ordering of the public sphere and his enemies its corruption. In this schema the Reformation becomes an
exemplary story of the dangers of flattery and, in particular, the dire
results likely to arise if the public sphere is corrupted by secret machinations and counsels. Juxtaposed with this story of the corruption of the
public by private counsels is the story of More's life. The structure of
Harpsfield's work mirrors its polemical thrust. The public world of
More's early career is slowly subverted by the private and corrupt
desires of the king. Once More is driven from this privately corrupted
public world Harpsfield's text discusses his private world and illustrates
the private basis of More's virtuous public persona. In Harpsfield's text

---

[35] Ibid., p. 181.
[36] Nicholas Harpsfield, *Harpsfield's Life of More*, ed. Elsie Vaughan Hitchock (EETS
o.s. 186, London, 1963), p. 40.

there is no separation between More's public and private personae; his public virtue is built on the private, while in the public sphere the royal divorce produced the opposite situation, the king's private desires and corruptions leading to a collapse of good and orderly public rule.

Having been driven out of a corrupt public domain More, like Wolsey, could now speak the truth of the events with which he had been involved, a truth validated in Harpsfield's text by More's status as the perfect humanist writer and loving family man. More tells the bishops who have come to persuade him to accept the Oath of Supremacy that:

> 'Nowe, my Lordes,' quoth he, 'it lyeth not in my powre but that they may deuoure me; but God being my good Lorde, I will provide that they shall neuer deflowre me.'[37]

More's rejection of the Oath of Supremacy is based on a refusal to be feminized and to therefore lose his status as a public man of virtue. He refuses, in effect, to become like Henry. This representation of the Reformation, as a process of defloration, constructs it as a corruption of the public sphere in the figure of the *man* of letters. For a man to accept the Oath of Supremacy is to be figured as having a grotesque 'feminine' body, one open to penetration and corruption; it is therefore to renounce one's right to be considered as a public person. It is thus no surprise to find that it is Anne Boleyn who, in Harpsfield's text, insists on the oath being administered to More:

> And albeit in the beginning they were resolued that with an othe, ... , he should be discharged, yet did Queene Anne by her importunate clamour so sore exasperate the king against him [More] that, contrary to his [Henry's] former resolution, he caused the saide othe of Supremacie to be ministered unto him ...[38]

This quotation makes clear that in the new post-divorce regime the world has been turned upside down and now women are telling men what to do. Indeed this construction of Anne Boleyn's role in forcing the issue by insisting More is confronted with the Oath of Supremacy conjurers up the image that it is she who is responsible for the defloration of the public, one that Harpsfield represents as involving the entire political nation.

> So then, as we were the first people that receaued the faith and the popes Supremacie with common and publicke agrement, so we were the first that with common consent and publicke lawe forsooke the vnitie of the Catholike Church, and gaue the Popes spiritual supremacie to a temporal king.[39]

---

[37] Ibid., pp. 149–50.
[38] Ibid., pp. 169.
[39] Ibid., pp. 212.

During the course of Harpsfield's text, however, the nature of the Reformation and More's relation to it subtly shifts. As the work progresses the Reformation takes on a greater importance and its meaning is universalized. From being the result of one man's ambition and desire for revenge, a mirror image of Cavendish's work, its status is expanded to encompass a larger, spiritual field. While Wolsey spoke the meaning of the Reformation, More performs it in his martyrdom. In a sense More's death rather than its cause is what produces this expansion of meaning. The Reformation's meaning is now not to be found in its historical precursors or in its role as a symbol of the eruption of the grotesque body within the body politic; the meaning of the Reformation is embodied in More's martyrdom. In Harpsfield's work the historical event of the Reformation finally has meaning in relation to the ultimately ahistorical event of martyrdom.

> But yet Sir Thomas Mores head had not so high a place vpon the pole as had his blessed soule among the celestiall holy martyrs in heaven. By whose hartie and devout intercession and his foresaide commartyrs ... I doubt not but God of late hath the sooner cast his pitiful eye to reduce vs againe by his blessed minister and Queene, Lady Mary ...[40]

At the end of his *Life of More* Harpsfield charges More's martyrdom with a meaning that shifts the whole import of the preceding pages. More, the exemplary virtuous politician, the writer of *Utopia*, the perfect family man, becomes More the martyr. His martyrdom allows Harpsfield to enact a similar escape from history to that Cavendish produced in his text in the person of Wolsey. More the martyr represents the eternal, ahistorical truth of the Church that Mary's succession guaranteed. With the return of Catholic rule the meaning of the Reformation has finished. More's martyrdom represents and affirms its ending and the deflowered body is made whole again through the sacrifice of its most precious member. Like Cavendish's work, however, Harpsfield's text is marked by the tensions implicit in the Royal Supremacy itself. More's death is exemplary, it is a martyrdom, because Henry's behaviour has universal meaning. The figure of the tyrannous persecutor is the shadow that dominates Harpsfield's work and which gives More's life meaning. It is the struggle with this figure and what it represents that provides the *Life of More* with narrative motivation. It is Henry's untruth that makes More's truth meaningful.

The scale of these two works is in a sense restricted by the topics which Cavendish and Harpsfield choose to write about and the issues

---

[40] Ibid., pp. 217–18.

on which they decided to concentrate. Clearly Cavendish's desire to protect Wolsey from any blame for the Reformation and Harpsfield's decision to construct the Reformation within the terms of More's own humanist critique of early Tudor government effectively led to a sidelining of spiritual and religious issues. For both these writers the Reformation appears to be a largely secular event that produced religious effects almost by chance. For the anonymous writer of the *Life of John Fisher*[41] the opposite was the case. This is a slightly later text than the other two and is perhaps marked more clearly by the strains and tensions of the Marian years. The *Life of John Fisher* is a radical and impassioned attack on Henry VIII and his religious policies. From its opening pages it makes clear that the Henrician attack on the Church, while perhaps in specific terms the result of Wolsey's ambition and his corruption of the king, was part of a larger, far more sweeping challenge to the Christian faith. In doing so the writer of this piece, like Harpsfield, is reproducing his subject's understanding of the Reformation.

John Fisher attacked Luther's teachings in print and in sermons from the moment they started to reach England. The writer of his life is certainly following in Fisher's footsteps when he comments that:

> Nowe approached the time wherin God was determined to make triall of his people, the manne of sinne (Antichrist) should be yet more manifestly revealed, for the verie mouth of hell was sett open, and out came the wicked spirit of Antichrist and entred into Martin Luther, an Augustin frier, an infamous heretick and execrable Apostate.[42]

For the writer of this work the contingent cause of the Reformation of England was, however, Henry's divorce of Catherine, 'the verie Spring from which so many lamentable & miserable tragedies have sponge, … '.[43] The royal divorce itself is represented as being initially caused by Wolsey and his immoderate power which meant 'that the king fell then to ydlenes and rest, gevinge his minde to wanton love and sensuall pleasure... '.[44] The immediate socially and politically disruptive effects of this corruption of the king are then symbolically illustrated by the make-up of the Reformation Parliament:

---

[41] *Life of Fisher*, ed. Rev Ronald Bayne (EETS e.s. 117, London, 1921). The dating of this work is difficult as it refers to Queen Mary as the ruling monarch but also gives the impression in places that both she and Cardinal Pole are dead. For the purposes of this paper it will be treated as a late Marian text that was perhaps completed early in Elizabeth's reign.

[42] Ibid., p. 33.

[43] Ibid., p. 40.

[44] Ibid., p. 47.

> in time times past, the Common howse was usually furnished
> with grave and discreet townes men, apparreled in comlie and
> sage furred gownes; now might you have seene in this parleament
> fewe others then roystinge courteours, servingmen, parasites, and
> flatterers of all sortes highly apparelled in short clokes and
> swordes, ...[45]

In this section of the work the writer of Fisher's life is clearly following
in Harpsfield's footsteps and constructing the Reformation as a corruption of the public sphere by the king's private desires and bodily lusts.
Having introduced the concept of the Reformation as an eruption of
Antichrist the writer of this life then proceeds to produce an account of
the divorce and the subsequent attack on the Church which is written
within the temporal historical tradition embodied in, for example,
Harpsfield's text. This creates a tension running through the text between an apocalyptic view of the Reformation as an eruption of the
Antichrist and the narrative account of the divorce that the work contains. This tension is given symbolic representation in the final section
of the work. Using similar discourses as Cavendish and Harpsfield but
pushing them further, this text's writer universalizes the meaning of the
Reformation, not purely in terms of Fisher's martyrdom but through
the representation of Henry VIII's status as a persecutor. The Henrician
Reformation is given meaning through a historical comparison with
other, ancient persecutions, in particular that of Nero. In a startling
image the writer of this text relates Nero's alleged literal patricide and
dismemberment of his mother with Henry's treatment of the English
Church.

> This kinge Henrie, an other Nero, did not only perpetrate parricide
> and sacriledge, but also that hainous treason of Heresie all at one
> clappe, whiles in ryppinge the bowells of his mother, the holy
> Church and verie spouse of Christ vpon earth, he labored to teare
> her in peeces, and dispisinge her authoritie (beinge but one of her
> rotten members) monstrously tooke vpon him to be her supreame
> heade; ...[46]

The text goes on to describe the story of how Henry's body was dropped
on to the floor while it was being prepared for the funeral:

> it chanced the said carcas by mishap and ouer boisterous liftinge to
> fall to the ground, out of which yssued such a quantitie of horrible
> and stinking filthie blood and matter, that it was no small trooble
> to a number about it to clense the place againe, ... But before all
> could be done there came into the place (as I have bene credibly
> informed) a great black dogge, no man could tell from whence,

---

[45] Ibid., p. 68.
[46] Ibid., p. 143.

which dogge ... filled himself so full as his side could hould with
lycking vp his filthie blood that was spilte ...[47]

It is interesting to note the similarities between this image of Henry's
body and its concealed corruptions and the one Cavendish used to
express the effect upon the body politic of the secret love between Anne
Boleyn and Henry. In this text the two meanings of the Reformation
coalesce in this image of the corrupt, filthy body of the king; the
Reformation is the filth that pours out of Henry's corrupt body. The
separation between the symbolic representation of the political nation
in the image of the body politic and the monarch's physical body are
collapsed in this work in order to represent the symbolic meaning of
Henry's crime in forcing his base corporeal desires into or on to the
public sphere. Like Cavendish and Harpsfield, however, the writer of
this work reproduces an image of the meaning of the Henrician Reformation that replicates the symbolic structure of the Royal Supremacy.
Again it is the figure of the monarch, of his body, that gives meaning to
the events of the 1530s. It is the corruption, the filth that pours from
this body that marks the return of an apocalyptic understanding of the
Reformation. In a corrupted state the body politic becomes the site and
the store of disease, a disease that needed to be purged and burnt out of
it to restore it to health.

George Cavendish's *Life of Cardinal Wolsey*, Nicholas Harpsfield's
Life of St Thomas More, and the anonymous *Life of John Fisher* are all
concerned with producing a meaningful, historical account of the Reformation around the figure of one of its central characters, Wolsey,
More and Fisher. All three texts use the discourse of publicness to
construct images of the Henrician Reformation as disordered and corrupting that simultaneously illustrate their post-supremacy status. By
representing the Henrician Reformation as the eruption of the private in
the person of the king these texts construct an image of its meaning that
implies that to restore order, and therefore to drive the private off the
historical stage, all that is necessary is to write Henry back out of the
history of the Church and to restore the separation of the two regimes,
secular and spiritual. This polemic, however, also has the effect of
constructing Henry as the source of the Reformation's meaning, as that
which makes the recent history of the English Church meaningful.
These works were all written by men committed to a doctrinal position
that rejected the Royal Supremacy and yet the way these texts produce
meaning, the images they use, illustrate their writers' inability to conceive of a Church in which the status of the monarch did not determine

---

[47] Ibid., p. 145.

its meaning. In George Cavendish's *Life of Cardinal Wolsey*, Nicholas Harpsfield's *Life of St Thomas More* and the anonymous *Life of John Fisher* the Henrician Reformation is given symbolic meaning through the use of images that effectively undermine the doctrinal positions these works express. Implicit in these works is a construction of the Marian Church as a non-Henrician one; a Church in which the events of the 1530s are still determining its structure and status. At the same time these works reflect a desire to write out, or historicize, the baneful effects of the previous two reigns. This desire, which is exemplified in Cavendish's text and in Nicholas Udall's play *Respublica*, was to escape the grip of history, to purge the past from the present and to find a place outside history from which to start rebuilding the English Church.

Mary's succession and Wyatt's rebellion: the Marian public sphere in action

John Proctor's *The historie of wyattes rebellion, with the order and maner of resisting the same* and Nicholas Udall's *Respublica* are histories of contemporary Marian events, Wyatt's rebellion and the queen's succession, and simultaneously are attempts to explain the Henrician and Edwardian Reformations. At the same time, while both texts draw on similar historiographic conventions as used in the *Life of Cardinal Wolsey* and the *Life of St Thomas More*, one of their primary concerns is the proper functioning of the Marian public sphere. *Respublica* represents Mary's succession as being produced by the appearance of a strong public whose disappearance is itself the motivation for the queen's appearance on stage. In Udall's text Mary's succession signals the end, not the beginning, of the purge of the private from the public sphere. In *The historie of wyattes rebellion,* the effects of heresy, as exemplified in the detailed account of Wyatt's rebellion that the text contains, necessitate the continuation of both the moment of crisis that motivated Mary's succession and the purge of the private that allowed it to happen. In Proctor's text Mary's succession signalled the start of a purge of the private that was far from over.

These differences over the meaning of Mary's succession are further reflected in Udall's and Proctor's texts through their different uses of the conventions of mid-Tudor history writing. In particular both writers play with the relation between history as circular, as a providential story of the rise and fall of public men, and history as apocalyptic, the stage upon which the truth of God's Word was enacted. In these terms Udall and Proctor were confronted with the same problems, but also possibilities, as Bale was in writing the truth of King John's martyrdom.

Did they emphasize the public historical nature of Mary's succession or its significance as representing part of the truth of God's simple promises? In *Respublica* and *The historie of wyattes rebellion* this choice is played out around two different models of history, the providential and the apocalyptic, the circular and the lineal; history chained to people and persons and history as the arena of Scripture's ultimately ahistorical truth.[48]

When he wrote *Respublica* Nicholas Udall took the morality play genre and related it directly to the events of the reign of Edward VI.[49] The text enacts the events of the Edwardian Reformation in order to celebrate the succession of Mary Tudor. Its vices are allegorical figures for the counsellors responsible for the ruinous state of the English commonwealth at Edward's death, and its virtues are their Marian successors. Like Cavendish, at one level Udall is writing within a providential discourse in order to illustrate the historical lesson of the transitory nature of fame and the continual rise and fall of commonwealths and people that is history:

> *The Prologue.*   To shewe that all Common weales Ruin and decaye
> from tyme to tyme hath been, ys, and shalbe alwaie,
> whan Insolence, Flaterie, Opression,
> and Avarice have the Rewle in theire possession.[50]

Udall, like Cavendish, gives his text the didactic aim of instructing its audience in the proper understanding of history as a continual round of rise and fall, of decay and reform. The vices may gain control of the commonwealth by deception and fraud 'yet tyme trieth all and tyme bringeth truth to lyght'.[51] This model of history, however, is juxtaposed with another, contradictory, historical narrative, that of the New Testa-

---

[48] The potentially antinomic relation between providential and apocalyptic history is starkly illustrated by George Cavendish's, *Metrical Visions*. This verse history, based on Lydgate's *The Fall of Princes* and dealing with all the major figures of the reigns of Henry VIII and Edward VI, manages to discuss such figures as Wolsey, Cromwell and Northumberland within an entirely providential framework without explicitly referring to the religious events of the period 1530–55 at all. See George Cavendish, *Metrical Visions*, ed. A.S.G. Edwards (Columbia, 1980).

[49] Nicholas Udall, *Respublica*, re-ed. W.W. Greg (EETS o.s. 226, London, 1969). For a discussion of why it is attributed to Nicholas Udall see pp. viii–xviii. Although the following analysis does relate *Respublica* directly to Udall it should be noted that there is no absolute proof that he did write this play. At the same time, however, the following reading is intended to reflect on the way *Respublica* as a text makes meaning and although the relation between Udall and the vice Adulacion is discussed in detail the conflicts that this relation reflects were common to many members of the mid-Tudor polity.

[50] Ibid., p. 2.

[51] Ibid., p. 2.

ment and of God's simple promises. Mary's coming, like Christ's, will not only reform present abuses but will forever banish them.

> *The Prologue.* Soo for goode Englande sake this presente howre
> and daie
> In hope of hir restoring from hir late decaye,
> we children to youe olde folke, both with harte
> and voyce
> maie Ioyne all togither to thanke god and Reioyce
> That he hath sent Marye our Soveraigne and Quene
> to reforme thabuses which hitherto hath been,
> And the yls whiche long tyme have reigned
> vncorrecte
> shall nowe foreuer bee redressed with effecte.[52]

The juxtaposition of the phrases 'from tyme to tyme' and 'shall nowe foreuer' in the opening speech of the play displays the conflicting nature of the play's two models of history. While the Edwardian Reformation is understood within a providential schema as part of the continuous round of rise and fall that is history, Mary's succession is written as a second coming, as a once and for all redemption, an apocalyptic event bringing history to an end.

The genre in which Udall choose to write, the morality play, highlights, but partially solves, these tensions. The allegorical nature of morality play language encourages, indeed demands, multiple levels of reading. This is because allegory privileges a dynamic textual relationship between a word's or image's outer and inner meaning, between the literal and the symbolic, the shell and the kernel.[53] Udall's use of this language in *Respublica* encourages the audience to perform the opposite historiographical manoeuvre to that demanded by Cavendish. In *The Life of Cardinal Wolsey* true history, providential history, is com-

---

[52] Ibid., pp. 2–3.

[53] The relationship between the various levels of allegorical writing is one fraught with critical disagreement. Indeed to talk in terms of levels is already to be in danger of reproducing a form of reading that privileges one level of the text over another. As Maureen Quilligan suggests:

> While the habit of talking about the action of allegorical narrative as simply a baseline for thematic translation into an *other* set of terms is an old one and therefore exceedingly difficult to break, break it we must if we are ever to perceive the organic coherence of a genre which consistently pays the most profound attention to the radical significance of that much dismissed literal surface.

Maureen Quilligan, *The Language of Allegory: Defining the Genre* (Ithaca, 1979), p. 29. Despite this necessary injunction, however, the methods to be used when reading what are now classed as 'allegorical' texts were a matter of debate during the mid-Tudor period precisely in terms of the need to valorize the kernel over the shell.

pared with false, rumour-based history and it is the reader's task to understand the true nature of Wolsey's fall and his resulting status as a prophet/historian restoring truth to the historical stage. In *Respublica* providential history is equated with the vices while true history is related to the virtues and in particular to Mary's succession, the historical event that brings history and the play to an end.

This structure produces a situation in which the audience needs to read Udall's allegory in an asymmetrical way; they must read the vices as shell and the virtues as kernel. To read the vices as kernel would be to open up a series of questions that Udall for one would have wished to be left unasked. In particular while it was essential that the audience read Nemesis as Mary it was potentially dangerous if they, courtiers and counsellors, read themselves as Oppression or Insolence. It is perhaps for this reason that Udall opens his play with an immediate disclaimer.

> *The Prologue.*   we that are thactours have ourselves dedicate
> with some Christmas devise your spirites to recreate
> And our poete trusteth the thinge we shall recyte
> maye withowte offence the hearers myndes delyte.
> In dede no man speaketh wordes so well fore
>   pondred
> But the same by some meanes maye be misconstred,
> Nor nothinge so well ment, but that by somme
>   pretence
> ytt maie be wronge interpreted from the auctors
>   sence.[54]

From this opening moment, however, the tension implicit in the separation between providential history and true history, between the surface world of the vices and the truthful world of the virtues, becomes increasing difficult to sustain. This tension becomes particularly apparent at the *gestic* moment when the virtues first appear on stage. At this point Udall uses a set of explicitly Marian strategies in order to mediate this potentially difficult moment when the two models of history his text contains come together; when 'from tyme to tyme' meets 'shall nowe foreuer'.

Udall's construction of the vices in the play illustrates the productivity of his approach and its potential dangers. From a polemical point of view the portrayal of the Edwardian Reformation as a time when vices ruled conforms very well with Marian constructions of Protestantism. For Udall the strictures of the morality play genre allowed him to deploy a model of history in which the rule of the vices could be

---

[54] Udall, *Respublica*, p. 1.

equated with both the time of the play and with a specific historical period. The vices exist, the play exists, history happens; the vices are banished, the play ends, history stops. Robert Potter suggests that the 'morality play, ... is an extreme manifestation of one perennial impulse of theatre, which is to embody, to verify, to create the acknowledged Truth'.[55] Truth banishes the vices, the vices' world and the play in one fell swoop. For Udall the end of the play, the end of history, is the restoration of truth. This moment radically alters the nature of the relationship between the world of the play, of history and the time after the play, after the advent of truth. In historiographic terms Udall's play constructs a profound, indeed total, discontinuity between the past, history, the time of the vices and the present.

The neatness of this formulation in polemical terms, however, serves to emphasize the extent to which Udall's representation of the Edwardian Reformation is in practice dominated by the political realities of the present. These realities were themselves the result of events and actions that took place during a period that the play implies had no meaning or status in the present. Indeed how could a time of untruth have any influence after the restoration of truth? *Respublica* demands a very specific form of reading from its audience. For example the moment when Avaryce 'names' his bags of gold to Adulacion to teach him how to be more rapacious is both amusing and potentially dangerous for Udall.

> *Avaryce.*   This is of Churche goodes scraped vpp withoute alawe,
> For which was as quicke scambling as ever I sawe,
> of their plate, their iewels, and copes, we made them
>   lowtes,
> Stopping peoples barking with lynnen rags and clowtes,
> Thei had thalter clothes thalbes and amices
> with the sindons in which wer wrapte the chalices.[56]

When this play was performed at court what would such men as Lord Paget or even the Duke of Norfolk have made of this equation of those who profited from the Church with the vices? In terms of the allegorical meaning of the text this may not matter. *Respublica* as a morality play enacts the inherent sinfulness of humanity; all are sinners, all are vices, in need of salvation. As history, however, the play implicitly criticizes the behaviour of the English gentry and nobility in the period 1536–53. It is perhaps for this reason that the appropriated lands of the Church and the monasteries are never specifically alluded to in the play. Like

---

[55] Robert Potter, *The English Morality Play: Origins, History and Influence of a Dramatic Tradition* (London, 1975), p. 16.
[56] Udall, *Respublica*, p. 30.

the Marian regime as a whole, Udall's *Respublica* shys away or fails to confront this issue. In the process Udall's play performs a moment of historiographical slippage. The discontinuous and denied past, the time of the vices, is still structuring the representation of the time of their rule even within a text written after the restoration of truth. The appearance of the virtues has not, despite the play's message, driven the vices completely off the historical stage; their effects are still being felt, like a bad smell that occasionally wafts into the text to remind the reader of something unpleasant best not discussed, or even acknowledged.

It is around the figure of Adulacion, however, that the greatest movement between the world of the vices, of history and that of truth takes place. This is primarily because at one level Udall writes himself into the play as Adulacion, the feckless but basically harmless vice who, alone among the vices, remains on stage after the advent of truth. The relation between Udall and Adulacion embodies the slippage between the world of the vices and that of the truth. In historical, vice, terms the relation between Adulacion and Udall is based on their identical roles during the period the play represents. Udall, like Adulacion, provided the arguments and words that justified the Edwardian Reformation, the rule of the vices. Indeed Udall implicitly draws attention to this similarity during the course of the play. For example when Avaryce asks:

> For who is so foolishe that the evell he hath wrought
> for his own behoff he wolde to light sholde be brought?
> or who hadnot rather, his ill doinges to hide,
> Thenne to have the same bruted on everye syde?[57]

the answer is of course, at one level, Udall himself in this play. At the end of the play Adulacion is forgiven by Nemesis on the basis of his confession and his pledge to work for the common good rather than his own.

> *Adulacion.* Nought in myne excuse, but submitte me to your grace.
> onelie this I promise if I maie mercye fynde,
> vtterlie for ever to chaunge my wicked mynde.
> I nere sought afore myne owne private gayne so muche,
> But I will ferther Commonweales tenne tymes so muche.[58]

The status of Udall/Adulacion is unsurprising in the sense that *Respublica*'s writer himself wanted, in fact needed, to have a position in the Marian regime while not being able to deny his involvement in the Edwardian one.

---

[57] Ibid., p. 3.
[58] Ibid., p. 65.

In practice *Respublica* contains three and not two historical models: the providential model of rise and fall, of the vices; an apocalyptic model in which the arrival of truthfulness in the figure Nemesis/Mary brings history, and the play, to an end; and a model in which there is movement between these two opposed worlds. In this model of history, by an act of contrition and through God's mercy, a person could escape from the world of the vices, from the circle of history, and become one with the truth. The need, however, to construct this third model of history, to argue for the possibility of such a move, reflects the flawed nature of the basic historiographic structure of *Respublica* in which the time of the vices is antinomic to that of the truth. The advent of truth creates a completely new state; one, however, in which the effects of the past still echo in the shape of those figures like Udall/Adulacion who are both vice and virtue, untruth and truth. Ultimately what *Respublica* illustrates is not the Marian regime's discontinuous relation to the past but its symbiotic relation to it, that the truth of the Catholic restoration only has sense in relation to the untruth it replaced. Udall's role under Mary, like Adulacion's under Nemesis, has meaning because of, and not in spite of, their previous status. Perhaps truth can only be the daughter of time if untruth was her father.[59]

Respublica is not, however, simply a historical morality play; it is also an attempt to create a polemical representation of Mary's succession as the end not the start of a purge of the public sphere. In conventional morality plays reformation often comes about when the central figure has, under the influence of the vices, sunk so low that the only choice seems to be between despair and death. It is at this point that the virtues intercede to teach the central character the error of his or her ways. *Respublica* does contain this structure but in a distorted form. The central character of the play is Respublica, an allegorical female figure for the realm of England. However Respublica does not herself sin or fall, except in her inability to see the vices for what they are. In a sense, therefore, Udall's play contains a Widowe Englande but not, at its opening, a King John. This produces a situation in which the narrative motivation of the play becomes not the vices' temptation of the central figure but their own behaviour. This in turn creates a problem in terms of justifying the appearance of the virtues. Udall's solution to this potential crisis in his text is a profoundly Marian one. Respublica's salvation is not produced, initially, by Veritas, Iusticia or Pax but by the sudden and unexpected appearance of Misericordia, mercy. While it is the arrival on stage of Veritas, truth, that spells the end of the vices'

---

[59] Mary's motto was 'Truth the Daughter of Time'.

power, it is Misericordia who signals their downfall. The advent of Mercy demonstrates God's infinite desire to forgive man's sinfulness.

> Miserico. wherein apeareth the graciousnesse of god
> more then ynfinitelye to excede mans goodnesse,
> but that he kepeth backe the sharpe stroke of hys rod
> whan man woulde rage in mooste furious woodenes?
>
> Scarce anie emendes maie mannes eagrenesse appeace,
> yea and thoughe he forgeve, he wilnot soone forgette:
> towardes true penitens gods warthe foorthwith doothe
> cease,
> and he their past sinnes, behind his backe dooeth sett.[60]

It is the assuredness of forgiveness, of God's mercy, that creates the space for Veritas. One is reminded of Cardinal Pole's advice to Henry VIII that the first step in what Pole hoped would be a return to the Catholic Church should be to 'do penance!'[61] Despite all the historiographical and political problems that Udall's play reflects the operation of mercy can transcend them all.

Indeed in this representation of mercy Udall constructs a figure that, like Adulacion but in a positive way, cuts through the play's various levels of interpretation to produce closure. The operation of mercy, dependent as it is on remembering the past in order to forgive it, explicitly links and overcomes the conflict between history and the present, between the shell and the kernel. At one level Udall's play reflects not the oppression of a sorrowful past but the possibility of escape from such a past through the operation of mercy; an escape that is both allegorical and historical, symbolic and literal; of the play and of the writer's own life.

The appearance of mercy at the *gestic* moment when the various levels of the play come together creates the space for the other virtues to appear and to reform the public sphere through the purgation of the vices. Only once the vices have been defeated can Nemesis, or Mary, take her rightful place on stage. In a sense this is a reversal of the comparable moment in Bale's *King Johan* in which the similar pivotal point takes place between or in the gap when John himself is dead but Imperyall Majestye has not yet appeared on stage. In both plays the

---

[60] Udall, *Respublica*, p. 40.

[61] Reginald Pole, *Pole's Defence of the Unity of the Church*, trans. Joseph C. Dwyer (Westminster, Maryland, 1965), p. 298. Due to the almost complete neglect of Marian literature there has been no recent work on the importance of the idea of mercy in the writing of this period. Eamon Duffy's brief discussion of the subject in *The Stripping of the Altars* (New Haven, 1992), pp. 529–37, is extremely interesting but clearly much more work needs to be done.

reform of the public sphere is initiated outside or before the advent of royal power. However in Udall's text the operation of mercy is required before the actual process of reformation itself can start to take place. Implicit in Udall's text is a construction of the strong public which propelled Mary to the throne, and the purge of the public sphere that it enacted, as being over once order has been restored. In this understanding of Mary's succession mercy has already been bestowed, and the purge of the private taken place, before the queen appears on stage. This construction of a radical discontinuity between Mary's reign and that of her brother clearly held attractions for those members of the political classes, probably the majority, who wished to see any purge of their ranks restricted in scope and duration.[62]

At the same time Udall's play enacts an identical claim to the position of veritas-producing historian as Bale did in *King Johan*. Indeed Udall's text makes this claim for its writer on the basis of the outrageous claim that Udall is ideally suited to play this role because he has known, indeed been, the untruth that is Protestantism. Udall offers, in the form of this text, to play Mary's veritas on the implicit basis of her construction as King John/Imperyall Majestye, the godly prince who nonetheless needs mediators like Udall to allow the public sphere to operate properly. Udall's Marian public sphere is identical to Bale's Henrician one, with the small difference that the names of the vices upon whose purgation it is based are different.

Proctor's *The historie of wyattes rebellion*[63] is a historical account of the events of January 1554 designed to enact a purge from the public sphere of those forces that motivated Sir Thomas Wyatt's rebellion against Mary Tudor's marriage to Philip of Spain. It contains a claim for its author to play the role of the veritas-producing historian on the basis of the continuing existence of the disorder, heresy, that required the strong public to appear which brought about Mary's succession. Proctor's text claims a position of cultural authority for its writer on a similar basis as Bale's *King Johan*. It offers its writer as a mediator

---

[62] For example, John Heywood's allegorical verse history of the twenty years between the dissolution of the monasteries and Mary's succession expresses a similar desire to see any Marian purge of the political classes restricted in scope and scale. See John Heywood, *The Spider and the Fly*, ed. John S. Farmer (London, 1908), STC 13308.

[63] John Proctor, *The historie of wyattes rebellion, with the order and maner of resisting the same* (London, 1554), STC 20407. John Proctor's *The historie of wyattes rebellion* is a more complex text then it is often credited with being. Unfortunately historians have tended to read the modern version of Proctor's text that edits the final third of the original text. See John Proctor, ' The History of Wyat's Rebellion', in *An English Garner*, ed. Edward Arber, 8 vols (London, 1896), vol. 8. For the standard historical account of Wyatt's rebellion see David Loades, *Two Tudor Conspiracies* (Cambridge, 1965).

between the forces that symbolically motivate the appearance of a strong public, England, and the monarch on the basis of its author's ability to play the role of veritas, to produce the truth of such disturbing events as Wyatt's rebellion.

Proctor's text creates an inherent relationship between heresy and rebellion similar to that found in other Marian works by using a traditional representation of heresy as a harlot tempting men to rise up against their natural rulers. The relationship between heresy and rebellion, however, was not a simple one for Marian writers. John Christopherson's text, *An Exhortation to all Menne,* represents rebellion as a basically secular act by constructing a separation between true and false subjects that relates to the latter's wickedness and selfish pursuit of personal gain and not to religious beliefs.[64] While Christopherson wishes to establish the sinful nature of rebellion first before deploying it as a sign of heresy's falseness Proctor reverses this structure. In his work, heresy is the cause not only of Wyatt's revolt, but, because of its false corrupting nature, of all rebellion. For Proctor Wyatt's rebellion is not simply a wicked, political act but was part of the eternal struggle between true religion and false, between Christ and Antichrist.

There is a potential conflict, however, between Proctor's representation of the causes of rebellion as being ultimately spiritual and his claim that the purpose of writing his account of Wyatt's rebellion was to teach the traditional providential lesson that pride comes before a fall.[65] Proctor had to find a way of uniting an ultimately scriptural understanding of the causes of Wyatt's rebellion with a relatively prosaic account of the events that took place in Kent in January 1554. To achieve this he created, like Udall, a text that demanded different levels of interpretation. In simple terms Proctor's text can be divided into three very unequal parts: the introduction in which the writer explains the reasons for writing his history, the narrative account of the rebellion and the final section in which Proctor draws the first two sections

---

[64] Christopherson draws on an Aristotelian, implicitly secular, discourse to explain Wyatt's revolt.

> The causes that specially moue men to rebellion, as the excellent and great learned Philosopher Aristotell writeth, are lucre, losse of goodes, honoure, dishonoure, welth, feare, contempt, and diuersite of maners or contryes, where vnto we may very well adde, the diuersitie of opinions and religion.

Christopherson, *An Exhortation to all Menne,* B.b(2v).

[65] Proctor also claimed that he was writing his history in order to defend Kent from the charge of supporting Wyatt. See Proctor, *The historie of wyattes rebellion,* a.iiii(1) and a.iiii(4).

together. In effect Proctor's text has a circular structure moving from present, to immediate past, and back to present. This structure is given coherence and meaning through the use of two allegorical figures, Heresy and Englande. These two figures give the narrative history of the text meaning. Between them the story of Wyatt's rebellion unfolds.

Proctor's representation of heresy as a sensual female temptress clearly draws on the discourse of publicness and religious imagery. His Heresy signifies sin, corruption and political disorder. Like an allegorical Anne Boleyn, from a Catholic perspective, Heresy stages 'entertainments' or rebellions within the public sphere by beguiling men through flattery and temptation.

> What a restlesse euil heresie is, euer trauailing to bring furth mischeif, neuer ceasing to protrude all those, in whose hertes she is receiued to confusion: by what plausible allurementes at her entrie she catcheth fauourable intertainement, with what waies of craft and subteltie she dilateth her dominion, [and] finally howe of course she toyleth to be supported by fraction, sedition, [and] rebellion, to the great perell of subuersion of that state where as a plague she happeneth to fynde habitation ...[66]

Having articulated this powerful, if conventional, image of heresy Proctor plunges into his detailed narrative of Wyatt's rebellion. In his account the revolt becomes a struggle between two stories, Wyatt's and his own. Throughout the course of the narrative Proctor constantly hammers home the point that Wyatt's support was based on a lie, on the traitor's deception in hiding the real heretical motivations for his revolt.

> [Wyatt] determined to speake no worde of religion, but to make the colour of hys commotion, onely to withstand straungers, and to auaunce libertie.[67]

Proctor claims that Wyatt's relative success was due to the failure of the loyal subjects of Kent to be heard and to Wyatt's deliberate suppression of their words. Proctor's text embodies a re-enactment of the rebellion and its inevitable defeat beyond Wyatt's lies and distortions. In telling the story of the revolt, however, Proctor is confronted with a historiographical dilemma; does he stress the danger of the rebellion in order to emphasize the providential nature of Mary's escape? or does he seek to minimize it in order to illustrate the futility of revolt?

The problems caused by this dilemma can be illustrated by one small incident that Proctor recounts. During the height of the rebellion, with Wyatt at the gates of London, Mary went to Guildhall to rally the citizens of London to her cause.

---

[66] Ibid., A.i.
[67] Ibid., A.iii.(v)

This done her grace retourned towardes white hall, and passinge thorowe the streates beinge full of people, pressynge to beholde her grace, wherein they hadde singular delite and pleasure: One amongest all moste impudent of all others, stepped fourth sayinge: youre grace maye doe well to make youre forewarde in battayll of your Byshoppes and Priestes for they be trusty and wyll not deceyue you. For whiche wordes he was commaunded to Newgate, who deserued to be hanged at the nexte boughe for example of all other, so impudentlye and arrogantlye to assaulte hys Soueraygne and Queene with suche seditious and trayterours language.[68]

Proctor's account of this episode is marked by a number of contradictory pressures. He wishes to emphasize the bravery of Mary in staying in London at this time and in making the journey to the Guildhall while at the same time he does not want to give a false impression of the dangers of Wyatt's revolt. The passage opens with the image of a harmonious, loyal city that, in the persons of its citizens, lauds the monarch during her return from the Guildhall. Suddenly from within this crowd of loyal subjects a man steps forward and, in a highly inappropriate manner, offers Mary some 'advice' on the best way of fighting the rebels, advice that is clearly anti-clerical and, possibly, treacherous. Strangely the actions of this one man seem to have a disproportionate effect on the whole crowd whose behaviour changes from being motivated by delight and loyalty to being impudent. In a sense this moment of rebellion acts as a metaphor for Wyatt's revolt, and perhaps Mary's reign as a whole. From the image of a harmonious, joyful, crowd/country united in welcoming Mary to the city/throne the actions of one person create a completely different image of one brave woman standing out against a crowd of threatening, impudent, hostile onlookers. Mary's symbolic status travels from beneficent monarch/Nemesis to innocent, wronged woman in one swift moment, from mother to daughter, from queen to virgin.[69] Proctor's account of Mary's visit to the Guildhall embodies two images of the Marian public sphere, one in which the members of the non-public, the crowd, know their

---

[68] Ibid., G.v(1v)–G.v(2).

[69] This slippage in roles is repeated in other Marian works. John Christopherson uses a number of images of Mary in order to condemn the act of rebellion. In particular the queen's status as a virgin is used by Christopherson to illustrate the cruelty of the rebels.

> But alas what harde hartes haue those, that if she were but a priuate woman, being so gentle of nature, so vertuouse and so merciful, coulde drawe theyr sworde agaynste her. For albeit that all bloudeshedde is cruel and horrible in the syght of god, yet the sheddynge of so a pure virgyns bloude, is of all moste cruell detestable.

Christopherson, *An Exhortation to all Menne*, O.iiii.

place, and another, hidden within this one, in which members of the crowd suddenly break ranks and step rebelliously outside their proper social position to demand attention. It is this moment of disruption that Proctor wishes both to record and deny, to display and to negate.

Having worked through his narrative account of Wyatt's rebellion Proctor then uses the final third of his work to stress the meaning of the preceding text. This section of the text is, in effect, a history lesson, an attempt to control the meaning of the events that Proctor has recorded. It is as though he is unsure or even doubtful whether his readers are capable of properly understanding his text. The first part of this concluding section is entitled, ' An earnest conference with the degenerates and seditious, for the search of the cause of their greate disorder'. One should not be misled, however, by this title into thinking that this text is a dialogue. It takes the form of an address from Proctor to the rebels, and in particular to Wyatt. In a sense the writer is at this moment creating the speech that should have been, and was not, shouted at Wyatt when he first issued his proclamation in Maidstone. However this is not enough to satisfy Proctor's anxiety over how his work will be understood. As the peroration of his 'conference' with the rebels Proctor brings on Englande to confront them with the cost of their deeds.

> O Englande Englande, if thou hadest wordes to speake as thou hast greife to co[m]playne. If thou couldest as well strike out eares with thy lamentable voice, as thou doest perce oure heartes with thy great and incomparable sorowes, wouldest thou not, if sobbinge teares letted not thie utteraunce, speake in this sorte and these wordes?[70]

Proctor's Englande shares many characteristics with Udall's Respublica and John Bale's Widowe Englande. In all these texts a feminine figure representing the English commonwealth is deployed as a voice of supplication. The use of this trope by these writers serves a number of polemical aims. It allows the articulation of a voice of the people in a way that avoids the potentially radical move of having them speak for themselves; it stresses the disordered nature of the times under discussion by implying that they are sufficiently desperate for such an aberrant figure to have a place within the public sphere; and it allows the creation of an effective dichotomy between the true voice of the commonwealth and the siren voices of its corrupters.

In Proctor's text a comparison is being drawn between the figure of Heresy and that of Englande. One needs to be careful, however, not to collapse Mary Tudor herself into this allegorical figure. Englande asks the rebels:

---

[70] Proctor, *The historie of wyattes rebellion*, M.ii(v)–M.iii.

> Be you so unwise to thinke that your malice towardes her [Mary]
> toucheth onelye her person, and not me, onelye molesteth her
> [and] not me? O you wicked children, if I may nowe call you
> children ...[71]

Englande then goes on to accuse the rebels of being responsible for her
present dishevelled and decayed state.

> You haue been the occasion, at the least, the mischiefe, whiche you
> with mischiefe striue nowe to defende, that these manye yeres I
> haue lost manye and diuerse of my liuelye and sounde membres,
> being cruelly cut from my politike bodie, and haue also susteyned
> the greate contempt and breache of godlye and wise orders deuised
> for preseruation of mine estate, and conseruation of my membres
> in their dewe and ordinarie course.[72]

Even this level of rhetorical framing, however, is not enough to satisfy
Proctor's desire to ensure that his text is properly understood. Finally
Englande brings on a Scottish nobleman to reinforce her accusations
against the rebels.

> I speake thus in this sorte not as a Scotte to an Englishe man, but
> forgetting al priuate quarrels as one christian to another, lamenting
> in my heart to behold the wretched condition and present face of
> this your [Englande's] realme ...[73]

Having been given this endorsement Englande returns to her theme and
recounts how

> as I was example to the whole worlde of all disorder, impietie and
> heresie: so now by her [Mary's] ministery and authoritie, he [God]
> meaneth mercyfully to cure and heale my mangled bodye, to repayre
> myne abased state, to restore my good and wholsome lawes, to
> reforme my disordered membres.[74]

Having used these various fictional voices to press home his argument
Proctor returns to his own narrative persona to conclude the work
with a final call for the rebels to repent and to return to 'better
gouernaunce'.[75] During the course of this final section Proctor has
used three authorial voices, Englande, Scotte and polemicist, in an
attempt to contain and control the meaning of the preceding narrative. The relationship between this section and his narrative history is,
however, problematical. If the history of Wyatt's revolt illustrates
through its failure the sinful and hopeless nature of rebellion why is it

---

[71] Ibid., M.iii(v).
[72] Ibid., M.b–M.b(v).
[73] Ibid., M.b(1v)–M.b(2).
[74] Ibid., M.b(2v).
[75] Ibid., N.ii.

necessary to spend so much time at the end of the text repeating and emphasizing this lesson?

Such a question, however, fundamentally misses the point of Proctor's text for it is precisely the need to continue the history lesson that this text demands. Proctor's performance of the three authorial voices of Englande, Scotte and veritas-producing historian advertises that he is ideally suited to give this vital history lesson to the Marian public. *The historie of wyattes rebellion* enacts an identical claim to authority to that produced by John Bale in *King Johan*. Proctor's status as veritas-producing historian is validated by the text's representation of the moment of crisis at which such a person is required as the Marian norm. Proctor's text produces an anxious, fractured image of the Marian regime in order to construct a position for its writer as mediator between the monarch and those forces that symbolically represent the legitimacy of a strong public. The presence of Englande and, moreover, of a Scotte as truth speakers within a Tudor public sphere reflects the continuing state of crisis and the need for a person who can safely mediate the authority they embody. The strong public that enabled Mary's succession is a continuing necessity because of the continuation of its other in the public sphere, and in such a situation the place of writers like Proctor is vital. In mid-Tudor texts a godly monarch always seems to need a veritas-producing historian, a person whose texts reflect and enact this very claim to cultural authority.

Miles Hogarde and Marian spiritual history

To talk of the historical works of Miles Hogarde is, in a sense, a misnomer. Hogarde's dream poems, *The assault of the sacrament of the Altar*[76] and *A Treatise entitled the Path waye to the towre of perfection*,[77] announce the failure of history or historical knowledge to add anything to faith while simultaneously using history to sustain this argument. Hogarde denies the status of history to add anything to faith and produces historical texts to prove his point.[78] However, it is poten-

---

[76] Miles Hogarde, *The assault of the sacrame[n]t of the Altar* (London, 1554), STC 13556.

[77] Miles Hogarde, *A Treatise entitled the Path waye to the towre of perfection* (London, 1554), STC 13561.

[78] This potentially paradoxical structure is repeated by the articulation in Hogarde's texts of the assertion that only priests should engage in debate over matters of belief in a text written by a layman; laymen have no place in debates over matters of faith as this text by a layman proves. Despite the apparent paradoxical nature of this line of argument, however, Hogarde's use of it replicates that of Thomas Hoccleve in his

tially reductive, and misleading, to highlight such apparent paradoxes. Hogarde adopts a radical position that not only engages in a polemical attack on Protestantism but extends this critique into the very form of their polemic. His texts, in their insistence on the status of reading as an act of faith, as a lived experience, are diametrically opposed to the anti-allegory, anti-imagery, polemic of much Protestant writing.[79] They articulate a view of the relation between meaning, image and reading incompatible with, for example, Robert Crowley's iconoclastic literary critical advice that in order to correctly understand the vision of Piers Plowman one needed to, 'breake the shell of the nuttte for the kernelles sake.'[80]

Hogarde's poetry contains a holistic view of God's relation to the world based on an understanding of reading as an act of faith. For Hogarde Protestantism, as a denial of this true faith, produced and required a form of textual analysis that inevitably led to the tearing apart of texts. In these terms Hogarde's work can be seen as part of a Marian cultural movement deliberately attempting to return to pre-1530 textual forms and poetics.[81] A notable aspect of this programme is the popularity during Mary's reign of the work of the early Tudor poet Stephen Hawes. In an 'Address to the Reader', not found in the earlier, pre-Marian, versions of Hawes's dream allegory, *The Pastime of Pleasure*, the relation between this holistic poetics and a return to a

---

fifteenth-century anti-Lollard poem, 'Address to Sir John Oldcastle', in which the writer argues that all discussions of faith should be left to priests, and produces his own translations of St Augustine to prove the point. See Thomas Hoccleve, 'Address to Sir John Oldcastle', in *Hoccleve's Works: The Minor Poems*, ed. Frederick J. Furnivall and I. Gollancz (EETS e.s. 61 & 71, London, 1970), pp. 8–24. For an interesting, albeit brief, discussion of Hoccleve's text and the cultural pressures that it reflects see Nicholas Watson, 'Censorship and cultural change in late-medieval England: vernacular theology, the Oxford translation debate, and Arundel's Constitutions of 1409', *Speculum*, 70 (1995), pp. 822–64.

[79] John N. King discusses briefly the traditional nature of Hogarde's poetry and its antithetical relation to the style of mid-Tudor Protestant verse. See J.N. King, *English Reformation Literature: The Tudor Origins of the Protestant Tradition* (Princeton, 1982), pp. 216–17.

[80] Robert Crowley, 'The Printer to the Reader', *The Vision of Pierce Plowman, nowe the seconde tyme imprinted by Roberte Crowlye* (London, 1550), STC 19907, *.ii(v). For Crowley's understanding of *Piers Plowman* and the way this poem was appropriated by Lollards and Protestants see John N. King, 'Robert Crowley's editions of *Piers Plowman*: A Tudor apocalypse', *MP*, 73 (1976), pp. 342–52; David Lawton, 'Lollardy and the "Piers Plowman" tradition', *MLR*, 76 (1981), pp. 780–93.

[81] For example Hogarde, in a move that David Lawton has suggested is typical of fifteenth-century poets, often opens his texts with a declaration of his own inadequacy as a writer. See David Lawton, 'Dullness and the fifteenth century', *ELH*, 54 (1987), pp. 761–99.

pre-Reformation state is made explicit.[82] This address opens by declaring that men naturally desire to spend their days in 'pleasure and delectable pastimes'. It goes on, however, to comment that:

> And yet neuerthless by the secrete inspiracion of almighty God (all men in general) so insaciately thirsteth for the knowledge of wisdome and learnyng, that some for the very earnest desire therof (though nature grudgeth) cease not to spend their dayes and houres, with such co[n]tinuall and importune trauayle in sekynge the same, that hauyng no regarde to the ouer pressyng of Nature, ... , do sodainely bryng forth their owne confusion. Some contrariwise ... beyng discomforted wyth painefull [and] tedious study, rather chose to be drowned in the stinkyng floude of ignoraunce, ...[83]

This Address presents its reader with a choice between ignorance and an insatiable desire for knowledge that will almost inevitably lead to heresy.[84] There is, however, a third option and that is ' to sayle (wyth a by wynde) into the pleasaunt Islande of wisdome and science ' – *The Pastime of Pleasure*.[85] The writer of this text claims that by reading Hawes' poem 'thou mayest easelye fynde (as it were in pastyme) wythout offence of nature that thyng ... whiche many great clarkes wythout great paynes and trauayle ... coulde neuer obteyne ... ' .[86] This Address draws a clear relation between the Hawes' poem, its status as an allegorical text demanding a specific kind of almost non-interpretative reading, and its ability, effortlessly, and without danger of heresy, to produce wisdom in its reader. The poetics expressed in this Marian understanding of *Pastime* are identical to those Hogarde advocates in his poems: the need to read with faith in order to understand the totality of the text, surface and depth. Hogarde's poems claim to be meaningful only when read with a faith that is beyond any historical or social boundaries – one that takes precedence over reason and knowledge.[87] In the process of advancing

---

[82] Ironically while this Address asserts even more rigorously than the original versions of *Pastime* the status of Hawes's text as containing its own glosses and guides to reading, it does not include the wood-cuts that were an essential part of the poem. Indeed none of the Marian editions of *Pastime* reproduce all the wood-cuts found in the original editions. One can perhaps see in this failure the effects that twenty-five years of iconoclasm had had on Tudor culture and its appreciation of the printed image.

[83] Stephen Hawes, *The Pastime of Pleasure* (London, 1554), STC 12950, *.iii.

[84] This Address's critique of those who actively strive to acquire knowledge, and its advocacy of a form of passive reading, draws on a similar understanding of the proper place of the individual in the process of interpretation as that advanced by James Brooks in his *A sermon very notable, fructefull and godlie*.

[85] Hawes, *The Pastime of Pleasure*, *.iii.

[86] Ibid., *.iii(v).

[87] In the process Hogarde explicitly aligns his polemical position with that of Reginald Pole as articulated in the latter's *Defence of the unity of the Church*. This text is a

these claims Hogarde's texts implicitly claim an authoritative position for their author that transcends the norms of mid-Tudor culture given Hogarde's status as an artisan.[88] It is Hogarde's faith that gives him the right to speak in public, and it is this faith that his poems are written to celebrate and defend.

In his text, *The Displaying of the Protestants*, Hogarde compares the living Spirit of God embodied in the Catholic view of tradition with the dead word of the Protestants. He writes:

> The maker myndes to mende eche mys
> That talke and tyme hath bred,
> Of heresies, and errors great,
> That fansies late hath fed.
>
> Which so with witte and wyll haue wrought
> As wronge hath wrested right,
> From frutefull faith, to fruteles wordes,
> And quenched vertue quyght.
>
> Belefe is brought to talke of tongue,
> Religion rackt amis
> Open praier, lyp labour cald,
> Fasting folysh fondnes,
>
> Prelacy is popishe pompe,
> Vertuous vowes are vaine,
> Ceremonies curious toys,
> Priesthod popery plaine.[89]

---

stunning attack not only on Henry VIII's policies towards the Church, but also on the whole theoretical basis of the Royal Supremacy and the Tudor Church-state. Pole rejects any role for reason in the running of the Church:

> All things that are contained in the leading dogmas of the Church, my Prince [Henry] are above reason ...

Instead he insists absolutely on the authority of the living tradition of the Church over the dead words of silent books.

> The dogmas of the Church ... and the decrees of the Church should be preferred by weight of authority to all writing and all dogma.
> ...
> Do you [Henry] think the truth should be sought from silent books always offering material for contention for man's ingenuity, rather than from the agreement of the Church that never lacks the Spirit of God?

Pole, *Pole's Defence of the Unity of the Church*, pp. 305, 326. and 327.

[88] Crowley made much of Hogarde's non-magisterial status at one stage producing the hilarious pun 'Hog-herd' to stress his opponent's relatively lowly social standing. See Martin, *Religious Radicals in Tudor England*, p. 98.

[89] Hogarde here defends almost all the main forms of religious practice that were the main targets of Protestant critique. The one that he omits, penance, is the central topic of

In these verses Hogarde constructs an image of heretical language as empty, disordered and distorting identical to that produced by John Skelton in his poem, *A Replycacion Agaynst Certayne Yong Scolers Adjured of Late*. In the process Hogarde, as Skelton did, is implicitly claiming an important public role for himself as a poet, as one whose language skills make him the ideal person to enact the purgation of heretical discourse from the commonwealth. Hogarde's assumption of this privileged role did, however, also have a positive aspect. As well as attacking heretics Hogarde also set out in his writing, and in particular his poetry, to promote true religious teaching. His poetry seeks to guide its reader between the twin rocks of ignorance and an insatiable desire for knowledge to the pleasant island of true Christian teaching.

In his poem *A Treatise entitled the Path waye to the towre of perfection*, Hogarde represents the journey of the narrator's soul towards perfection through the process of penance. During the course of the poem the concept of penance is explicitly historicized and simultaneously rescued from the historically based attacks of Protestants. As the dream narrator approaches a rugged stone wall he sees in it a gate which he must pass through, but which is guarded by a woman who fills him with dread.

> Who art thou quod I of so great vertue.
> I am quod she perfite confession
> Which doth mannes soule truly renewe.[90]

Confession then goes on to justify her status in historical terms that locate her firmly in the Garden of Eden, at the beginning of history.

> Our lorde which is auctor of all goodnes,
> Ordained me when the first man did sinne,
> Causinge him his faute plainly to confesse,[91]

Accepting her Biblical provenance the narrator then brings up the Protestant rejection of auricular confession. He accepts Confession's authority while still holding doubts over her age.

> Thus I [Confession] am nedefull and also aunciente,
> And therefor I trowe thou wylt me not refuce,
> To alowe the quod I, I am content,
> But yet at thin age somwhat I do muse,
> For some wryt that man of olde did the not use,
> Thou wast made they say in Latrense counsell,[92]

A Treatise. Miles Hogarde, *The Displaying of the Protestants* (London, 1556), STC 13557, unpaginated.

[90] Hogarde, *A Treatise*, D.i(v).

[91] Ibid., D.i(v).

[92] Ibid., D.ii.

His faith is justified, however, because Confession can completely rebut the Protestant argument that she is a corrupt papal innovation.

> Thei are deceiued quod she, which that tale doth tel
> For auncient writters diuerse ther be,
> Which wrot before that councell many daies,
> The whiche for very godly doth alowe me,
> Beinge rygthly used as the doctours saies,
> But that counsell stablisht me, no man denaies,[93]

This episode illustrates the scale of Hogarde's historical vision and its paradoxically essentially ahistorical nature. Confession does have a history in this schema. The actions of the Lateran Council are a historical fact and yet they have no direct bearing on the status of the sacrament. The poem's narrator first believes, then turns to history; a move which is itself entirely motivated by the attacks of the Protestants. For Hogarde the desire to historicize is an inherently suspect one based on a failure of faith. With faith one does not need history.

In *The assault of the sacrament of the Altar* the historical and the heretical become one in opposition to the ahistorical truth of the Mass.[94] This poem is in two parts with the first section providing a detailed polemical defence of the doctrine of transubstantiation, and the status of the priesthood, on the basis of Biblical reference, while the second part tells the history of the various heretical attacks on the sacrament of the altar. In effect it is heresy that produces history and it is reason that, in opposition to faith, leads all the attacks on the sacrament of the altar. Indeed there is a level at which it is precisely the narrator's faith that calls up reason as its other, as that which makes it meaningful.

> On my knees to Christ I kneled by and by,
> And with diuine honour as God in one assence,
> With the father and the holy ghost truely,
> I did him there worship in that mystery.
> Then reason in a corner spied me right soone,
> And calde me Idolater, for that I had done.

---

[93] Ibid., D.ii.

[94] The opposition truth/Scripture versus untruth/history was a common Augustinian inheritance that sixteenth-century Christians shared. R.A. Markus suggests that for St Augustine it was the Fall that made history necessary. He writes:

> But for man's primal sin and fall from the condition of grace there would have been no need for God's saving work. Nor would man's existence in that state, had he continued in it, have been fully historical. Both sacred history in particular and history itself as experienced by men arise from this primal tragedy.

R.A. Markus, *Saeculum: History and Society in the Theology of St Augustine* (London, 1970), p. 10.

> Then, [cry] I to him, why dost thou reproue me
> For geuing honour, where honour is due?
> I would agree, quod he, if I could se,
> But til then, I wyll not thinke it to be true.[95]

It is the implicitly unreasonable act of faith demanded by the doctrine of transubstantiation that motivates the appearance of reason and the launching of attacks on Lady Faith. The text's historical account of these assaults opens with that of Berenganious and works through those of Wycliffe and Luther before reaching that of the Edwardian Churchmen, Cranmer and Ridley. In the process it articulates a relation between truth and reading that privileges the allegorical over the literal. The figure of Lady Faith, whose imagery requires interpretation and understanding on a number of levels, represents truth while her attackers, signified by their bald historical names, are the representatives of untruth. In Hogarde's text truth is located in the allegorical and the ahistorical while untruth resides in the literal and the historical. Given these associations it is inevitable that the text constructs the various assaults on Lady Faith in terms of a conflict between stasis and change, between defence and attack. While Faith and her defenders adopt a purely defensive static posture, one that nonetheless is completely impervious to the various assaults, the attackers are represented as aggressive, changeable and violent.

This structure becomes particularly marked when the narrator of the poem refers to Cranmer's scholastic methodology as exemplified in such works as *A confutation*,[96] to illustrate the fury and the disordering nature of the attack on the sacrament of the altar.

> Then sawe I the cheife byshop [Cranmer] of them all,
> Rushe to the doctours unreuerently,
> And rent out of their bookes in gobetes small,
> Peices for his purpose, which peruersly,
> He chewde with his teeth, and then spitefully,
> Shot them at lady faieth in pellet wyse,
> And beastly did the sacrament despise.[97]

Hogarde's representation of Cranmer's methods deploys them as a sign, a metonym, for the effects of heresy and its violence towards the text of the Church.[98] Like Crowley's view of the proper reading strategy to

---

[95] Hogarde, *The assault*, C.ii(v).

[96] Thomas Cranmer, *A confutatio[n] of vnwritte[n] verities, both bi the holye scriptures and moste auncient autors*, trans. E.P. (Wesel?, 1556?), STC 5996.

[97] Hogarde, *The assault*, E.ii.

[98] Hogarde's text contains a radical attack on Protestantism through its representation of the sacrament of the altar as the allegorical sign that makes sense of, indeed produces, wholeness in the body of the text, and in the entire Christian community. The Mass

adopt towards allegory, texts like Cranmer's *A confutation* are, according to Hogarde, based on a reductive violent attitude to the homogeneity of the Church's teachings, a homogeneity that can only be understood within the context of a prior faith in their unity and truthfulness. Hogarde's texts privilege a form of faithful and truthful reading that Cranmer's scholarly methodology inherently undermines and attacks. Indeed, despite the role of reason in motivating all the heretical attacks on the Mass, the extent to which the assaults are all written as furious, violent and self-evidently unreasonable is clearly ironic. Hogarde's text represents human reason as that which corrupts or distorts the truth and in the process produces the untruth of history. In the process it deploys a neo-Augustinian structure in which history is the field on which man's sinfulness is played out. Without sin there would be no history; without the attacks of heretics there would be no need to write the history of their assaults on the sacrament of the altar. Hogarde's construction of the relation between truth and history therefore, in a curious way, mirrors that of Anne Askewe in the sense that for both these writers the truth was before and outside history. Clearly there are large and important differences between the texts of these two writers, and yet one wonders if their shared characteristic of being not of the public allowed them to produce understandings of the past more radical then those of their magisterial supporters.[99]

At the end of *A Treatise entitled the Path waye to the towre of perfection* the narrator is confronted with a vision of numerous groups of pilgrims trying to make their way to the tower.

> The saw I before me diuers bye wayes,
> In the whiche diuers men diuersly did go
> Making in the way many stoppes and stayes
> Lyke people ouerseene, wandryng to and fro,[100]

Among these crowds of people the narrator sees a group clearly intended to represent all heretics.

> Then sawe I an other great rablement,
> Whiche busseled togither out of quietnes,

---

becomes the site of Christian unity and textual meaning. This strategy illustrates the extent to which Hogarde is drawing on discourses associated with the Mass, and with the festival of Corpus Christi. For a discussion of these discourses, and in particular of the use of the body of Christ to produce images of social cohesion and, at the same time, as a site of social conflict, see Sarah Beckwith, *Christ's Body: Identity, Culture and Society in Late Medieval Writings* (London, 1993).

[99] As I have argued above in Chapter 2, one of the aims of John Bale's glosses on Anne Askewe's words was to make her a part of an authorizing Church history, the validity of which her own testimony had implicitly denied.

[100] Hogarde, *A Treatise*, D.iii(1v).

> Not one of them was with another content,
> Many pathes thei had which I can not expresse
> Going out of that, where they wêt ther progresse
> Of the which eche of them contrariely
> Affirmed to be the right way to the towre hye.[101]

However it is not only heretics who fail to make it to the tower. The narrator comments,

> Then in this thornye way wherin I did go
> I sawe some people walke, but in number smal,
> Alacke quod I for paine, that I see no mo,[102]

Hogarde's stress on the difficult and highly selective nature of the 'thornye' path to the tower of perfection rejects the view implicit in most Marian histories of the Henrician and Edwardian Reformations which invariably stressed that redemption and escape from heresy were open to all loyal subjects. For Hogarde the succession of Mary did not clear the route to the tower of perfection, it simply made an inherently difficult journey slightly less perilous; the pathway to perfection was still one open only to the few, the chosen, the godly.

Hogarde, the Catholic artisan and religious polemicist, is perhaps the true voice of Marian radicalism. In his texts a new, dark, Catholic mysticism can be seen emerging, only to be stifled by the advent of Elizabeth. Hogarde's texts implicitly contain an image of a godly[103] Marian public sphere in which the status of one's faith determines an individual's membership of the public. In Hogarde's texts the private is not driven out of the public sphere by words or the actions of men. There is, and can be, no historical moment at which the public is purged given that in Hogarde's texts the private is in the hearts and souls of people and, as such, can only be fought with the truth, defeated by faith and purged by fire. Hogarde, like his arch enemies the Protestant activists, created an image of a purged public sphere, and of the act of reading, which valued godliness over the social order and which placed faith before reason. This Catholic public sphere embodied the radical move of separating publicness from the political classes and the

---

[101] Ibid., E.i(v).

[102] Ibid., E.ii.

[103] The use of the word 'godly' in this passage requires some explanation given its more normal use to refer to those in the Elizabethan Church who wanted to continue the Reformation after the settlement of 1558. The term godly is used here quite deliberately to illustrate that despite the fundamental doctrinal differences between such men as Foxe and Hogarde their relation to the orthodoxy of their day and the subject position that this relation led them to adopt was remarkably similar. The piety and radicalism of godly Catholics marked them out from their fellow Catholics just as surely as that of godly Protestants marked them out from their fellow Protestants.

polity. Hogarde, as did a fellow mid-Tudor historian, John Foxe, ultimately placed godliness before publicness.

The texts that this chapter has addressed adopted different strategies in
order to produce meaningful accounts of the Henrician, Edwardian and
Marian Reformations. However they were all, at one level, written to
enact and celebrate the escape from a heretical, disordered past. This
escape might have been partial and compromised but it was nonetheless
real and potentially lasting. Perhaps not many more years needed to
have passed since the veil had been lifted for its shadow to disappear
from the face of truth. Perhaps a sorrowful past was making way for a
joyful future.

Miles Hogarde at the end of *The assault of the sacrame[n]t of the
Altar*, pointed to the failure of the Edwardian attack on the Mass as
proof that the judgement of history had gone against heresy. He argued
that while the Protestants might deny the truth of Scripture they could
not ignore the facts of history. Bale makes an identical claim in *The
Actes of Englyshe Votaryes* writing that:

> I haue ... thought it best, seing they [the papists] regard not the
> sacred Scripture, to lay before them theyr abhomynable practyses
> and examples of filthines, by their own lege[n]ds, Chronicles, and
> sainctes liues, that al men may know what legerdemaines they haue
> used, and what lecherous liues they haue led here in Englande
> sence the worlds beginning.[104]

The papists reject the truth of Scripture so Bale claims he will confront
them with an alternative truth of their untruths drawn from their own
historical texts. Hogarde repeats this polemical strategy at the conclusion of *The assault of the sacrame[n]t of the Altar*. In a polemical move,
often seen as inherently Protestant, Hogarde argues that while the
heretics might reject the truth of Scripture they cannot deny that of
history. He writes:

> But sith as I do say before,
> That James and Paule they do deny,
> And by Christes wordes to passe nomore,
> Then they do now, no cause se I,
> To meruaile though they say I lye,
> And only dreame all that I tell,
> Though first and last, they knowe full well.

---

[104] John Bale, *The first two partes of the Actes or unchaste examples of Englyshe
Votaryes, gathered out of theyr owne legendes and Chronicles* (London, 1560), STC
1274, Part I, A.iiii(1).

Cheiflye they knowe whiche learned be,
That these assaultes hath trulye been,
As for the laste, all we did see,
Tyll God did sende our noble quene,
Which nowe wyll haue as hath been seene,
The christen faieth truely confest,
As Gods worde hath it plaine exprest.[105]

A poem which denied the place of history in matters of faith turns to the immediate past to conclude its argument. And yet it was not the past but the future that was to determine the truth of Hogarde's history, a future in which Hogarde's truth became John Foxe's lie and his heretics the Elizabethan writer's martyrs. As the final entry in Robert Parkyn's 'Narrative of the Reformation' illustrates, the sorrowful for Marian historians was not in the past but in the future; one veil had been lifted but another was about to fall.

This gratius Qweyne Marie continewally preserving & maytenynge wholly Churche att laste departtide this transitorie lyffe in the 6 yeare of her reigne, anno domini 1558.[106]

---

[105] Hogarde, *The assault*, E.ii(1v)–E.ii(2).
[106] Robert Parkyn, 'Robert Parkyn's narrative of the Reformation', ed. A.G. Dickens, *EHR*, 62 (1947), pp. 58–83, p. 83.

CHAPTER FOUR

John Foxe and the Writing of History

Now if men commonly delite so much in other Chronicles which entreate onely uppon matters of policy, and reioyce to behold therin the variable euentes of worldly affaires, the stratagemes of valiant captaines, the terror of foughten fields, the sacking of Cities, the hurly burlies of Realmes and people. And if men thinke it such a gay thyng in a common wealth to commit to history such old antiquities of things prophane, and bestow all their ornamentes of wyt and eloquence in garnishyng the same: how much more then is it meete for Christians to conserue in remembraunce the liues, Actes and doings, not of bloudy warriours, but of mylde and constant Martyrs of Christ, which serue not so much to delight the eare, as to garnish the lyfe, to frame it with examples of great profite, and to encourage men to all kinde of Christian godlynes?
John Foxe, 'To the true Christian reader, what vtilitie is to be taken by readyng of these Historyes', *Acts and Monuments* (London, 1570) p. *iii[1]

John Foxe's historiographical endeavour is based on a desire to radically rewrite history and to alter its heroes and stories. Foxe argues that while men may be happy to read about the acts of princes and about the rise and fall of empires, a Christian should read history not for pleasure but as an aid to leading a godly life. In particular Christian history should privilege the testimony and example of the members of Christ's invisible but true Church. Foxe asserts that it is the memory of Christ's humble martyrs, the excluded or silenced of traditional history, that should have pride of place in Elizabethan culture. He writes:

me thinks I have good cause to wish, that like as other subiectes, even so also Kings and Princes, which commonly delite in heroicall

---

[1] The two editions of John Foxe's text that this chapter is concerned with are, *Actes and Monuments of these latter and perilous dayes, touching matters of the Church, wherein ar comprehended and described the great persecutions and horrible troubles ... Gathered and collected according to true copies and wrytinges certificatorie, as wel of the parties them selues that suffered, as also out of the Bishops Registers, which wer the doers therof* (London, 1563), STC 11222. and *The Ecclesiastical History, Contaynyng the Actes and Monumentes of Thynges passed in euery Kynges tyme in this realme especially in the Church of England principally to be noted* (London, 1570), STC 11223. To avoid unnecessary footnotes references to these texts will be given in the body of the chapter.

stories, would diligently peruse suche monumentes of Martyrs, and lay them alwayes in sight, not alonely to read, but to follow and would paint upon their walles, cuppes, ringes [and] gates. For doubles such as these, are more worthy of honour then an hundreth Alexanders, Hectors ... (Ibid., p. *iii.)

Foxe claims that the symbolic space traditionally occupied by classical gods and heroes should be filled with pictures and texts that record the testimony of Christian martyrs. He produces an image of a public sphere whose *telos* is the production and valorization of texts like *Acts and Monuments*, a public sphere that is continually invigorated and purified by the symbolic presence of the Marian martyrs at its centre. In 1563 Foxe constructs the Marian martyrs as embodying the past, the present and the future of the Elizabethan regime. He makes them the meaning of Elizabeth's reign.

This chapter is not an attempt to produce a new reading of Foxe's entire corpus of writing. Nor is it intended to add to the already excellent work undertaken by historians on Foxe's accuracy, his use of sources, or his religious beliefs.[2] The aim of the first section of this chapter is the more modest one of examining the 1563 edition of *Acts and Monuments* as a text in its own right by looking at the way it produces historical meaning. The second part of this chapter will then go on to analyse a small number of exemplary changes and revisions made to the text of *Acts and Monuments* during the period 1563 to 1570. The polemical thrust of this chapter is that rather than discussing a non-existent complete version of Foxe's work, the text of *Acts and Monuments*, one should be examining a number of different, discrete texts. In 1563 *Acts and Monuments* is a prophetic text, aimed at the public and confident of its effect on the public sphere, while in 1570 it has lost confidence in the course of history, in its role in the public sphere and in the public as a whole. In 1563 *Acts and Monuments* constructs itself as within the public and as part of the public sphere, in 1570 it addresses itself to a public and a public sphere.

---

[2] See Richard Bauckham, *Tudor Apocalypse* (Oxford, 1978); Catherine Randall Coats, *(Em)bodying the Word: Textual Resurrections in the Martyrological Narratives of Foxe, Crespin, de Beze and d'Aubigne* (New York, 1992); Katherine R. Firth, *The Apocalyptic Tradition in Reformation Britain: 1530–1645* (Oxford, 1979); W. Haller, *Foxe's Book of Martyrs and the Elect Nation* (London, 1963); John R. Knott, *Discourses Of Martyrdom in English Literature, 1563–1694* (Cambridge, 1993); J.F. Mozley, *John Foxe and His Book* (London, 1940); V.N. Olsen, *John Foxe and the Elizabethan Church* (Berkeley, 1973); Helen C. White, *Tudor Books of Saints and Martyrs* (Madison, 1963); Warren Wooden, *John Foxe* (Boston, 1983).

Anticlericalism, religious reform and history, 1563

When in 1563 Foxe produced the first English edition of *Acts and Monuments* it was not the first attempt to write a history of the persecutions of Mary's reign. Thomas Brice and Robert Crowley, two other Edwardian survivors of the Marian persecution, had already produced historical accounts of Mary's reign. Indeed the 1563 edition of *Acts and Monuments*, like Brice's and Crowley's texts, can be read as part of the swan-song of a radical Edwardian Protestantism temporarily reinvigorated by Elizabeth Tudor's succession, a radicalism that was confident in its message, the rightness of its cause and in the inevitable victory of the Word of God. This confidence, however, was already out of date by 1563. The assumption contained in the 1563 edition of *Acts and Monuments* that the inevitable result of Elizabeth's succession would be the complete and radical reform of the English Church was not one shared by the queen[3] or by many of her leading advisers. Indeed while the Elizabethan religious settlement certainly did return the English Church to the Protestant fold it also embodied a potentially extreme Erastianism[4] fundamentally at odds with the agenda of such godly Protestant writers as Foxe or Crowley. The Elizabethan religious settlement holds a unique place in the history of the English Reformations as the only one to be enacted exclusively by lay people. As John Guy has commented:

> The Acts of Supremacy and Uniformity ... imposed religious change without a single churchman's consent, making constitutional history. Whereas many bishops had supported the Crown during the 1530s, the Elizabethan settlement was enacted by laity alone.[5]

This result, while at one level being the effect of opposition to the proposed settlement by the bishops in the House of Lords, also reflects the kind of anticlericalism[6] embodied in such texts as *A Speciall grace*,

---

[3] The nature of Elizabeth's religious beliefs is open to debate. However, as Andrew Pettegree points out, most contemporary observers were in no doubt that her succession was 'a golden opportunity for Protestantism, and a disaster for Catholicism'. Andrew Pettegree, *Marian Protestantism: Six Studies* (Aldershot, 1996), p. 137.

[4] This Erastianism was, however, itself a source of conflict between Parliament and Elizabeth. Patrick Collinson points out that 'Nothing made the queen less Erastian than the Erastianism of the House of Commons'. *The Religion of the Protestants: The Church in English Society, 1559–1625* (Oxford, 1988), p. 5.

[5] John Guy, *Tudor England* (Oxford, 1991), p. 262.

[6] For two very different views of the status of anti-clericalism during the sixteenth century, and its role in the English Reformations, see A.G. Dickens, *The English Reformation* (London, 1989), pp. 316–25, and Christopher Haigh, 'Anticlericalism and the English Reformation', in Christopher Haigh (ed.), *The English Reformation Revised* (Cambridge, 1992), pp. 56–74.

appointed to haue been said after a banket at Yorke, upo[n] the good nues and proclamacion thear, of the entrance in to reign ouer us, of our soveraign lady Elizabeth.[7] This text amounts to an attack on all clergymen, Protestants and Catholics. It asks:

> And why, [and] why, I pray ye, all these their merveilous persecutions, cruelties, [and] tyra[n]nies? But onely (as I said) for the self same doctrine that thei afore had taught us the[m]-selues.[8]

However, while this question may appear to be Protestant in the sense that it is criticizing the Marian clergy for persecuting people for holding beliefs they themselves had enforced during Edward VI's reign, a subsequent question appears to be articulated from a Catholic position.

> Who taught us to pluck images out of churches for dout of idolatrie?[9]

Indeed the main polemical point of this text is that the clergy as a whole are constantly changing the teaching of the Church, and persecuting those who fail to follow their dubious lead. The opening section of *A Speciall grace* claims that the most noticeable thing about the clergy's behaviour at the opening of Mary's reign was their desperate desire to win back Church lands from the laity. The writer of this text, referring to Mary's relatively generous treatment of the Church in financial terms at the time of her succession, comments that:

> And yet this great profusion of their Prince, did so samlli serue their hu[n]gri guts as like storuen tikes, [that] wear never conte[n]t with more then inough, at all their collacions, assembles, and sermones, never lind yellyng and yalpyng, in pursuit of their pray: Restore, Restore.[10]

Finally this text concludes with the hope that under Elizabeth the country will see the 'quenchyng of the Clergies execrable thirst of tyranny, reduction of them to the knowledge of the[m]selues and to a woorshipful estate after Gods lawe moste meetest for them ... '.[11] *A Speciall grace* tars all clergy, Protestant and Catholic, with the same brush. Although it is clearly written from the perspective of those who profited from the sale of Church lands it does not spare Protestant clergymen from its critique of the effects of religious change in the

---

[7] *A Speciall grace, appointed to haue been said after a banket at Yorke, upo[n] the good nues and proclamacion thear, of the entrance in to reign ouer us, of our soveraign lady Elizabeth* (1558), STC 7599.

[8] Ibid., C.b(2v).

[9] Ibid., d.ii.

[10] Ibid., a.iiii(2).

[11] Ibid., e.b(2).

period 1540–58. Ironically, given the historical commonplace that this period saw a fundamental shift of power away from the clergy and the Church to the monarchy and the gentry, *A Speciall grace* represents this period as one in which clerical power and interference in lay concerns had grown and had therefore become increasingly unacceptable.[12]

This critique of the role of the clergy, Protestant and Catholic, is also reflected in the openly pro-Elizabethan settlement text *The declaracyon of the procedyng of a conference, begon at Westminster the laste Marche*.[13] In this account of the Westminster Conference the role of the Protestant opponents of the Catholic disputants is far less important than the latter's failure to obey the rules of the conference, and by implication the commands of the monarch.[14] Indeed the three propositions that this text claims were to be discussed at the conference, while undoubtedly being primarily designed with the polemical aim of forcing the Catholic disputants to argue on their opponents' chosen ground, are also potentially anticlerical. The propositions were:

1. It is against the worde of god, and the custum of the auncient church, to use a tong unknowen to the people, in common praier, and the admynistration of the sacramentes.
2. Euery church hath authoritie to appoint take away [and] change ceremonyes and ecclesiastycall rites, so [the] same be to edificacio[n].
3. It cannot be proued by [the] word of god, that ther is in the Masse offred up a Sacrifyce for the quicke and the dead.[15]

If one accepted all three of these propositions one would produce an understanding of the clergy as teachers, speaking the same language as the laity and implicitly occupying a similar relation to the Word of

---

[12] *A Speciall grace* can be read as at one level supporting Haigh's suggestion that 'Anticlericalism … was not a cause of the Reformation; it was a result'. Haigh, 'Anticlericalism and the English Reformation', p. 74.

[13] *The declaracyon of the procedyng of a conference, begon at Westminster the laste Marche, 1559. concerning certiane articles of religion and the breaking up of the sayde conference by default and contempt of certyane Byshops, parties of the sayd conference* (London, 1560?), STC 25286.

[14] In these terms it is interesting to note the differences between this apparently government-inspired account of the Westminster disputation and the almost identical one printed in the 1563 edition of *Acts and Monuments*. Although Foxe's text contains that of the declaration in its entirety it also prints what it claims is the response of the Protestants to the first proposition and a detailed account of the Lord Keeper's debates with the Catholics when they allegedly refused to dispute in the pre-arranged format. For Foxe the teaching of the Protestants, and perhaps the role of the Lord Keeper, is as important as the failure of the Catholics to go along with a disputation ordered by the queen.

[15] Ibid., no pagination.

God as other literate people. One could argue that these three propositions express an understanding of the role of the clergy that relates directly to the desire articulated in *A Speciall grace* that they be reduced to a role 'moste meetest for them'. Constructing the clergy's role in these terms implied a restriction of the clergy's influence and authority in the public sphere to their performance of their pastoral role as teachers. Give them any more than this, *A Speciall grace* implies, and they will be changing religion again, persecuting and demanding their lands back. In particular both these texts represent the behaviour of the clergy, Protestant and Catholic, as disruptive when it is allowed expression in the public sphere. The proper position for the clergy is clearly one in which their role as teachers reduces drastically their status within the public as a whole.[16] Although a public sphere purged of papist influence had long been an aim of Protestant polemicists these texts express a desire to produce one in which no clergyman has any influence or even voice.

There were, however, other texts being produced in this period that contained a very different understanding of the relationship of the clergy, the public sphere and religious authority. Robert Crowley's 'Continuation' to *An Epitome of Cronicles*[17] describes the events of the years 1547–58 in such a way as to emphasize the need for further reform during Elizabeth's reign by denying that the Protestant clergy had any part in the troubles of Edward VI's reign. For Crowley the people responsible for the failure of this regime to complete the process of religious reform, and therefore to prevent the advent of God's wrath in the person of a persecuting monarch, were Northumberland and the court. Crowley writes that after the fall of Somerset the young king:

> was entised to passe time in maskeyng and mumminge. And to that ende there was piked oute a sorte of misrulers to deuyss straunge spectacles in the courte, in the tyme of Christmas to cause the yonge kynge to forgette, yea rather to hate, hys good uncle, who

---

[16] The relation between English Churchmen and the monarchy in terms of the former's right to speak with authority within the public sphere was a source of conflict throughout Elizabeth's reign. Margaret Christian comments that:

> While Elizabeth tended to see the Church as an instrument of policy, the preachers saw secular power as an instrument of the Gospel.

Margaret Christian, 'Elizabeth's Preachers and the Government of Women: Defining and Correcting a Queen', *SCJ*, 24 (1993), pp. 561–76, p. 563.

[17] Robert Crowley, *An Epitome of Cronicles ... continued to the Reigne of Quene Elizabeth by Robert Crowley, Thomas Copper and Thomas Languet* (London, 1559), STC 15217.5.

had purged the courte of all suche outrage, and enured the kynge vnto the exercyse of vertuouse learninge, and hearynge of sermons. This was the high waye, firste to make an ende of the kynges uncle, and after of the kyng hymselfe.[18]

Crowley is distancing here the Protestant endeavour from the regime of Northumberland. Indeed, as this quotation makes clear, there is a level at which Crowley is implying that the fall of Somerset, and not the succession of Mary, was the moment of crisis for English Protestantism. Certainly his later claim that Edward was effectively poisoned by Northumberland reflects this interpretation of the Edwardian period. Crowley writes that:

The sommer folowyng, the kyng wente in progresse into the weste countreye, wherein his yonge affections were fedde by them that were about hym, not withoute great daunger of his lyfe, by outragious ridyng in haukyng and huntyng. Towardes wynter he retourned to London, [and] fro[m] thens he went to Grenewich, wher was prepared matter of pastyme, a sort couterfaited, riding at the tylte, and goodly pastimes at Christmas, tyll the kyng had gotten a cough that brought hym to his ende.[19]

Crowley puts all the blame for the death of Edward on the behaviour of Northumberland and the Edwardian courtiers who plotted to usurp Mary's right to the throne. Crowley argues, however, that, despite the accuracy of the usurpers' claim that Mary's succession would bring a return to popery, God would not allow his truth to be protected by such an obviously unlawful act. He writes:

But God, who wil not haue his truth mayntayned by puttyng heyres from theyr right co[n]founded their wisedom. And by that woman who[m] they wold haue shuldred fro[m] her right, he punished their unsaciable gatherynge of tresure under theyr good kyng. For he so turned the hertes of the people to her [and] against them, that she ouercam them without bloudshed ...[20]

For Crowley the period of Northumberland's rule was one in which courtiers abused their status in order to amass worldly goods, while the court itself became the home of masques, plays and false games. Crowley's account of Edward's reign privileges as proper a court in which the main activities are listening to sermons and the pursuit of virtuous learning. It is also clear from this section of Crowley's text that the sins of which Northumberland and his supporters were guilty were not

---

[18] Ibid., E.eee.2(1).
[19] Ibid., E.eee.2.(1v).
[20] Ibid., E.eee.2.(2).

religious so much as worldly, and that when they tried to ignore the right of inheritance God confounded their plans.

Having described the later half of Edward's reign as a period in which the Protestant reformers were banished from the court, and having represented their opponents as the people who were being punished by God through the advent of Mary, the way is open for Crowley to construct the Marian persecution in explicitly religious terms as the reign of the Antichrist. Crowley comments that after Mary's marriage to Philip and the reception by Parliament of Pole's absolution from the Pope:

> Nowe was the kyng, the quene, and all the commons at a good poynt, and in case mete to procede to the adua[n]cyng of Antichriste, and treadynge Christe under fote in his members, as thei dyd, in that they renued thre statutes for the punisshement of Christes people (whome they call heretikes) and in repealynge statutes made agaynst the apostolike sea of Rome, as they terme it.[21]

From this moment two features dominate Crowley's account of Mary's reign, a listing of all those who died as martyrs and the status of the queen's body.

Crowley's text represents itself as containing a complete and inclusive listing of the victims of the Marian persecution. It achieves this by listing people even when their names are unknown. The text implicitly claims that the material inscription of the names, or at least the time and place of the burning, is important in and of itself. Unlike other chronicles in which a few representative, and well-known, victims might be listed,[22] Crowley's text constructs itself as listing everyone regardless of rank or importance. For example it contains entries as unspecific as:

> The firste of August there was burned at Exceter an olde woman. The. rriiii. of September were burned at Mayefielde, John Hart, Thomas Rauesdall, Nicholas holden, and two other. And the morowe after was bourned at Bristowe a yonge man a glouer.[23]

The implication of history written in this way is that all those who were burnt are of the same status. Crowley's history contains a similar ten-

---

[21] Ibid., G.ggg.i.

[22] For example the 'Catholic' *Chronicle of the Grey Friars of London* contains the following entry.

> Thys yere [1556] was dyvers burnyd in many places in Ynglond. And the xxvii.day of January was burnyd in Smythefelde v. men and too women for gret heryse.

Chronicle of the Grey Friars of London, ed. John Gough Nichols (Camden Society, o.s. 53, 1852), p. 96.

[23] Crowley, *An Epitome of Chronicles*, G.ggg.2(v).

sion to that found in such works as Halle's *Chronicles*, in that at one level it is clearly magisterial[24] while at the same time representing the act of martyrdom as transcending the usual hierarchical distinctions over who is a proper person to be a named historical actor. The effect of Crowley's privileging of these martyrs from outside the acceptable circle of named historical personages is radically to change the meaning of the text to which his final section is only a continuation.[25] In the first two parts of *An Epitome of Chronicles* the focus is on the traditional view of history as providing a set of examples for rulers and magistrates. Within such an understanding of the role of history, recording the fact that an old woman was burnt at Exeter is of little or no meaning. Crowley's text therefore implicitly critiques the chronicle's earlier concentration on the deeds and affairs of monarchs and suggests that a new kind of history, with different events and people as its principal concern, needs to be written. In effect this section of *An Epitome of Chronicles* advocates a history in which the determining principle of selection is the status of a person's religious beliefs and their place in the playing out of God's will on earth.

It is for this reason that the other main focus of Crowley's history of Mary's reign is the queen's body and the phantom pregnancies that she experienced. Crowley uses the image of these failed attempts at conceiving a child as a metaphor for the sterility and corruption of the Marian regime. In doing this Crowley is drawing on an understanding of the Mass as a failed or corrupt moment of liminality and relating it to an image of the body politic through an emphasis on the queen's physical body and her failure to conceive. Perhaps not surprisingly Bale is an exemplary user of this construction of the Mass. In his 'Epistle Dedicatory' to Elizabeth Tudor's *The Glass of the Sinful Soul* Bale writes:

> A priest may every day both beget Him and bear Him, whereas his mother Mary begat Him (bore Him they wold say) but once ... O blasphemous belly-beasts and most idle-witted sorcerers! How idolatrously exalt they themselves above the eternal living God and His Christ![26]

---

[24] Crowley's reputation as a social radical is based on such texts as *The Way to Wealth*. However the social critique contained in this text is entirely conventional in terms of the discourse of publicness, the status of the voices of the public's others and the authorial role that Crowley claimed for himself as mediator of this voice. Robert Crowley, 'The Way to Wealth', in *The Select Works of Robert Crowley*, ed. J.M. Cowper (EETS e.s 15., London, 1872), pp. 129–76, STC 6096.

[25] See above, pp. 10–12, for a discussion of the relation between Crowley's text and Thomas Copper's 1560 version of the same chronicle.

[26] Elizabeth Tudor, 'The Glass of the Sinful Soul', in *Elizabeth's Glass*, ed. Marc Shell (Lincoln, 1993), p. 86.

Crowley's emphasis on Mary's failure to conceive a child, and the effects of this failure, is designed to draw on a similar discourse. Of the first rumours that Mary was with child Crowley writes:

> Aboute this tyme, greate preparation was made for the queenes chyldbedde, Mydwiues, rockers, and other sortes of women in great numbre taken into the quenes lodgyng at Hampton Courte and not suffered to come home to their husbandes. Besydes that, great preparation of al thyng pertaynyng to nursery, for it was plainly affirmed out of the mouths of the queenes phisitions, that she was great with a man chylde, and some sayde with two. But in conclusion there was borne neyther manchild nor woman, that could be knowen.[27]

The implication in the final words of this passage is that perhaps Mary did have a child but it was so deformed that it was impossible to determine its sex.[28] The effect of this failed pregnancy is the disruption to the natural order, women taken away from their husbands, and a corruption of the English polity. Crowley goes on to comment that people were punished for not celebrating this non-pregnancy and for saying it was a lie. However:

> after it was manifestlye knowne to be a lye, the people were verie desyrous to se what shulde be borne to the staye of the succession of the crowne, for the whole number of mydwyues and rockers were retayned still at the courte. But at the laste all were sente alwaye, and neyther prince nor princesse borne.[29]

Crowley uses the image of Mary's false pregnancy to illustrate the corrupt nature of the Marian polity in which people are persecuted for saying a lie is a lie. Mary's pregnancy is false but pretends to be the truth and in its pretence reveals its true nature. In an ordered or truthful public sphere the conception and delivery of a royal child would be an occasion for rejoicing and social harmony; in an untruthful, corrupt one like Mary's everything is turned upside down, a false pregnancy produces nothing, or nothing that is truthful, it causes illogical punishments and dissension instead of joy and celebration. Crowley's emphasis on the story of Mary's failed pregnancies serves to indicate the disordered or untruthful nature of her rule. As in the Marian histories of the reign of Henry VIII the appearance of the monarch's physical body, particularly when its corporeality is emphasized, is a sign of political corruption. A public sphere in which a non-pregnancy produces the kind of disor-

---

[27] Crowley, *An Epitome of Chronicles*, G.ggg.h(v).

[28] It is interesting that an identical charge is made against Anne Boleyn in Nicolas Sanders' *Rise and Growth of the Anglican Schism*, trans. David Lewis (London, 1877).

[29] Crowley, *An Epitome of Chronicles*, G.ggg.h(1).

der that Crowley ascribes to Mary's is clearly one in desperate need of reform and purgation.

The final section of Crowley's text asserts the true nature of Mary's reign, the writer's expectations for Elizabeth's rule and the status of the people who had died.

> Thus dyd the Lord of his mercy take from his people his sharpe rodde, wherwith he had duringe the dayes of Quene Mary chastised them, as it may appeere by the noumber of theym that suffered in the tyme of her reigne, which were manye mo in noumber then are in this brefe chronicle reme[m]bred. But god hath theyr name in his boke, and theyr teares in his bottell, and when the number shalbe fulfylled, he will be reuenged uppon the murtherers. The Lord graunt us grace so to walke in his feare, that our vertuous Queene maye continewe with us, and sette forthe Goddes truth, to hys glorye and our saluacion.[30]

This passage asserts that the Marian persecutions should be viewed in the context of the eternal struggle between the forces of good and evil. It suggests that the purpose of history is the recording of the names that are themselves going into God's book of martyrs. In the process this understanding of the role of history valorizes the spiritual over the worldly and changes the place or site of history in the public sphere. While the introductory sections to *An Epitome of Chronicles* constructed history as a protection for rulers and magistrates against flatterers, Crowley's final words conceive of history in far more spiritual terms as the recording of the actions of God and Antichrist. The extent to which such history can also express a magisterial understanding of the naturalness of the social order is highly debatable. If it is godliness that determines one's historical status what place has the magisterial in determining who are, and who are not, appropriate historical agents? One returns to the *gestic* moment of King John's martyrdom in *King Johan*; is this event valorized because John is a monarch or because his name will be entered in God's book?

Thomas Brice's *A compendius regester in metre, conteining the names, and suffryngs of the members of Jesus Christ*,[31] published in 1559, has a tripartite structure that embodies a similar set of concerns over the relation between history and the status of the martyrs. The first section of this text is a conventional dedication and an introduction describing how in mathematical terms the compendious register should be read. This is necessary because Brice provides each martyrdom with a

---

[30] Ibid., G.ggg.3(3).

[31] Thomas Brice, *A compendius regester in metre, conteining the names, and suffryngs of the members of Jesus Christ* (London, 1559), STC 3726.

mathematically precise date. He tells his readers that these figures, and the instructions on how to read them, are 'done (gentle Reader) that thou shouldest understande, the yere, moneth, and day, wherin euerye person dyed (accordynge to the knowledge that I have learned)'.[32] Brice expresses a desire that everyone should take part in his travail, in the production of a list of martyrs and in keeping it at the forefront of their minds, so that the martyrs' sacrifice will remain in the collective, political memory of the public sphere. This intention is made explicit by Brice's insistence that his text is designed to remind Elizabeth of the sacrifice of the martyrs and of who were their persecutors. Brice expressly hopes that his work will be placed in the queen's hands:

> wherein her grace mighte see, what unmercyful ministers had charge over the poore shepe, who, wolvishely, at theyr wylles, deuoured the same, And also what ruyne and decay of her graces subiectes (that myghte have been) they have broughte to passe ...[33]

Brice claims that Elizabeth should feel robbed of loyal subjects by the actions of the clergy who persecuted during Mary's reign. This is a clear polemical move to make the events of the past determinate in the present. Brice's text seeks to make the past the meaning of the present and therefore a continuing determining factor at the centre of the Elizabethan public sphere.

The second section of Brice's text has this aim even more at heart. It consists of the verse catalogue explained in the introduction giving the names of those martyred under Mary.

1555
July
When Bradford, beautified with bliss
With yong John Least, in Smithfield died
When they like brethren, both did kisse
And in the fyre were, truely tried
Whe[n] teares were shed, for Bradfords deth,
We wyshte for our, Elizabeth.[34]

The intention of this section of the text is to provide a tool for the memorizing of the names of the martyrs. At the same time the refrain, repeated at the end of every verse, again makes the polemical claim that there was, and is, a relation between the sacrifice of the martyrs and Elizabeth's succession. The use of the word 'our' to designate the monarch in this context amounts to an attempt to appropriate Elizabeth, and the meaning of her monarchy, to a religious agenda personified in

---

[32] Ibid., B.iii(v).
[33] Ibid., B.iii(1)–B.iii(1v).
[34] Ibid., C.ii.

the persons of the martyrs. After the advent of Elizabeth's succession the refrain changes and the verses take on a panegyric aspect.

> That goddes treu word, shall placed be
> The hungrie soules, for to sustaine
> That perfite love, and unitie
> Shalbe set in, their seate agayne
> That no more good me[n], shalbe put to deth
> Seeing God hath sent Elizabeth.[35]

At one level these final verses are a conventional pæan to Elizabeth. They also express, however, an understanding of who are 'good men' and of what their 'goodness' consists. The implication is that the combination of good men, the creation of unity, the advent of God's word and Elizabeth's rule are causally linked. It is not Elizabeth, as monarch, who will produce the hoped-for restoration of peace and unity, but God working through her in order to ensure that no more good men are burnt. As in Crowley's text, the polemical claim being advanced here is that the meaning of Elizabeth's succession relates directly to the suffering of the martyrs and that the queen will, or perhaps even should, make this true; that a true Elizabethan public sphere is one that retains the memory of the Marian martyrs at its centre.

The final section of Brice's text, however, turns away from this insistence on the need to remember the martyrs as named individuals within the public sphere. Indeed given the meaning that the text had just given to Elizabeth's succession the first lines of this final part of the text are strangely contradictory.

> Whe[n] shal this time, of trauail cease
> Which we, with woe sustain:
> Whe[n] shal the daies, of rest [and] peace
> Returne to us agayne.
>
> ...
>
> When shall Jieriusalem reioyce
> In him, that is their kyng:
> And Sion hill, with chereful voyce
> Sing Psalmes with triumphyng.[36]

What does it mean to produce this set of questions after having written verses to Elizabeth which suggested that a return to peace and the end of persecution were a function of her succession? At one level one could argue that this section of Brice's text expresses an uneasiness over the reality of the preceding construction of Elizabeth. At another level,

---

[35] Ibid., D.v(v).
[36] Ibid., D.v(1v).

however, what this section also embodies is a discourse altogether different from that which Brice had earlier associated with the queen. While the remembering of the named martyrs is an important political goal in terms of their continuing presence in the public sphere, this section of the text is drawing on a spiritual discourse akin to that of Askewe's ballad. It embodies a yearning for certainty and unity with the absolute that is incompatible with the agenda of the rest of Brice's text. 'Our Elizabeth' is undoubtedly capable, indeed in her God-given role cannot but be capable, of stopping persecution and restoring the gospel. However she, and the discourse within which this construction Queen Elizabeth is articulated, cannot bring about the resolution looked for in this final section of Brice's text. The final three verses of the text exemplify the potential conflict between the discourse of the world and that of the spirit.

> Whe[n] shal the trumpe, blow out his blast
> And thy deer babes reuiue:
> When shal the Hoare, be headlong cast
> That sought us to depryne.
>
> When shall thy Christ, our kyng appeare
> With power and renowne:
> When shall thy sainces, that suffer here
> Receyve their promest crowne.
>
> ...
>
> When shall the faithful, firmely stande
> Before thy face to dwell:
> When shall thy foes, at thy lefte hande
> Be caste into the hell.[37]

The discourse of godliness embodied in this text, as in Askewe's work, transcends, or at least has no place for, the world and the public sphere. Brice's apocalyptic verses enact an authoritative intervention in the public sphere based on godliness and not publicness. The martyrs are remembered in the second section of the text as that which gives Elizabethan culture its meaning and in the final section this meaning is specifically located outside or beyond history in the Word of God. In a world in which the 'when' of Brice's apocalyptic poem is answered with 'now', the words of his verse martyrology become redundant or are transformed. When the Word of God becomes immanent, enters the world, the martyrs will no longer need to be remembered, their names are already of and in this Word.[38]

---

[37] Ibid., D.v(2v)–D.v(3).
[38] Avihu Zakai comments that:

The intention of Brice's text is that the memory of the martyrs should, and must, be the purpose of the Elizabethan polity, and that in order for Elizabeth's rule to stay true to its God-given meaning it must amount to an embodiment of the cause of the martyrs. This view of the truth of Elizabeth's rule implicitly demands a privileging of the spiritual over the worldly. Clearly there is a level at which such a demand is in direct contradiction to the attitude towards the religious and the clergy embodied in *A Speciall grace*. If an ordered public sphere as constructed in this text is one in which the clergy have been reduced to their proper pastoral, perhaps passive, condition, then what status did such clerical martyrs as John Rogers or John Hooper have? Equally, if the example of these men should be the *telos* of the Elizabethan polity, a public sphere in which their role was not valorized would surely be a corrupt one?

Acts and Monuments in 1563

The 1563 edition[39] of *Acts and Monuments* not surprisingly contains identical themes and polemical strategies to those articulated in the texts of Crowley and Brice. Perhaps more unexpectedly, however, Foxe's text also bears the marks of a similar weariness and even hostility to clerical power to that expressed in *A Speciall Grace*. Foxe's text depicts the act of martyrdom within a narrative that privileges martyrs over and against clergymen and magistrates. Unlike Bale, Foxe positions himself within, not above, the text and creates a space for the testimony of the martyrs that allows it far greater narrative autonomy than that given to Askewe by Bale. In Foxe's text the testimony of the witness bearers to Christ is the narrative motivation, it is the privileged text and the magisterial historian's own words are unimportant in comparison. The 1563 edition of *Acts and Monuments* contains a relatively optimistic attitude to the continuation of Reformation in England on the basis

---

Protestant apocalyptic historiography implied that a point would come when prophecy and history would be irrevocably joined. This was to be the eschatological day of judgement, Christ's second coming, or the millennium.

One could argue that one sign of the advent of this eschatological event would be the symbolic coming together of two sections of Brice's text. See Avihu Zakai, 'Reformation, History, and Eschatology in English Protestantism', *History and Theory*, 26 (1987), pp. 300–318, p. 312.

[39] There were two earlier Latin editions of *Acts and Monuments*. Foxe, however, explicitly constructs his English editions as written within a different discourse and as aimed at a different audience from these more scholarly texts.

of the salutary and exhortatory effect of the words of the martyrs perfectly and lovingly preserved in the reliquary of Foxe's text.[40]

In his 'Dedication to Queen Elizabeth' in 1563 Foxe articulates a number of polemical points that mirror those expressed in *A compendius regester in metre*. Although Foxe notoriously compares Elizabeth with Constantine in this piece,[41] the text as a whole is far from being a simple acclamation of the new queen. Indeed as the piece progresses it becomes clear that it contains a discourse that is at least potentially critical of the Elizabethan regime. For example Foxe draws a parallel between Elizabeth and himself, and Constantine and Eusebius. Foxe goes on to comment on the latter pair:

> In whiche Historie (moste excellent and noble Queene) twoo thynges put me in a variable doubt, whether of these two rather to co[m]mend and extolle: good Emperour, or godly Byshoppe: the one for his Princely proferre, the other for his godly and syncere peticion. The Emperour for his rare and syngular affection in fauouring and furtherynge the Lordes churche, or the Byshoppe in zealyng the publique busines of the Lord, before the priuate lucre of hymselfe. Certes in bothe together may to vs appeare, what all maner estates may learne to knowe: not onelye what in those dayes was done, but also what ought nowe to be followed. *Acts and Monuments* (1563), pp. B.i–B.i(v))

Not only is Foxe not sure which of the two, historian or Emperor is most worthy of praise, he also explicitly relates the lessons of his own history to the authority of that of Eusebius in terms of its status as a manifesto for practical worldly government. The implication of the text at this point is that in a godly polity histories, like those of Eusebius or Foxe, are an integral part of the formulation of the aims and practices of government.[42] Foxe goes on, in a way that would surely have appalled the writer of *A Speciall Grace*, to implicitly criticize the Tudor plunder of the Church, or at least the queen's failure to return some of the wealth and lands stolen over the preceding thirty years.

---

[40] Catherine Randall Coats discusses this aspect of Protestant martyrologies in her study, *(Em)bodying the Word*, p. 6.

[41] Frances Yates discusses the implications of Elizabeth's symbolic pairing with Constantine in *Astraea: The Imperial Theme in the Sixteenth Century* (London, 1975).

[42] In this context one could argue that this text already contains the potentially divisive polemical structure that John Guy has argued was produced as the result of the Admonition Controversy, 1572. Guy suggests that this controversy, and its sequels, created the situation in which the 'far-reaching discovery was made that to argue *for* one form of Church government was to deny the legitimacy of a related form of civil administration'. John Guy, 'The Henrician Age', in J.G.A. Pocock, assisted by Gordon J. Schochet and Lois G. Schwerver, (ed.), *Varieties of British Political Thought 1500–1800* (Cambridge, 1993), pp. 13–46, p. 43.

> In the Emperour ... we beholde howe studiously the Nobilitie in those dayes were set to te[n]der the state and vtilitie of the Churche, and the Ministers of the same: in geuyng to the[m], not in takynge from them ... (Ibid., p. B.i(v))

The 'Dedication' reproduces the message of Brice's text that Elizabeth's succession was an act of God and that therefore for her rule to remain true to itself it needs to continue to fulfil this God-given role. In particular Foxe relates this aspect of Elizabeth's rule to the maintenance and advancement of the Reformation abroad. Foxe writes:

> Here nowe if it were not for suspicion of flatterie, I could recite, not onely what we at home, your natural and louing subietes: but also what ouer forraine Realms abroade haue receiued by your grace, or rather by Gods grace in you: as neyther the Realme of Scotlande, nor yet of Fraunce to this daye wyll or can deny the same. (Ibid., p. B.ii)

For Foxe, as for Crowley and Brice, the relationship between Elizabeth and the ending of persecution is a deterministic one; the fact that the succession and the ending of burnings was simultaneous creates not a causal relationship from one to the other but an equality of meaning. Elizabeth's succession did not lead to the end of persecution but was part of the same God-given happening and as such its meaning remains directly related to the status of this homogenous event. In this understanding of the meaning of Elizabeth's rule there can be no acceptable separation of the godly from the dynastic or political; in the moment of succession all are made one, of the same status and therefore of an equal, continuing validity.

This creates a situation in which Elizabeth's rule should be fundamentally different from that of past monarchs, with the possible exception of her brother. Indeed the latter's reign could be used as a measure of the extent to which Elizabeth was fulfilling her godly role,[43] while her sister's reign could be deployed in a similar dynamic as the other that Elizabeth's rule must not be. It is in this context that Foxe's construction of Mary's reign is of particular interest. Like Crowley, Foxe uses the fact of Mary's false pregnancies as a sign of the corruption at the heart of the English polity. Foxe's use of this rhetorical device is, however, more subtle and far reaching than Crowley's. Foxe interprets the way the political nation and the court reacted to this non-event as a sign of the corruption of both these sites of political power. While Crowley's use of Mary's false pregnancies implied that they corrupted the operation

---

[43] Margaret Aston has recently discussed this Elizabethan deployment of Edward VI in her work, Margaret Aston, *The King's Bedpost: Reformation and Iconography in a Tudor Group Portrait* (Cambridge, 1993).

of the public sphere because of their specific effects, Foxe implies that
they revealed structural problems in the constitution of the public sphere
itself.

Foxe's account of Mary's pregnancy opens immediately after he has
recounted the story of Parliament's submission to Cardinal Pole. Foxe
goes on to recount the acceptance by the council and Parliament of the
truth of Mary's pregnancy. Clearly there is the potential in this structure
for the reader to see a structural similarity between the acceptance of a
restoration of Catholicism and the acceptance, by the same people and
institutions, of Mary's false pregnancy. Foxe then prints a letter he claims
was from the council to Bonner that states Mary is 'quicke with childe'
(*Acts and Monuments*, 1563, p. 1014). This letter goes on to ask Bonner
to instruct his clergy to perform Masses and sing praises for Mary's
pregnancy because 'good hope of certaine succession in the crowne is
geuen unto us, and consequently the great calamites, which (for want of
suche succession myght other wyse haue fallen vpon us, and our prosteritie)
shall by Gods grace be well avoyded ... ' (ibid., p. 1014). Having emphasized the general expectation that Mary was indeed pregnant Foxe does
not return to the story for another forty pages. This is despite the fact
that all his readers will have known that Mary never gave birth. This
creates a textual situation in which Foxe has introduced a theme into the
narrative that implicitly tars all the actions of the Marian public sphere as
suspect. The false pregnancy is left rattling around Foxe's account of the
other events of this year while the reader knows the truth but the text has
not yet articulated it. Mary's false pregnancy embodies a metaphoric
structure in which the corruption of her regime is reflected in the general
public acceptance of the truth of its falseness. The monarch's falsifying
body infects the whole of the public sphere.

Foxe's discussion of the universal acceptance of the truth of Mary's
pregnancy by those constituting the public sphere relates directly to his
discussion of the innate untruthfulness of the Mass, and the doctrine of
transubstantiation, which itself draws on the same discourse of sterility
and stalled liminality that Bale deployed in his construction of papists
as 'belly-beasts'.[44] Foxe's account is placed at the very beginning of

---

[44] The representation of the Mass as a failed moment of liminality expresses a clear
development from earlier anti-clerical attacks on the doctrine of transubstantiation.
While Bale represents the Mass's complete sterility in the image of a man giving birth the
Lollard Margery Backster, in the mid-fifteenth century, rejected transubstantiation on
the grounds that although something does happen during the Mass the result is filthy
and disgusting. Backster claims that having celebrated the Mass, and made their Christs,
the priests 'afterward eat them, and void them out again by their hinder partes filthely
stinking under hedges, wheras you may find a great many such Goddes ... ' (*Acts and
Monuments*, 1563, p. 355).

Mary's reign, before any narrative of the events surrounding the episode of Lady Jane Grey and Mary's succession. Foxe claims he adopts this textual strategy because in the forthcoming section persecution for denying the Mass will be the central theme. He writes that he has decided to 'set forth to the reader the great absurditie, wicked abuse, and perilous idolatory of the Popish masse, declaring how [and] by whome it came in ... ' (ibid., p. 889). Foxe then goes on to discuss the Mass in great detail, in particular emphasizing the arguments of its supporters over its nature, history and even over its name,[45] before concluding:

> or what terme soeuer it be els, either Laten, Siria[n], Doutch, or French: or how so euer els it taketh his appellation, as there is no certainty emonges the[m]selues that most magnify the masse, so it is no matter to us that sta[n]d against it. (Ibid., p. 889.)

This is a typical piece of Foxian historiography in that the implication is that the preceding lengthy discussion is of no real importance or note because its only aim is to show what does not need showing, in this case that the Mass is a 'perilous idolatory'. Although Foxe never makes explicit the link between the status of the Mass as a corrupt, disordered perversion, an inherently stalled moment of liminality that never rises above or beyond the material, and Mary's non-pregnancy, there are clear structural and polemical similarities between the falseness at the centre of Catholicism in the shape of the Mass and that created at the heart of the public sphere by Mary's 'pregnancy'.

Foxe returns later in his narrative to Mary's pregnancy in order to reproduce the polemical point made by Crowley that people were punished for saying it was false, for calling a lie a lie. He prints a version of the Lord's Prayer with lines praising Mary inserted between those of Scripture in order to illustrate simultaneously the corruption inherent in Catholicism and its effect on the public sphere. Having reminded the reader of the prayers that Bonner had asked his clergy to say for the queen's pregnancy Foxe goes on to comment:

> And for so much as prayer is here mentioned for Quene Mary: here foloweth to be sene the Pater noster then sette forth in Englishe meter, compiled or rather corrupted by one W. Forest. Whyche when thou shalt see (good reader) I referre the matter to thy

---

[45] D.R. Woolf suggests that for Foxe 'unity is the watchword of the Reformed, division is that of the Rome'. See D.R. Woolf, 'The rhetoric of martyrdom: generic contradiction and narrative strategy in John Foxe's *Acts and Monuments*', in Thomas F. Mayer and D.R. Woolf (eds), *The Rhetorics of Life Writing in Early Modern Europe: Forms of Biography from Canandra Fedde to Louis XIV* (Michigan, 1995), pp. 243–82, p. 259.

discretion to iudge of these catholikes, what men they are, and how
contrary to themselues, which fynde faulte with the Pater noster,
song in meter in oure churches: and yet they them selues haue
doone the same before, much more worthy of rebuke, whiche not
only haue intermired their own sense with the wordes of the lord,
but also haue so wrasted and depraued the same, that the thyng
which the lord hath set forth for publique and generall petitions,
they haue turned to priuate request. (Ibid, p. 139.)

Foxe here is relating Forest's verses, Mary's phantom pregnancy and the
Catholic support for private Masses in a structure that implies they are
all distinguished by their privateness and untruthfulness. As the effects
of Mary's sterile pregnancy spread so they reproduce and increase corrupt tendencies within the whole Catholic endeavour. A public prayer is
turned into a 'priuate request' and the words of Scripture are used to
flatter the monarch.

At this point, however, Foxe's critique of the effects of Mary's pregnancy and what it implicitly embodies potentially extends beyond the
specific to take in the whole of court culture. Although one of the
poems that Foxe prints as exemplary of the private corrupt texts produced by W. Forest is a paraphrase of the Lord's Prayer, the other poem
he prints at the same time is a standard piece of court panegyric that
would not have looked out of place at the court of Elizabeth, or any
other sixteenth-century English monarch.[46]

> Vouchsafe this day, from sin, and crime
> To gouerne us we praye,
> Our quene graunt here to reygn lo[n]g time,
> And to obserue thy waye.
>
> ...
>
> Thy mercy (Lorde) let on us light,
> As we do trust in thee:
> And saue our Quene both day and nighte,
> In high prosperitie.
>   (*Acts and Monuments*, 1563, p. 1141)

Foxe implies that the situation in which such corrupt poems as Forest's
can be written relates directly to the restoration of Catholicism and to
Mary's false pregnancies. A public sphere in which such texts as Forest's

---

[46] Jane Facey has suggested that 'For Foxe true order was a matter of non-popery. Any
authority, clerical or lay, which lapsed into popery became in some sense illegitimate'.
The implication of Foxe's construction of this kind of courtly poetry as papist is that
court culture was itself popish and therefore illegitimate. See Jane Facey, 'John Foxe and
the Defence of the English Church', in Peter Lake and Maria Dowling (eds), *Protestantism and the National Church in Sixteenth Century England* (London, 1987), pp. 162–92,
p. 182.

were acceptable was for Foxe a potentially corrupt one in which the cynosure of the public sphere was not the worship of God but the lauding, indeed flattery, of the monarch. In this context Foxe's claim that he could not tell who was more worthy of praise, Constantine or Eusebius, was not a simple piece of self-promotion but represented a cultural programme that implied a complete rewriting of the centre and purpose of the Tudor public sphere. To focus one's attention on the martyrs was to not focus it on something, or someone, else. For Foxe, and Crowley, the privileging of the Marian martyrs produced in their texts a corresponding subversion and critique of the central place of the court and by implication the monarch in constructions of the public sphere.[47]

This is not to suggest, however, that Foxe was in any sense a clericalist.[48] Indeed it is surprising to find similar feelings towards the clergy, or perhaps more accurately clerical power, in the 1563 editions of *Acts and Monuments* to those articulated in *A Speciall Grace*. In his discussion of the histories of John Wycliffe and John Huss, Foxe produces a number of significant digressions. He prints what he claims is a 'paraphrase' of a sermon by Wycliffe in which the latter discusses the example of a godly magistrate. This section then continues with the following words:

> But now while that the Princes, do attende and geue eare vnto blinde prophecies, the Byshoppes play the tirauntes. The deuines drowned in ambition. The Prophettes are slayne. The noble menne fall into all kynde of lascivious wantonesse. The magistrates winke at vice unpunished. The common people runeth hedlong unto all kynd of lice[n]cyousnes ... (Ibid., p. 100.)

The nature of the text at this point, however, makes it unclear what the status of these words is. Are they Wycliffe's? Foxe's? or Foxe's

---

[47] Thomas Brice, in his tract, *Against filthy writing and such like delighting*, also attacks court culture. In particular, he criticizes the privileged place Greek and Roman figures occupied within it. Brice writes:

We are not Ethnickes we forsoth, at least professe not so
Why range we then to Ethnickes trade? come back, where will ye go?
Tel me is Christ, or Cupide Lord? doth God or Venus reigne?
And whose are wee? whom ought wee serve? I aske it, answere plaine

Thomas Brice, *Against filthy writing and such like delighting* (London, 1562), STC 3725, no pagination.

[48] Helen C. White suggests that: 'it may be said roughly that the only bishop that seemed good to Foxe was a bishop burned for Reforming principles'. *Tudor Books of Saints and Martyrs*, p. 154. Although White's view is an exaggeration Foxe clearly felt that the role of a bishop should be restricted to that of a teacher and spiritual guide. As such it was almost inevitable that any practising Tudor bishop would fail to match up to Foxe's standards given their role as enforcers of clerical and lay religious conformity.

Elizabethan version of a fourteenth-century sermon? What is interesting is the separation they express between on the one hand the divines and the bishops as corrupt and worldly and on the other the prophets.

A far more significant digression, however, in this section of the text occurs when Foxe discusses the relation between persecution and the Church. In this section Foxe advances the almost Foucaultian view that the persecution of heretics is not the result of their heresy but the effect of the production of religious articles.[49] In a complete reversal of John Bale's earlier position Foxe argues that the production of written accounts of true religious beliefs not only do not guard against heresies, they effectively produce them by making one person's belief another's heresy. Foxe, however, like Bale, prefaces his discussion of these points with an assertion of his personal antipathy to heresies.

> But before I will take this quarrel in hand, I do once again admonishe the, gentle reader, of that which I must oftentimes repeat in thie argument. Firste of all that you do not interpreat any thinge whych shall be here spoken, in suche manner, as thoughe I woulde maintaine anye unproued doctrine: for as I doo not fauoure heretickes, which are heretickes in dede, euen so muche lesse do I not fauoure false Byshoppes. (Ibid., p. 131.)

Despite this disclaimer, however, it soon becomes clear that Foxe is not prepared to accept the right of one group of people to define another as heretics. In particular Foxe criticizes the clergy's persecutory practices.

> Who was the first that brought in amongst Christians, these recantations, faggottes and fire, and these lamentable funeralles by burninge of the liue bodies of menne, under the name of heretikes, who but only this stocke of religious menne, and clergye? (Ibid., p. 131.)

This criticism of the role of the clergy in the process of making people heretics is not, however, a historical point. Foxe explicitly links the production of such Tudor formulas of faith and religious practice as, for example the Thirty-Nine Articles, to this critique, commenting that:

> For if we shuld say the truth, wheruppon commeth it, that the world is so ful of dissention, but only that al thinges are so intricate [with] so many articles, so many censures cautions [and] scole pleas ... (Ibid., p. 134.)

Foxe's radical solution to this problem is to 'require doctrine the whiche should rather bridle the heresies than the Heretikes' (ibid., p. 135). One

---

[49] Thomas S. Freeman has found, in as yet unpublished research, that this section on heresy is largely a translation of a similar discussion in Foxe's two earlier Latin versions of the text and that it is almost certainly his own work. It also fails to appear in any of the subsequent editions of *Acts and Monuments*.

should note that, as he promised, throughout this section Foxe insists on his opposition to heresy.[50] Despite this, however, Foxe's text does contain an understanding of the relationship of an individual's personal faith, heresy and the enforcement of religious orthodoxy that undermines the moral authority for any corporeal punishment of people on the basis of their beliefs. Foxe's view as expressed in this text is that the clergy's proper, indeed Christian response to heresy should be one of preaching and teaching, to attack the heresy not the heretic.[51] The implication of this section is that Foxe, like the writer of *A Speciall Grace*, felt it was unwise, indeed dangerous, to allow the clergy any more power than that they themselves earned through the performance of their pastoral spiritual role.

This attitude to the place of the clergy in the Tudor public sphere as teachers, and not bigoted enforcers of religious conformity, also impacted directly on Foxe's self-understanding as a historian. This is reflected in the structure of the 1563 text and in its construction of its author. The intention of the 1563 edition of *Acts and Monuments* is almost identical to that of Crowley's earlier account of the Marian persecution. Although Foxe was quite capable of taking very large liberties with the testimony of the martyrs,[52] the main emphasis of the text is the moral imperative of materially fixing and preserving their words and acts. This produces a situation in which Foxe makes entries that are almost without detail apart from the fact that a martyrdom took place. For example Foxe writes that:

> A litle before this was bre[n]t at Tunbridge a certain woman, named Jone Polley, much about the time of the burning of M. Bradford of whom I should have made mention before. (Ibid., p. 1249.)

---

[50] Foxe refers to the conservative Henrician bishop John Stokesley when discussing the abusive nature of the persecution of heretics in terms of the clergy's proper role as teachers and not, in Foxe's terms, tyrants. One could argue that this leaves the possibility that it is only against Catholic bishops that Foxe's critique is directed. However this text certainly does not make this point explicit and leaves the clear impression that any attacks on heretics, by any bishop, are unChristian.

[51] This aspect of Foxe's beliefs as expressed in *Acts and Monuments* relates to the strong influence that Erasmus had over the Elizabethan martyrologist. V.N. Olsen comments that, 'Many of Foxe's thoughts on toleration are specifically reminiscent of Erasmus'. V.N. Olsen, *John Foxe and the Elizabethan Church*, p. 199.

[52] See the changes and rewrites that Foxe engaged in when dealing with John Rogers's written account of his examination by Stephen Gardiner below pp. 193–9, and in Joseph L. Chester, *John Rogers: The Compiler of the First Authorised English Bible; The Pioneer of the English Reformation and its First Martyr* (London, 1861). See also Patrick Collinson's seminal article on Foxe's rewriting of Marian examinations, 'Truth and legend: the veracity of John Foxe's *Book of Martyrs*', in *Elizabethan Essays* (London, 1994), pp. 151–77, p. 168.

It is almost as though the text is laying claim to be a reliquary, a depository in writing of those moments of extreme spiritual courage and certitude that Foxe represented the deaths of the Marian martyrs as being. All this entry articulates is the fact of martyrdom. It lacks all other details *except* the one fact that is absolutely vital. Like a relic the text is the material embodiment of Jone Polley's martyrdom that guarantees its continuing efficacy, and, therefore, her status as a witness bearer to Christ. In order to fulfil this role, however, the textuality of the text needs to be obscured or denied to give readers the impression that they are reading an unmediated truthful account of the testimony of the martyrs. It is for this reason that this edition of *Acts and Monuments* constantly constructs itself as a chronicle, as having a mimetic, unproblematic relation to the events that it records. So in the quotation above Foxe feels the need to confess to a lapse in his historiography due to his failure to record Jone Polley's death in its proper chronological place in the text, one that should correspond exactly to its actual one in the past. At the same time the primary aim of Foxe's text, transcending its status as a chronological account of the Marian persecution, is clearly to be an inclusive record of the name of every martyr whose details Foxe had. Like Crowley's text, Foxe's embodies the desire to place the acts and words of the martyrs unembroidered into the public sphere so that their example will inevitably work on the members of the Elizabethan public to produce reform and spiritual renewal.

This creates a situation in which interventions by Foxe himself as the text's narrator have to be carefully negotiated. In the earlier example the intrusion of the authorial voice into the text is meditated by the need to explain a failure of the chronological order. In his account of Bishop Hooper Foxe's interventions are made as a participant in the events that the text is representing.[53] Such moments, however, of authorial intervention often need detailed and convoluted narrative motivation. For example after Foxe has told the story of King John's reign and his struggle with the papacy he goes on to recount the events of the pontificate of Innocent III. After a digression through the story of Francis of Assisi and the creation of the order of the friars Foxe comments that:

> And forsomuche as we haue here entred into the matter of these two orders of Friers, by the [o]ccasion hereof I thought a lyttle by the way to digresse from our story, in reciting the whole cataloge or rableme[n]t of mo[n]ks Friers, and Nunnes, of al sectes, rules, and orders set up and confirmed by the Pope. (Ibid., p. 70(v).)

---

[53] See below, p. 203, for a discussion of this aspect of Foxe's account of Bishop Hooper.

Foxe then lists all the religious orders that he can find in alphabetic order.[54] The digression, however, does not end here as he goes on to comment that:

> Now as I haue reckoned up the names and varieties of these prodigious sectes, it commeth to mind co[n]seque[n]tly to inserte the prophecy of Hildegardis ... (Ibid., p. 71.)

Here, as with Wycliffe's text, the space between the voice of the prophet and Foxe's own authorial persona is blurred by the latter's insistence on the need for this obviously potentially papist text to be suitably glossed. Finally the text returns to its stated intention by recounting the suffering of the Cathars. While the listing of the martyrs provides the text with its explicit narrative motivation, Foxe's polemic against their papist persecutors has to be inserted alongside this narrative in a space created by the deployment of an explicit authorial voice. This voice is ultimately antithetical to the formal and textual conventions of the chronicle genre in which the account of the martyrs is written. Unlike Bale, however, who when confronted with a similar textual problem made Askewe's words the reason for his polemic, Foxe places his polemic specifically in the same textual place, and with the same status, as the papist acts of corruption it discusses. While Bale used Askewe's words to motivate his polemic, Foxe constructs a text in which his words, and their polemical target, are separate from and of a different order to those of the martyrs. Bale's historicization of Askewe makes her speak his language, Foxe's history clears a space for the martyrs to speak.

The 1563 edition of *Acts and Monuments* enacts precisely the programme set out in the 'Dedication' to Elizabeth with which it opened. Its textual motivation is the creation of an unembroidered textual space in which the words and example of the martyrs can be read. Implicit in this text is a relatively optimistic attitude towards the progress of continuing Reformation: one that assumes that having allowed, indeed insisted on, the testimony of the martyrs being heard the effect of their words reverberating through the public sphere will be to inevitably produce the desired reform of the English Church. In the 1563 text the writer's role is simply that of an archivist, a teacher, setting out a lesson to inherently insightful and godly pupils. In 1570 the teacher's estimation of his pupils had changed so drastically for the worse that his methods, material and indeed status had to change. The movement from 1563 to 1570 is one from bright pupils to delinquents and from teacher to preacher.

---

[54] The polemical point here is identical to that Bale made in *King Johan* which contains a similar list; papistry leads to diversity and inappropriate linguistic productivity.

From the prophetic to the apocalyptic, 1563–70

Changes in the title of the text and in the content, although not the form, of the 'Dedication' to Elizabeth are two exemplary instances of the differences between the 1570 and 1563 editions of *Acts and Monuments*.

As has already been suggested, in 1563 Foxe constructs his work as one of compilation, of bringing together the records of the past. So the title of the 1563 edition is *Actes and Monuments of these latter and perilous dayes, touching matters of the Church, wherein are comprehended and described the great persecutions and horrible troubles ... Gathered and collected according to true copies and wrytinges certificatorie, as wel of the parties them selues that suffered, as also out of the Bishops Registers, which wer the doers therof*. In the title to the 1563 edition Foxe stresses his role as a 'gatherer' and 'collector' of 'true copies' and 'writings certificatorie' and completely fails to claim the role of historian or either author. The title of the 1570 edition, *The Ecclesiastical History, Contaynyng the Actes and Monumentes of Thynges passed in euery Kynges tyme in this realme especially in the Church of England principally to be noted*, however, explicitly claims for its writer the role of historian, and for itself the status as history.[55]

The 'Dedication' to Elizabeth retains its distinctive italicized print and the placing of Elizabeth within the C of the first word of the text. However, in 1570 it is the C of Christ not of Constantine. This in itself is a perfect illustration of the shift in emphasis in 1570 towards the spiritual and away from the worldly. Gone from this 'Dedication' is any mention of the state of the English Reformation, or those of France and Scotland. Instead the reader is regaled with the trials and tribulations that Foxe has suffered as a result of publishing the 1563 edition. Gone as well is any notion that *Acts and Monuments* will as a text produce reformation within or through the actions of men. In this 'Dedication' Foxe makes an equation between the status of his history and that of the Bible in terms of the efficacy of both in spreading light in times of darkness.

---

[55] The distinction between a chronicle and a history is discussed in *Carion's Chronicle*, a text Foxe would certainly have known, which comments that while histories contain 'all thynges that are done in one realme', chronicles 'do brefely shewe thynges done, and settyng the order of the tyme before, seme onely to aduertyse the wyse reader, to marke some of the notablest thynges'. This passage also articulates the view that the writers of such chronicles, as defined here, 'ought not to take vpon them the name of History wryters'. *Carion's Chronicle: The Thre Bokes of Chronicles and Carion gathered wyth great diligence of the beste athours: Whereunto is added an appendix by John Funcke*, trans. G. Lynne (London, 1550), STC 4626, C.c.i.

> For as we see what light and profite commeth to the Church by histories in the old tymes set forth of the Iudges, Kinges, Machebeis, and the Actes of the Apostles after Christes tyme: so likewise may it rebound to no small use in the Church, to know the Actes of Christes Martyrs now since the time of the Apostles. (*Acts and Monuments* (1570), p. *ii(v).)

The 1563 'Dedication' ends with a promise by Foxe to protect the words of the martyrs from the inevitable attacks of their, and his, opponents. In 1570 the 'Dedication' ends with Foxe the Old Testament prophet preaching the lesson that history teaches of God's will and power:

> in preseruing his Church, in ouerthrowyng tyrants, in confoundyng pride, in alteryng states and kingdomes, in conseruyng Religion agaynst errours and dissentions, in relieuyng the godly, in bridelyng the wicked ... (Ibid., p. *ii(v).)

From Constantine to Christ, from teacher to preacher, the change between the 1563 and 1570 editions of John Foxe's *Acts and Monuments* is one from the archivist to the historian, from chronicle to history and from the world to the spirit.

These changes can be usefully explained in terms of a movement from a prophetic to an apocalyptic perspective, in particular because such a development is one that was often enacted by English Protestant writers when confronted by adversity.[56] John F. Wilson has written about a similar development in the Fast Sermons preached before Parliament during the English Civil War. Wilson suggests that:

> In its classical usage 'prophecy' did not primarily signify 'prediction' but rather the delivery of a 'word' from the Lord. The 'word' was usually one embodying both judgement and mercy.[57]

He goes on to comment that the 'prophetic perspective at bottom presupposed that God's providence was working in and through mundane events toward the realization of divine purposes'.[58] In prophetic thought or discourse human agency is invited to respond to divine

---

[56] The relation between prophetic and apocalyptic history that this section discusses has been subject to a number of recent historical studies. In particular, Paul Christianson has discussed the tension within Protestantism over who were the proper or natural agents of Reformation and has related this discussion to apocalyptic views of history in sixteenth- and seventeenth-century England. See Christianson, *Reformers and Babylon: English Apocalyptic Visions from the Reformation to the Eve of the Civil War* (Toronto, 1978), p. 11. See also Bauckham, *Tudor Apocalypse*; Zakai, 'Reformation, history, and eschatology in English Protestantism'.

[57] John F. Wilson, *Pulpit in Parliament: Puritanism during the English Civil War 1640–1648* (Princeton, 1969), p. 198.

[58] Ibid., p. 206.

purposes and is therefore based on a relatively optimistic understanding of the ability of humans to respond to God's message. This in turn produces a form of history that stresses the continuity between past events and future 'reformation', and the role of human agents in producing such change. While the apocalyptic grew out of, and, in a sense, depended on the prophetic it was based on a far more pessimistic attitude to humanity and the course of history. Wilson writes, ' By contrast to classical prophetism, apocalypticism developed as a proclamation of hope in Israel's darkest hours.'[59] Apocalypticism emphasized

> not ... an open future but ... the declaration that, appearances to the contrary notwithstanding, God ruled the course of historical events and *would* bring out of the ominous present a glorious future quite independently of human agency.[60]

While prophetic history stressed continuity, apocalyptic thought constructed the future as radically discontinuous to the present and as unknown to 'the worldly wise but delivered to the faithful (elite).'[61] In *Acts and Monuments* developments in form, from chronicle to narrative, the increased role of the author as the 'explainer' or shaper of the past and the subtle changes in the status of the martyr all illustrate a similar movement. While a chronicle form implies continuity a narrative one creates discontinuity. Emphasizing the role of the author in shaping the past implies that it is no longer enough simply to display the events of the past to provoke reform, one must also shape them. Subtly changing the status of martyrs from human prophets to almost Biblical ones, figures in a grand historical narrative, allows Foxe to use them in support of an apocalyptic construction of the past that stresses God's, and not humanity's, role in determining its progress and conclusion.

At the same time the move from the prophetic to the apocalyptic embodied a radical rewriting of the position of Foxe's text as regards the public sphere, and the monarch. In 1563 Foxe's text, like those of his fellow Protestant historians of the Marian persecution, constructed itself as within the public sphere. Indeed it was this positioning that gave the text its intentionality. In 1563 *Acts and Monuments* constructed itself as a constant provocation towards a strong public motivated by the memory of those who had died during Mary's reign. This construction, however, was premised on its efficacy; it depended on its already successful operation. A public that accepted its implicit construction in the 1563 edition as godly and as having learnt the

---

[59] Ibid., p. 199.
[60] Ibid.
[61] Ibid.

lessons of the mid-Tudor period, was, in a paradoxical sense, ready to listen to Foxe's words because it had already read them. In 1563 Foxe took for granted that the Elizabethan public sphere was sufficiently godly for all that was necessary to provoke the public to act and produce further reformation was for him to place the facts of the past before them. In 1570 Foxe had effectively lost this faith in his own history. *Acts and Monuments* is now addressed to the godly, and to a sinful nation of non-godly. It is no longer placed in *the* public sphere, but is instead directed at *a* public sphere, one defined on the basis of godliness and not publicness.[62] The 1570 edition of *Acts and Monuments* is addressed to a godly public whose existence the text is designed to nurture and sustain. In 1570 it is the dark future of Elizabethan Protestantism that is shaping Foxe's text, not its past.

From chronicle to narrative

These changes in the nature of Foxe's history can be illustrated by examining the concluding sections of the 1563 and 1570 editions of *Acts and Monuments*. The final sections of the prophetic 1563 edition express a relatively optimistic view of the possibility of continuing reformation in England. In 1563 the final part of *Acts and Monuments* represents the English Church and people as set on a continuing process of renewal and reform. It opens with an extended comparison between the lawlessness and rigour that, according to Foxe, marked the opening of Mary's reign and the moderation and clemency of Elizabeth's first years as queen. Foxe writes:

> In prosecuting the matter [of this comparison] I mighte here speak of the heady hastines in quene Maries daies in proceding without and before any lawe by mere affection.
>
> ...
>
> Nowe wee see thinges done with moore aduisemente, and lesse haste, no man nowe presuminge to violate orders godlye taken, or styre the people to chaunge what they lyst before order bee pubishled by lawe. (*Acts and Monuments* (1563), pp. 1708–10.)

---

[62] Thomas Freeman points out that 'most of the material encouraging Elizabeth to godliness was only inserted in the second edition [1570] of Foxe's work (or even later) ... '. One does not need to exhort a godly prince to be godly, but one might have to resort to such exhortations if the prince appeared to be less godly then she ought to be. See Thomas S. Freeman, 'Research, rumour and propaganda: Anne Boleyn in Foxe's "Book of Martyrs"', *HJ*, 38 (1995), pp. 797–819, p. 815.

Having made this comparison Foxe goes on to write an extended eulogy on Elizabeth in which he discusses her childhood and schooling, before going on to recount the story of her tribulations during her sister's reign. He then continues his history, again referring to the singularly peaceful succession of Elizabeth:

> yet I coulde neuer finde in english Chronicle the like that may be written of this our noble and worthy Quene, whose comminge in, not only was so calme, so joyful, so peaceable, without sheding of any bloud ...

> ...

> In speaking whereof I take not upon me the part here of the morall or the diuine Philosopher, to judge of thinges done, but onelye kepe me within the compasse of an historiographer, declaring what hath bene before [and] comparing thinges done, with thinges nowe present, the like whereof as I saide, is not to bee found lightly in Chronicles before. (Ibid., p. 1716.)

Having restated this comparison, Foxe carries on with his work producing an account of the conference between Catholics and Protestants staged at the beginning of Elizabeth's reign.

Foxe's account of this conference expresses an understanding of the Elizabethan religious settlement as the result of public debate and the actions of an informed reforming Parliament. Although the conference was staged at the behest of the queen, the actual mechanics of it are dominated by a confrontation between the Lord Keeper and the Catholic disputants.[63] Foxe emphasizes the desire of Parliament to attend the conference in order to aid their deliberations on religious matters (ibid., pp. 1717–18). Finally, as Foxe writes:

> Although in this parliament some diuersyty there was of iudgement and opinion betwene parties, yet not withstandinge through the mercifull goodnes of the Lord, the true cause of the gospell had the upper hand, the papistes hope was frustrate, and their rage abated, the order and proceading of king Edwards tyme concerning religion was reuiued agayne, the supremacye of the Pope abolished, the articles and blouddye statutes of Queene Marye repealed ... (Ibid., p. 1728.)

---

[63] The refusal of Catholics to debate in an orderly fashion was a common element of Protestant polemics. It expressed an understanding of Catholicism as unable to sustain itself through public reasoned debate, and therefore as incompatible to the proper functioning of a public sphere. An example of this polemic which reproduces all the main elements of Foxe's account of the Westminster conference can be found in Nicholas Ballasus, *A True report of all the doyngs at the assembly co[n]cernyng matters of Religion, lately holden at Poyssy in France*, trans. J.D. (1561?), STC 6776.

At the end of the 1563 edition of *Acts and Monuments* the reader is presented with the image of the passing of the Elizabethan religious settlement that stresses the role of Parliament and reduces the queen's to that of an onlooker. Foxe shows the reformation of religion proceeding through Parliamentary processes, after a public discussion between Catholics and Protestants used to inform the house's deliberations. Implicitly, in this construction of the 1558–59 religious settlement, the role of the monarch is minimal. In 1563 religious reform is represented by Foxe as being the result of a process of discussion and debate by the body politic under the guidance of its godly religious leaders. The chronicle form of this section of *Acts and Monuments* implies that these events will, or can, be ongoing; that the process of reform, like the 'sequele of history', will continue into Elizabeth's reign.

The end of the 1570 edition of *Acts and Monuments* is completely different from that of 1563. There is no sixth book detailing the events of Elizabeth's reign, nor an extended comparison between the calm at the start of her reign and the lawlessness when her sister, Mary, succeeded. Even more noticeable is the absence of an account of the Westminster conference and, by implication, of the setting up of the Elizabethan religious settlement.[64] In 1563 Foxe constantly refers to the way the pressure of history, 'the sequele of events', makes him continue his story into Elizabeth's reign. Indeed the 'conclusion' of this edition is very messy and disjointed, ending as it does with after-notes and a list of corrections (*Acts and Monuments*, 1563, pp. 1703–42). In 1570 *Acts and Monuments* comes to an abrupt end with Foxe's 'Admonition to the Reader' (*Acts and Monuments*, 1570, pp. 2300–02). In 1570 there is, for Foxe, no 'history' to be written after Elizabeth's succession, or perhaps there was none that it was worth the risk to write.[65] While the chronicle form of the 1563 text implies a continuing history of reform in England during Elizabeth's reign the 1570 text's more narrative style creates a clear-cut ending.

This is not to suggest, however, that Foxe regarded the succession of Elizabeth as the end of religious struggle in England. Indeed given the

---

[64] An account of the Westminster Conference, however, is printed in the 1583 edition of *Acts and Monuments*.

[65] Foxe does refer at the end of the 1570 edition to a possible further book or section dealing with 'the great styrres and alterations which haue happened in other foreine nations, and also partly among our selues here at home, ... '. However this work never appeared and it is of course ironic that this comment, in textual terms, occupies the same place as the account of the Westminster conference did in 1563 (*Acts and Monuments*, 1570, p. 2296).

pessimism of his 1570 sermon *A Sermon of Christ Crucified*,[66] it would be difficult to sustain this argument. In this sermon, when Foxe wishes to compare heavenly messengers, the apostles, with those of kings he uses the example of Cardinal Pole's return to England in 1555. He goes on to point out that Pole was 'welcomed' by the country, including 'the priuy Counsell (of whom some are yet aliue) ... '.[67] Foxe certainly thought the English Church, and people, needed more 'Reformation'; the narrative style of the ending of the 1570 edition suggests that he had given up on earthly powers and was trusting in the inevitable processes of divine history – a process that was not open, dependent on human actions and continuous with the past – but one that was discontinuous, beyond human understanding and driven by apocalyptic revelation.

This darkening of Foxe's view of the possibility of continuing reform in England, and of the future course of history itself, also affected his use of historical comparisons to elucidate the message of his work. In 1563 Foxe often uses contemporary historical figures to stress the lesson of his history; in 1570 he tends to deploy Biblical, or mythic, ones. For example, in the 1570 edition of *Acts and Monuments,* Foxe compares Edward VI, at the time of his succession, with Josias, the iconoclastic Old Testament King. Foxe writes:

> And here to use the example of Plutarch in comparyng kynges and rulers ... if I should seeke with whom to match this noble Edward, I finde not with whom to make my match more aptely, then with good Josias. (*Acts and Monuments* (1570), pp. 1483–4.)

In 1563, however, Foxe had been happy to use a far more contemporary monarch to compare Edward with, his father. Needless to say the comparison was not flattering to Henry. Foxe makes the perfectly reasonable point that from a Protestant perspective Henry's Reformation was only half finished.

> Although it cannot be denied, but kinge Henry the noble father of this worthy Prince deserued also prayse [and] renown for his valiant and vertuous beginninge: Yet if he had proceded so hardeli, according as happely he begonne; ... Then had his actes ioyning a perfect ende to his godly beginning, deserued a firme memory of much co[n]mendation, with the sauinge of many a poore mans life.

---

[66] John Foxe, 'A sermon of Christ crucified', in *The English Sermons of John Foxe*, ed. Warren Wooden (New York, 1978), STC 11242.

[67] Ibid., B.ii. Foxe goes on to claim later that:

> They which be frendes and louers of the Byshop of Rome, although they eate the fatte of the land, and haue the best preferrementes and offices ... yet are they not therewith content. They grudge, they mutter and murmure, they conspire and take on agaynst us ... (Ibid., T.ii).

> But that which the father eyther could not, or durst not bring to prefectio[n], that the son most worthely did acco[n]plish, or rather the grace of Christ by him. (*Acts and Monuments* (1563), p. 675.)

A similar development can be seen in the case of William Tyndale.[68] In 1563 Foxe's account of Tyndale is relatively prosaic, by 1570 it has become almost Biblical in places. In 1563 Foxe explicitly mentions Tyndale's row with Joye over the latter's plagiarism of his work; in 1570 Foxe makes much more of Tyndale's self-assumed role as the father of the English Bible but 'forgets' to mention the dispute with Joye. Indeed there is an almost sacrilegious feel to the way Foxe claims that the production of Tyndale's New Testament provoked a similar reaction in the ungodly as the birth of Christ, with Satan singling out Tyndale for his particular attention to the extent of engineering a storm at sea in which Tyndale lost all his books (*Acts and Monuments*, 1570, pp. 1226–7.)

As with Edward, and Elizabeth, the way Foxe constructs Tyndale in 1563 and 1570 shows a clear development away from historical imagery towards the mythic and the Biblical. The scale of his history increases, it becomes more universal and simultaneously less human and less worldly. As Foxe's view of the possibility of continuing reform carried out by worldly human actions darkens so the imagery he uses in his history becomes more Biblical and apocalyptic. If, as Foxe claimed in his 1570 sermon, Catholics held all the main positions at court then further godly reform was unlikely to be produced by political action and instead it would have to be guaranteed by revelation. If the worldly powers, personified in a queen who was beginning to look more and more like her father, were again about to betray the godly cause again then history itself would have to be brought into the fight.

From words to signs: John Rogers's martyrdom in 1563 and 1570

These changes in the nature of Foxe's history affected even those events that appear in both the 1563 and 1570 editions of *Acts and Monuments*. In particular the darkening of Foxe's thought during the 1560s fundamentally changed the way he constructed the act of martyrdom. In 1563 Foxe was confident that martyrdom, and persecution, were things of the past for English Protestants but by 1570 he had reversed this judgement. Indeed the temporal status of the act of martyrdom constantly changed throughout the sixteenth and seventeenth centuries

---

[68] The suggestion that there might be interesting differences between the 1563 and 1570 accounts of Tyndale's life was first made to me by Professor Patrick Collinson.

and with it the meaning of *Acts and Monuments*. Was it a record of the past, history, or was it a nightmare vision of the future?[69] Unfortunately the nature of martyrdom, and its place in Christianity, can encourage the construction of it as a transhistorical category, with a fixed, self-evident meaning. Certainly John R. Knott is right to suggest that:

> All Christian martyrdom is in some sense an *imitatio Christi*, be-cause the crucifixion and resurrection of Christ established the pattern of winning spiritual victory through suffering and thereby overcoming worldly strength through apparent weakness.[70]

It is also essential, however, to place the act of martyrdom in a clear historical and cultural context. As Miri Rubin points out:

> the act of martyrdom is twofold: it is a choice taken in testing circumstances by an individual, or a group; but its is also a social-collective act, that of martyr-making, of martyr-naming. Thus a double-edged perspective is necessary in order to contain the vari-ety of contexts in which martyrdom is practised: in the intention of the martyr/victim, and in the interpretation of those who will declare a given demise to be the crowned death of a martyr. As we enter the area of interpretation we must perforce step into fields of authority and dissent, of perspective and subjectivity; of meaning, as one man's cult of a martyr is another woman's superstition.[71]

As Rubin suggests, it is important not to impose a false homogeneity on the act of martyrdom, but rather to stress why each specific event took place, what were the cultural pressures, the different subject positions and the different discourses that produced an act of martyrdom, and that were produced by it. For example, John Rogers's martyrdom was an exemplary one for Foxe. Here was a man whose 'crimes' were that he had translated the Scriptures into English and had been a hard-working London preacher. Rogers's martyrdom set a pattern that was to be repeated over and over again during Mary Tudor's reign. Or rather Rogers's martyrdom created an orthodox English Protestant model of martyrdom that could be unambiguously endorsed by most, if not

---

[69] The 1631 edition of *Acts and Monuments* contains a text entitled 'A Treatise of Afflictions and Persecution of the faithfull', that instructs the godly on the need to put on the armour of God and thereby creates the impression that persecution has returned, or is about to return, to England. For a more detailed discussion of this point see Damien Nussbaum, 'Appropriating martyrdom: fears of renewed persecution and the 1632 edi-tion of *Acts and Monuments*', in David Loades (ed.), *John Foxe and the English Reformation* (Aldershot, 1997), pp. 178–91.

[70] John R. Knott, *Discourses of Martyrdom in English Literature, 1563–1694* (Cam-bridge, 1993), p. 2.

[71] Miri Rubin, 'Choosing death? Experiences of martyrdom in late medieval Europe', in Diane Wood (ed.), *Martyrs and Martyrologies; Studies in Church History* (33 vols, Oxford, 1993), 30, pp. 153–83, p. 153.

all, his fellow believers. Clearly Rogers was performing an instantly recognizable role as the Christian martyr standing out against the attacks of the world and winning victory in death. The meaning of his act, however, was ultimately determined by the events of 1558 and after. Without a Protestant Church Rogers would not have become an officially endorsed martyr, and Foxe's view of the nature of this Protestant Church structured and determined how he constructed Rogers's martyrdom.

The story of Rogers is very similar in both the 1563 and 1570 editions of *Acts and Monuments*. Foxe recounts the story of Rogers's examinations, his confession of faith and his condemnation. The main difference comes with a piece entitled 'Further matter by the sayd Maister Rogers ... ' printed in 1563 but largely edited from 1570. This is interesting given the way the 1570 edition self-consciously constructs itself as more complete, more voluminous than the earlier version. So what does Foxe choose to leave out of his account of Rogers in 1570 that he included in 1563? He leaves out a text in which Rogers replies to two questions that Gardiner had asked him during the day but which he had not been given a chance to answer. Rogers writes:

> Two thinges I purposed to haue touched. The one how it was lawfull for a priuate man to reason and write agaynst a wicked acte of Parliament, or an ungodly counsell, which the Lord Chauncelor the daye before denyed mee. Thother was to proue that prosperity was not alwayes a token of gods loue. (*Acts and Monuments* (1563), p. 1031.)

However, these are not Rogers's own words, they are a paraphrase of what he originally wrote.[72] The entire opening section of this text was largely rewritten by Foxe. This makes its almost total exclusion in 1570 even more interesting because Foxe was editing out a text that he had already adapted and paraphrased. Why should he do this? If one returns to Rogers's original words one can suggest a number of reasons for both Foxe's rewriting and his eventual suppression of this piece. The section that appears to have caused the martyrologist most concern is that in which Rogers discusses the relationship between acts of Parliament and the law of God. Rogers's text contains an explicit attack on the status of Parliament that relates the corruption of its democratic nature over a long period to the behaviour of kings and counsellors. Rogers writes:

---

[72] For Rogers see Chester, *John Rogers*. In this work Chester prints a copy of John Rogers's account of his examinations taken from Lansdowne Mss 389 H. 190–202. When quoting from this text I have left it as close as possible to the original while at the same time adding modern words when this explicates the meaning. Knott discusses the nature of Foxe's changes to Rogers's words in *Discourses Of Martyrdom*.

> I say, (& many other who so wold read [the] chronikles of england,
> ...) ... [that] our pliame[n]tes are & have bene, specially, for [the]
> most [part], in these latter 100 yeares, but [the] will & pleasure of
> one, or of a very fewe of [the] heades, [either] of [the] kynges or of
> [the] cou[n]sailours ...[73]

Rogers's words give the impression that even the Protestant acts of
Henry VIII and Edward VI are of relatively little value because of the
debased nature of Parliament.

> As in [Henry] eightes dayes, ye [Gardiner?] in you[r] pliamentes
> folowed only his wyll & pleasure, even to grau[n]te [the queen
> majesty Mary] to be a bastard, (god it well knoweth, agai[n]ste
> you[r] willes &, as ye well knowe, agai[n]ste [the] willes of [the]
> whole realme ...[74]

The martyr is quite clear that the Word of God should explicitly and
publicly take precedence over any act of Parliament.

> wherfore I may co[n]clude [that] I, or any [other] ma[n], havinge
> [the] word of god on ou[r] sydes, may speake agai[n]ste such an
> acte, & oughte to be heard, & [the] pliame[n]tes to geve place to
> [the] worde of [the] [ever] livi[n]ge god, & not god to [the] acte of
> pliame[n]te ...[75]

Foxe's paraphrase of Rogers's words still makes most of these points,
albeit in a more muted way. What he does change is Rogers's implicitly
critical construction of the Henrician and Edwardian Reformations
making them justifiable both in terms of the law of God and of Parliament. This makes the conflict between acts of Parliament and the law of
God, which appears almost inevitable in Rogers's text, much less striking. So although Foxe still constructs Rogers as criticizing Mary Tudor's
Parliaments he makes this critique far more historically specific. Foxe's
Rogers comments that:

> And as it is most true that Actes of Parliament haue in these latter
> dayes bene ruled by the fantasies of a few, and the whole Parlia-
> ment house, contrarye to their myndes was compelled to consent
> to suche thinges as fewe had conceiued. (*Acts and Monuments*
> (1563), p. 1032.)

In the original text the impression given is that 'these latter dayes' refers
to anything from the last 100 years to the period from the Norman
Conquest. In Foxe's version it is implicit that 'latter days' is a reference

---

[73] Chester, *John Rogers*, p. 321.
[74] Ibid., p. 319.
[75] Rogers appears to be specifically referring to any act that re-established papal
authority in England, however, he is also clearly making a more general point about any
act or law that contradicted what he saw as the Word of God (ibid., p. 322).

only to Mary's reign. One should note, however, that the main point of the Foxe/Rogers text is still to assert that 'we ought more to obeye God then man' (ibid., p. 1032). So Rogers/Foxe writes:

> I saye it is not onely laufull for any priuate man, which bringeth gods word for hym, and the autoritye of the primatiue and best churche, to speake and write against such unlaufull lawes, but it is his dutye and he hys bounde in verye conscience to do it ... (Ibid., p. 1032.)

Of course in Marian terms this is not a particularly radical argument. As Gerry Bowler has argued:

> From the first to the last days of her reign Mary Tudor was faced with Protestant subjects who felt themselves justified, on both religious and political grounds, in taking up arms against her regime.[76]

Clearly neither Rogers or Foxe/Rogers is suggesting armed resistance, however the status of this text, or texts, is altered by their inclusion in *Acts and Monuments*. Arguments that in a Marian perspective might appear quite mild could appear radical in an Elizabethan one. In particular the thrust of Rogers's argument that the laws of God took precedence over those of man and that the godly had a duty to publicly proclaim and enact this doctrine had radical implications given the Elizabethan regime's denial of the right of the godly to perform this role, for example when opposing the injunctions to wear vestments.

Indeed the events of the 1560s suddenly make Rogers's original words more relevant, and more provocative, than they were in 1563. When Foxe rewrote Rogers's demand that Parliamentary acts should give place to the Word of God he may have felt that this point was irrelevant now England had returned to Protestantism. Far from being redundant, however, Rogers's original words had been shown to be more pertinent than Foxe's own rewrites.[77] The conflicts of the 1560s made godly people again confront the potential conflict between the Word of God and the laws of man. The last two paragraphs of both the original and the 1563 version of Rogers's text are a warning of what will happen if the English continue to place man's laws before those of God.

> If God loke not mercifully upon Englande, the seedes of utter destruction are sowen in it already, by these hypocriticall tyrauntes,

---

[76] Gerry Bowler, 'Marian Protestants and the idea of violent resistance to tyranny', in Peter Lake and Maria Dowling (eds), *Protestantism and the National Church in Sixteenth Century England* (London, 1987), pp. 124–43, p. 124.

[77] For a discussion of the godly experience of the decade 1560–70 see Patrick Collinson, *The Elizabethan Puritan Movement* (Oxford, 1990), pp. 21–97.

and Antichristian prelates Popish Papists, and double traytours to
their naturall countrey.

...

If the righteous shal scant be saued, where shall the ungodly and
sinfull appeare? Some shall haue their punishment here in this
world and in the world to come, [and] they do escape in this world,
shall not escape euerlasting damnatio[n]. This shalbe your sauce, O
ye wicked Papistes, make ye mery here as long as ye may.
(*Acts and Monuments* (1563), p. 1036.)

It is only this last section of the text that Foxe reprints in 1570. In the
process he obscures its status as the conclusion to a piece making a
number of explicitly political points. Instead the reader is told the
edifying story of how Rogers's words were found by his wife and son
after his martyrdom in his cell.

For notwithsta[n]ding that duryng [the] tyme of his imprisonme[n]t
strait search there was to take away his letters [and] writyngs: yet
after his death his wife [and] one of her sonnes called Daniell,
comming into the place where he lay, to seeke for his bookes [and]
writyngs, [and] now ready to go away, it chau[n]ced her sone
aforenamed, castyng his eye aside to spy a blacke thing (for it had
a black couer, belike because it should not be knowe) lying in a
blynd corner under a payre of stayres. Who willing his mother to
see what it was, found it to be the booke writte[n] with his owne
hand ... (*Acts and Monuments* (1570), p. 1663.)

Foxe then goes on to frame the final section of Rogers's writings in a
completely different manner to that he had used in 1563.

In the latter ende [of the book] whereof this also was conteined,
which because it co[n]cerneth a Propheticall forwarning of things
perteinyng to [the] Church, I though here to place [the] same his
words, as they be there writte[n], which are these: If God looke ...
(Ibid., p. 1663.)

By constructing Rogers's words in this way Foxe changes their meaning.
A text that contained potentially subversive political ideas, evidence of
Protestant divisions in Edward's reign and rejected a providential understanding of history has been truncated and turned into an apocalyptic
warning.[78] In textual terms the space occupied by the edited section of

---

[78] In response to Gardiner's criticism of the Edwardian regime Rogers writes:

it maye please your Lordshyppe to understande, that we poore Preachers,
whome ye so euill allow, did moost boldly and playnlye rebuke their euill
gouernaunce in many thynges, specially their couetousnes, and neglecte
and small regarde to lyue after the Gospell: ... (*Acts and Monuments*,
(1563), p. 1033.)

Rogers's text has been replaced by the evocative story of the finding of the martyr's words. The 1570 story of the finding of Rogers's words creates a metonymic relationship between the blackened body of the martyr and that of the book containing his writings. At the same time the story of how Rogers's testimony is rescued, symbolically, from the flames implicitly emphasizes the role of the historian. The martyr's words have to be dug up, searched out and brought to the notice of the world by the dedication of his son, his wife and his martyrologist. In 1563 it is the martyr, or the historian speaking through him, who creates his own testimony, who writes down his thoughts in answer to Gardiner's questions in order to speak in public and be heard. In 1570 it is his son, and wife, who save his prophecy from the ashes. In 1563 the martyr's words are precious because in them he addresses England as a prophet speaking in worldly terms and warning the people to mend their ways. In 1570 it is pointless to expect a godless country to heed such a call.

The changes Foxe made in his account of Rogers's martyrdom follow the pattern of moving away from the prophetic to the apocalyptic. In 1563 the prophetic construction of the meaning of Rogers's death and testimony was based is on the possibility of humanity heeding the words and example of the martyr while in 1570 this possibility had been discounted. Now Rogers must speak as a voice of warning to the godly, to those who will and can understand the true nature of his apocalyptic warning to England.

Edwardian bishop, Marian martyr and Elizabethan radical: the journey of Bishop Hooper 1563–70

Finally, by looking at the way Foxe revises the story of Bishop Hooper between 1563 and 1570 one can support the contention that many of these changes are the result of an increased pessimism about the possibility of continuing reform. One of the first points that needs to be made is that Foxe edits and changes his account of the opening of the year 1555. In 1563 Foxe starts his record of this year with a discussion of the repeal of the Acts of Supremacy by Parliament and the passing of laws against heresy. Foxe then goes on to claim that the papists lost no time in making use of their new laws.

Rogers goes on to call on those he criticized as witnesses to his claim:

> Therefore lette the Gentlemen and Courtiers them selues, and al the Citezens of London, testifie what we dyd. (Ibid., p. 1033.)

> When these things were once obtained, [and] that the Papistes had
> gotte[n] the laws on their side, [and] the swerde put into their
> handes, to kill [and] murther whom they would: there was then no
> delay made on their behalf, to accomplishe the effecte of their long
> hidden infestred and cankred tyranny ... (*Acts and Monuments*
> (1563), p. 1019.)

This did not prevent, however, people meeting to hold Protestant serv-
ices:

> All which not withsta[n]ding the children of God, having the law-
> ful oportunitie of seruing of God, take[n] up by this crueltie from
> them, yet in sundrie times and places secretly assembled them
> selues, to the comforte of their co[n]sciences [and] instructio[n] of
> their soules. (Ibid., p. 1020.)

In the context of this quotation Foxe's earlier comment that the papists
'had gotte[n] the laws on their side' is potentially ironic. What does it
mean to say that under the papists it had become 'unlawful' to serve
God? The implication of course is that in an 'unlawful' country the law
is not law, for how could it be lawful to forbid the worship of God?

Foxe then goes on to recount the story of one of the secret London
congregations, how it met on New Years Day in Bowe Churchyard, was
betrayed and its members arrested. It is at this point that Hooper enters
the story as the congregation wrote to him, from prison, recounting their
trials. This letter is interesting because of the way it summons up the
possibility that the meeting in Bowe Churchyard was treasonable, or at
least illegal, in the act of denying any such intentions. The letter claims
that the congregation at Bowe 'prayed for the magistrates and estates of
the Realme' (ibid., p. 1020). At precisely the point that they were on their
knees praying for the worldly powers the representatives of the most
immediate one, the Lord Chancellor, entered and everyone was arrested.
When the Sheriff ordered the worshippers to stay, 'they humbly obeyed:
for they came not thether weaponed, to conspire or make any tumult, but
onely like Christians, Christianly to pray ... ' (ibid., p. 1020). The letter
writer then goes on to explain why these Londoners were gathered in
secret against the orders of their social superiors. The congregation met,

> to be instructed in the vulgar tongue, be reading and hearing of
> Gods word, as their consciences did enforce the[m], without the
> displeasure of God, to doo. For (as you well knowe) there is
> nothing so greuouse to the pacient in this worlde, as the gnawyng
> and bytyng worme of a troubled conscience, being accused by
> Gods lawe, for the wylfull transgressing of the same ... (Ibid.,
> p. 1020.)

Their consciences made them obey God's law before that of man.
Indeed the whole letter expresses a central contradiction at the heart of

Protestantism, that between the need to obey the law of the world, personified in the godly, or not so godly, magistrate, and the need to obey the law of God working through the individual's conscience. Hooper's reply expresses his joy that in this perilous time people are still turning to God. He also stresses the absolute necessity of passivity in the face of persecution.

> So dothe the worde of God commaunde all men, to pray charitably for them that hate us, and not to reuyle any Magistrate with wordes, or to mean him euill by force or violence. (Ibid., p. 1020.)

Despite all these protestations Foxe's account of the beginning of 1555 leaves the reader with the image of a secret congregation obeying the law of God before that of man. Indeed there is a sense in which the new laws Foxe says were passed at the beginning of this year caused the separatism that the Bowe meeting represents.

The letter from the Bowe congregation to Hooper is not printed as part of Foxe's 1570 version of the opening of 1555. In 1570 Foxe's account of 1555 starts with a brief account of the arrest of the members of the Bowe congregation, mentions the repealing of the Act of Supremacy, and then quickly moves on to recount a fight between the Spanish and the English before relating the story of Mary's 'pregnancy'. Foxe then discusses a number of acts recently passed by Parliament, in particular an act celebrating the royal conception and one against praying for Mary's death. Finally he prints Hooper's reply to the letter from the London congregation because 'the copy wherof I thought here not to overpasse' (Acts and Monuments, 1570, p. 1654). Given that he has just 'overpassed' the letter to which Hooper's was a reply one wonders if there is not a touch of irony in this comment. Clearly the meaning of Hooper's letter changes in this account of the first months of 1555. His letter now appears, to the reader, to be a response to a law against praying for Mary's death. Also the status of Parliament is subtly undermined here by Foxe's printing of an act showing its acceptance of what he, and his readers, would have known was a phantom pregnancy. Was it in 1570, in a way it was not in 1563, unpolitic, if not dangerous, to print a letter describing the meeting of a secret Separatist congregation in London in the way Foxe had done in 1563? Did Foxe want to protect one if his heroes, Hooper, from the taint of encouraging such Separatism in 1570? If so why was this not an issue in 1563?

In 1563 and 1570 Foxe uses the example of Hooper to criticize the office of bishop in general. In 1563 he writes, in a passage edited from 1570:

> I am ashamed when I compare examples, howe muche hys [Hooper's] trade and institucion, differeth from the common sorte

of the Popishe Bishoppes, whose life and exaumple, as I woulde
God oure Bishoppes would followe: so I woulde wishe that the
thother prynces [and] rulers would imitate the good trade and well
doynges of them. And as I greately desyre ydlenes to bee eschewed
of all Bishoppes seruauntes: so more I wyshe to be auoyded of the
Byshoppos themselues, riote and to muche wealthe. And yet I
speake not this, for that I woulde haue the Byshoppes by and by to
be brought to bagge and wallette, and extreme pouertye: but that it
were better for them selues [and] the Church to, yf they could
reduce [and] call themselues to Hoopers meane and moderation ...
(*Acts and Monuments* (1563), p. 1053.)

However it is not simply a question of Foxe removing passages critical
of bishops from the 1570 edition. In the latter versions of Hooper's
story the Edwardian bishop is still held up as an example but the nature
of the critique Foxe wishes to make has changed. So in 1563 Foxe
writes the following:

he [Hooper] lefte out nothing appertaining to their saluatiuon.
Other men were wonte for lucre sake, to take Bishoprikes upon
them: but he nothing abhorred more, the[n] desire of gain ... (Ibid.,
p. 1052.)

In 1570 Foxe expands this passage so it reads:

So careful was he in hys Cure, that he left neither paynes untaken,
nor wayes unsought, how to trayne uppe the flocke of Christ in the
true word of saluation, continually labouryng in the same. Other
men commonly are wont for lucre or promotion sake to aspire to
Byshoprikes, some hu[n]tyng for them, and some purchasing or
bying them as men use to purchase Lordshyps, [and] whe[n] they
haue them, are loth to leaue them, and thereupon loth also to
commit that thyng by worldly lawes, wherby to lose them.
     To this sorte of men M. Hoper was cleane contrary ... (*Acts and
Monuments* (1570), p. 1677.)

The subtle shift of tense between the two versions of this passage, in
1563 men *were wonte* to seek bishoprics for the sake of money while in
1570 men *are wont,* alters the time of Foxe's criticism of the office from
the past to the present. Equally important is the way the passage that
appears in 1563 but is cut in 1570 extends the scope of Hooper's
exemplary status. In this section Foxe uses Hooper as an image of a
godly bishop and a godly prince. Foxe implies that the Elizabethan
bishops should follow the example of Hooper and, presumably, that
Elizabeth should follow theirs. In this schema the authority of the
martyr, the prophet, extends across both the spiritual and secular landscape. In 1570 this extension of the martyr's role into the secular realm
has been edited; however, at the same time Foxe's use of Hooper to
criticize the present Elizabethan bishops has increased. Indeed one of
the main grounds of this critique is now their worldliness, their hunting

for clerical preferment and their treatment of their office as a secular lordship. So on the one hand Foxe removes a passage from Hooper's story that is implicitly critical of worldly powers, a passage that reverses the Erastianism that was such a marked feature of the Elizabethan Reformation by implying princes should follow the lead of pastors, while simultaneously increasing those parts of the text that explicitly attack the behaviour of the Elizabethan bishops. These changes illustrate Foxe's disillusionment with the progress of reform under Elizabeth and a growing desire to separate the spiritual from the secular realms. What is the point of holding Hooper up as an example in a public sphere full of worldly bishops ruled over by a monarch whose role as a reformer is at best in doubt and in which the process of reformation appears to have stalled? In this situation the example of martyrs, like Hooper, is most effective, most pertinent, when directed towards the godly and kept within the spiritual realm.

There are many other important, but subtle, changes in the story of Hooper. In 1563 the reader is left in no doubt that much of Foxe's account of Hooper comes from his personal acquaintance with the martyr. Foxe laces his account of Hooper with such comments as 'For I my selfe haue ben oftentymes present', or 'which I wished', or 'but I dout not this to bee done in him', constructing himself as both author and witness (*Acts and Monuments*, 1563, p. 1050). In 1570 all these phrases are cut. Instead, within the same passage and in the same form, that is in the first person, Foxe comments on Hooper in a way that explicitly distances him from the earlier, more personal, portrayal. As with Tyndale or Edward VI, in 1570 Foxe introduces a Biblical example to buttress his construction of Hooper.

> Briefly, of all those vertues and qualities required of S. Paule in a good bishop in his epistle to Timothe, I know not one in this good bishop lacking. (*Acts and Monuments* (1570), p. 1675.)

So one has an account, that in 1563, reads as almost a personal recollection of what Hooper was like being subtly changed into a far more apocalyptic or universal story. At the same time this corresponds to the developments in Foxe's historical form between 1563 and 1570. While in 1563 Foxe's persona in the text is that of a facilitator, whose role is simply to create a textual space for the words of the martyrs to be heard, in 1570 his role has become far more authorial, now he needs to shape the meaning and status of the martyrs' testimony by placing them within their proper discursive narrative. In 1570 Foxe must tell his readers that Hooper was a model of a New Testament bishop, he could no longer leave it to the martyr's own words and behaviour to make this point.

Finally one should note the extent to which many of these changes may be the result of self-censorship on the part of Foxe.[79] Hooper was a potentially problematical figure in the Elizabethan Church. Here was a martyr who had refused to wear the very vestments that the episcopacy were forcing on the Elizabethan clergy. In 1563 Foxe describes how Hooper initially refused to wear clerical dress comprising:

> First a Shemer, and under that a white rochette, and a foure forked cappe. (*Acts and Monuments* (1563), p. 1050.)

He then recounts the story of Hooper's eventual capitulation to the pressure of his fellow bishops, Ridley[80] and Cranmer.

> The Byshopps hauyng the upper hande, Hoper was fayne to agree to this poynte, and condicion. That ones he should in a Sermon shew hym selfe apparayled as other the Byshopps were. Wherefore, as a new player in strange apparayle, he commeth foorthe on the stage: hys upper garments was a long Shemer, downe to the foote, and under that a whyte lynnen rochet, that couered all his shoulders, his cappe uppon hys heade was foure cornerde. (Ibid., p. 1051.)

In 1570 Foxe makes the following significant changes to these two passages. Instead of simply describing the hat Hooper had to wear as four cornered, Foxe writes:

> then a Mathematical cap with iiij. angels, dividyng the whole world into iiij. partes. (*Acts and Monuments* (1570), p. 1676.)

One effect of this addition is to make the popish meaning of the hat Hooper had to wear more explicit. In Elizabethan terms this could have two effects. Firstly one could argue that it would make it harder for the

---

[79] By 'self-censorship' I am referring to the concept as suggested by Annabel Patterson in her work *Censorship and Interpretation: The Conditions of Writing and Reading in Early Modern England* (Wisconsin, 1984).

[80] Despite Ridley's role in forcing Hooper to wear these vestments at his degradation prior to his martyrdom Ridley expresses a view of them similar to that of Hooper. Both the 1563 and 1570 editions of *Acts and Monuments* contain the following passage.

> they [the Marian clergy] put upon the sayde Doctor Ridley the surples with all the trynkettes appertayning to the Masse. And as they were putting on the same, Doctor Ridley did vehemently invey against the Romyshe Byshop, and all that folyshe apparell, calling him Antichrist, and all the apparell folyshe and abhominable, yea to fond for a Vice in a play, in so much that Brokes was exceading angrie with him, and bad him holde his peace. for he did but raile. (*Acts and Monuments* (1563), p. 1374; 1570, p. 1924.)

It is interesting to note the identical theatrical metaphor being used to describe Ridley's appearance in clerical dress and that Foxe uses in the passage quoted above regarding Hooper. Indeed in Bale's plays clerical and monastic dress would have been used as costumes for the papist vice figures. See Peter Happé, 'Properties and costumes in the plays of John Bale', *Medieval English Theatre*, 2 (1980), pp. 55–65.

godly to relate their troubles with clerical dress to Hooper's. Although the actual items of clothing might be very similar the meaning attached to them was clearly very different. This gloss of Foxe's, however, could have the opposite effect, insofar that by stressing the popish meaning of the four-cornered cap Foxe was ensuring that Elizabethan clergy could not forget the provenance of their robes of office. The changes Foxe makes to the longer passage show perhaps a similar tension. In 1570 Foxe writes:

> that [the] Byshopps hauyng [the] upper hande, M. Hooper was fayne to agree to thys condition, that *sometimes* (ones) he should in hys sermons shew hym selfe apparelled as [the] other Byshopps were. Wherefore, *appointed to preach before [the] king* as a new player in strange apparell, he co[m]meth foorthe on the stage. Hys upper garment was a long *scarlet* Chymere, downe to the foote, [and] under that a white linnen Rochet, that couered all hys shoulders. *Upo[n] hys head he had a Geometriall, that is, a foure squared cap, albeit that hys head was round.* (his cappe uppon hys heade was foure cornerde.) [Words in italics added in 1570. Words in round brackets cut in 1570.] (*Acts and Monuments* (1570), p. 1676.)

Again one can see a distancing of the relation between the cap Hooper had to wear and the one that the Elizabethan clergy were expected to wear. Surely it was impossible to view the clothes they were expected to wear in such a humorous way? or was it? Were their heads not round too? Why was it important to stress in 1570 the relation between Hooper's appearance as a stage player and the times when he was 'appointed to preach before the king'? In 1570 Foxe increases the amount of comedy, the role of the monarch and the extent of Hooper's capitulation. In 1563 the impression given is that Hooper only has to wear clerical dress once, in 1570 he has to wear it sometimes, or perhaps occasionally, when appearing in the presence of the monarch.

If Foxe's changes to his account of Hooper's refusal to wear clerical dress were a form of self-censorship they again reflect the effects of the events of the 1560s on the text of *Acts and Monuments* and its writer's lack of faith in the godliness of the Elizabethan public sphere. The changes made between 1563 and 1570 are not just an increase, an accumulation of more stories and more facts. They reflect the relation of *Acts and Monuments* to the Elizabethan public sphere, and to Elizabeth herself. In 1563 the text constructed itself as part of and a provocation to *the* public sphere, in 1570 its scope has been reduced and its polemic focused as it constructs itself within *a* public sphere.[81]

---

[81] At another level this movement reflects a tension that Jane Facey suggests was inherent in Foxe's view of the English Church. See Facey, 'John Foxe and the defence of the English Church', p. 184.

Foxe's role between 1563 to 1570 changes from that of an archivist to that of a veritas-producing historian, whose labour is now, however, addressed to a specifically godly public and, perhaps, to a godly queen. Unlike Halle and Bale, Foxe does not attempt to make his text or his historiography fit a non-debatable, homogenized image of the public. Instead Foxe constructs a public, an audience for his text, that is both public and godly, one for whom the lessons of John Rogers will have meaning, one for whom Bishop Hooper's rejection of clerical dress will ring as a rallying call and one for whom godliness ultimately might, and indeed should, take precedence over publicness.

In 1584 the Bond of Association committed its signatories to hunting down, trying and punishing anyone guilty of assassinating the queen before a new monarch could be chosen by the body politic.[82] In effect the Bond of Association embodies an institutionalized, delayed strong public. Its signatories were committed Protestants, its aim was to ensure that in the horrific event of Elizabeth's assassination the strong public that would inevitably be required in such a crisis would be a Protestant one. In a sense the Bond of Association was designed to prevent a repetition of 1553. If the succession was going to be decided by the public, it would be a public defined both by their publicness and their Protestant godliness. The Bond of Association is an embodiment of the public that Foxe addressed in his 1570, a public defined divisively in religious terms. This public was one that Elizabeth, as a result of the Pope's excommunication, could not but be a part of and be at its centre. The potential hiatus between godliness and publicness illustrated by the *gestic* moment in Bale's *King Johan*, John's spiritual and temporal martyrdom, was solved by the Pope's inscription of Elizabeth as irredeemably non-popish and therefore godly. The Pope in 1570 made Elizabeth the centre of a Protestant public sphere in a way that was non-debatable, absolute and which combined godliness with publicness.

---

[82] This discussion of the Bond of Association relies heavily on the Patrick Collinson's analysis of it in 'The monarchical republic of Queen Elizabeth I', in *Elizabethan Essays* (London, 1994), pp. 31–57.

Conclusion: History and Persecution

> This thyng dothe God, whiche thynge all wyse menne accompte to be the most foolyshe and unwyse part that can bee. Wyll the wyse of the worlde (trowe ye) put theyr moost dere frendes and tenderlye beloued chyldren, into their enemies handes, to kyll, flaye, burne etc that is unto them a madnes aboue al madnes. And yet dothe God use this order, and this is an hyghe and syngular wysdome in his syght, which thei worlde taketh to be moost extreme madnes.
>
> Words attributed to John Rogers in John Foxe, *Acts and Monuments* (1563), p. 1033

Two more editions of *Acts and Monuments*, in 1576 and 1583, were produced during Foxe's lifetime. In both there were numerous changes with material being added, rearranged and quietly dropped. By looking at the concluding pages of the 1576 and 1583 editions it is possible to sketch out a narrative of change between these versions of *Acts and Monuments*.[1] The 1576 edition concludes with a new section, addressed 'To The Christian Reader', that explicitly constructs *Acts and Monuments* as a source of useful, indeed necessary, facts for those wishing to lead a Godly life. This short passage comments that the index 'of most notable thynges', also produced for the first time in 1576, is designed for those who have read the entire work, and for those who have not, 'for the memory of the one', and 'for the speedy and certiane knowledge of the other'.[2] This text goes on to represent the reading of *Acts and Monuments* as a kind of textual pilgrimage with the new index playing the role of guide. The writer of this passage encourages the reader to persevere with using the index and advises them that if,

> in this [the index] ... thou shouldest wander at the first, looke under the syrname, not the proper which we cal Christia[n]. So shalt thou at the first easely finde, which I in long tyme hardly haue sought.[3]

The address 'To The Christian Reader' that concludes Foxe's work in 1576 represents *Acts and Monuments* as having an active part to play

---

[1] For the differences between the 1573 and 1583 editions see Jesse Lander's excellent article, 'Foxe's *Books of Martyrs*: printing and popularising the *Acts and Monuments*', in Claire McEachern and Debora Shuger (eds), *Religion and Culture in Renaissance England* (Cambridge, 1997), pp. 69–92.

[2] John Foxe, *The Ecclesiastical History, Contaynyng the Actes and Monumentes of Thynges passed in euery Kynges tyme in this realme especially in the Church of England principally to be noted* (London, 1576), STC 11224, p. 2009.

[3] Ibid., p. 2009.

in the continuing Protestantization of England. It expresses an explicit incitement to further religious study and debate. In particular, this passage holds up *Acts and Monuments*' account of the Primitive Church as a model that, with the help of the augmented index, can be applied directly to the situation of English Protestants. This final section is, at one level, designed to encourage the use of *Acts and Monuments* as a source of authoritative facts within disputes over the nature of English Protestantism. Significantly the intended audience of this piece's incitement to study are those 'which are not altogether of a stayed iudgement'.[4] It is also notable that the author of this text claims that the example of the Primitive Church is of particular use in dealing with two kinds of adversaries; Popish Pagans and Paganish Papists.[5] The ideal readers of *Acts and Monuments* in 1576, as imagined in its final pages, are simultaneously those who are struggling against popery, paganism and papistry and also those who are not yet of a 'stayed judgement'. Is it simply coincidence that this edition therefore seems to fit perfectly within the religious agenda implicit in the Archbishop Grindal's programme of public disputation and godly debate?[6] In 1576 the final words of *Acts and Monuments* place it within an Elizabethan public sphere as part of an ongoing struggle to complete the reformation of the English Church and turn England into a fully reformed Protestant nation.

In 1583 *Acts and Monuments* changed again from constructing itself as an active participant in religious debate to presenting itself as a historical text, the overriding lesson of which is the need for Protestant unity and solidarity. Jesse Lander comments that:

> Unlike the 1576 edition, which had implicitly sanctioned further argument, the 1583 edition seeks to foreclose debate and urge discontented Protestants to count themselves lucky for the present dispensation. The 1583 edition does allude to disputes between Protestants, but it urges quietism and discourages further contention.[7]

The increase in size of *Acts and Monuments* in 1583, although not of the same scale as that which had taken place between 1563 and 1570, was part of this new emphasis on English Protestant stability.[8] The

---

[4] Ibid., p. 2009.

[5] Ibid., p. 2009.

[6] For Archbishop Grindal and prophesyings see Patrick Collinson, *The Elizabethan Puritan Movement* (Oxford, 1990), pp. 159–90.

[7] Lander, 'Foxe's *Books of Martyrs*: printing and popularising the *Acts and Monuments*', p. 81.

[8] Joseph Black has recently argued that the Martin Marprelate Tracts were an attempt to incite debate within an Elizabethan public sphere. One can see the violent reaction against these texts as part of an assertion of the absolute need for Protestant unity in the

addition of more notes, letters and details served to reinforce the work's status as a textual reliquary: a finished, complete monument to the past sufferings of the English martyrs. In particular, the addition of more incidental details from the Marian persecution articulates a desire for historical completion and for a historization of martyrdom in England. The 1583 edition is a self-consciously historical text, its monumentality implying that the records it contains are fixed and final. While the editions of 1563 and 1570 looked towards the future this edition's gaze is located firmly on the past. The restoration of the account of the Westminster Conference in the 1583 edition fits into this pattern. The placing of this narrative at the end of the text in 1563 implied a continuing history of reformation in England. Its dropping in 1570 illustrated Foxe's lack of faith that such a continuation was likely or even possible. In 1583 *Acts and Monuments* constructs the Westminster Conference as no longer having a direct topical meaning. It achieves this textual effect by deploying this account as one more detail in a summing-up of the facts of the Marian persecution. In 1583 the Westminster Conference is represented as part of the past, an aspect of the tradition of English Protestantism. The final Foxian edition of *Acts and Monuments* asserts a sense of completion of Reformation, if not of reform, that is lacking from the earlier versions of the text.

This sense of completion is, however, partially undermined by the addition of a new section at the end of the text recounting the events of the St Bartholomew Day Massacre and of the resulting civil war in France. In the Dedication to Elizabeth in 1563 Foxe had confidently held up the success of reformation in France and Scotland as part of a pan-European Protestant success story. Such optimism would have seemed completely out of place in the 1580s. During this decade, and for the next 100 years, English Protestantism viewed the continent as a place of threat and not of possibilities.[9] It no longer seemed likely that the Reformation was about to be exported to France but rather that Catholicism was about to import itself back into England. This apparent, and at times real, foreign threat provided the motivation for English Protestantism to unite around the religious settlement of 1559. Indeed

---

1580s. See Joseph Black, 'The rhetoric of reaction: the Martin Marprelate tracts (1588–89), anti-Martinism, and the uses of print in early modern England', *SCJ*, 28 (1997), pp. 707–25.

[9] The idea of a popish plot was used throughout the early modern period in England to explain political and social conflict. One should note, however, that in symbolic terms the nature of popery did not change from 1530–1688. Popery was not a peripheral side-effect of the English Reformations but was an integral part of its basic content, its waste product.

the Bond of Association and the 1583 edition of *Acts and Monuments* can both be seen as part of this unifying agenda.

The account of the St Bartholomew Day Massacre produced in the 1583 edition of *Acts and Monuments* introduces a new note into Foxe's text. Despite all the accounts of papist persecutions that make up *Acts and Monuments* this text is noticeable for its brutality and violence. Although it is centrally concerned with the St Bartholomew Day Massacre, this piece also refers to other alleged papist atrocities. In a typically Foxian motif a claim to brevity is used to justify presenting the reader with the details of these massacres.

> And first for breuity sake, to ouerpasse the bloudy bouchery of the Romish Catholikes in Orynge agaynst the Protestantes, most fiercely and unawares breaking into theyr houses, and there without mercy killing man, woman [and] child: of whom some being spoyled and naked they threw out of theyr loftes into the streetes, some they smothered in theyr houses with smoake, with sword [and] weapon, sparing none, the karkases of some they threwe to dogges ...[10]

The St Bartholomew Day Massacre is constructed in the 1583 edition of *Acts and Monuments* as being part of a policy of violent, disordered but paradoxically planned persecution of continental Protestants. The events of 1572 are depicted as being simultaneously arbitrary and the result of papist plotting. Foxe claims that the French Catholics 'foreseing no good to be done agaynst the Protestantes by open force, began to deuise how by crafty meanes to entrap them.'[11] These 'crafty means' included the drawing up of lists of supporters of Admiral Coligny and the marriage of Henry Navarre and Marguerite Valois. The actual events of the massacre reproduce the image of papist popular violence, albeit on a far larger scale, expressed in Luther's *The Burning of Brother Henry*. Foxe recounts that:

> After the Martyrdome of this good man [Coligny], the armed souldiours with rage and violence ranne upon all other of the same profession, slaying and killing all the Protestantes they knew or coulde finde within the Citty gates inclosed. This bloudye slaughter continued the space of many dayes, but especially the greatest slaughter was in the three first dayes, in which were numbred to be slayne, as the story writeth, aboue [ten] thousand men and women, old and young, of all sorts and conditions ... So great was the outrage of that Heathenish persecution, that not onely Protestantes

---

[10] John Foxe, *Acts and Monuments of matters most speciall in the Church. Newly reuised and reorganised, partly also augmented, and now for the fourth time published* (London, 1583), STC 11225, p. 2152.
[11] Ibid., p. 2153.

but also certayne whom they thought indifferent Papists they put
to the sword insted of Protestantes.[12]

This fearful image of popular chaotic violence combined with meticu-
lous secret papist planning remained a staple element of English political
praxis throughout the sixteenth and seventeenth centuries.[13] It embodies a representation of popery as the fantastical other of English
Protestantism.[14]

Placing an account of the St Bartholomew Day Massacre at the end
of *Acts and Monuments* also implied that the fate of English Protestants
was directly tied to that of continental Protestantism. In particular, the
way the text merges events in Paris in 1572 with those that took place
in the following years in France, for example the siege of La Rochelle,
creates the impression of continuous conflict between Protestants and
their Catholic adversities within an explicitly European context. Far
from Foxe's work being a nationalist text,[15] in 1583 it concludes with a
narrative that encourages its readers to compare and equate the embattled state of Protestant England with that of their besieged fellow believers
in La Rochelle. The scale of the St Bartholomew Day Massacre, however, initially makes it appear out of place at the end of the 1583 edition
of *Acts and Monuments*. The juxtaposition of the Mass of particular,
incidental details and notes relating to the Marian persecutions with the
grand story of thousands being killed in France, of miraculous sieges
and bloody assassinations, appears rather discordant. This apparent
discord, however, incites the reader to make the connection between
recent events on the continent and the details from England's past. The
'failure' of the text to integrate in textual terms the French and continental material with the incidental stories recounting the past struggles
of English Protestants means the reader has to perform this role: to
produce the lesson that Protestant England's past sufferings are the

---

[12] Ibid., p. 2153.

[13] For the place of popery within seventeenth-century English politics see Peter Lake,
'Anti-popery: the structure of a prejudice', in Richard Cust and Ann Hughes (eds),
Conflict in Early Stuart England: Studies in Religion and Politics, 1603–1642 (London,
1989), pp. 72–106. For a late seventeenth-century text that contains an almost identical
representation of popery to that expressed in the 1583 edition of *Acts and Monuments*;
see *The Grand Designs of the Papists, in the Reign of our Late Sovereign Charles the
First, and now carried on against His present Majesty, his Government and the Protestant Religion* (London, 1678).

[14] For the status of fantasy/enjoyment within symbolic structures and discourses see
Slavoj Zizek, *For they know not what they do: Enjoyment as a Political Factor* (London,
1991); Slavoj Zizek, *The Plague of Fantasies* (London, 1997).

[15] The myth of Foxe the nationalist has been thoroughly critiqued by Patrick Collinson.
See Patrick Collinson, *The Birthpangs of Protestant England: Religious and Cultural
Change in Sixteenth and Seventeenth Centuries* (London, 1991), pp. 12–17.

present of European Protestantism. The last pages of the 1583 edition of Foxe's text encourage an understanding of English Protestantism within the context of a European-wide struggle between the forces of good and evil.[16] To be a godly English Protestant in terms of *Acts and Monuments* in 1583 is to feel the sufferings of the French Huguenots as one's own.

The final version of Foxe's text published in his lifetime concludes with an image of a Elizabethan Protestant public sphere encompassing almost all sections of the community constructed against a Catholic threat now located explicitly, although far from exclusively, on the continent. The addition of the short account of the St Bartholomew Day Massacre at the end of this edition leaves its reader with the message that persecution and martyrdom exist beyond the borders of Elizabethan England.[17] Unlike the earlier editions the 1583 version places the act of Reformation in the past. The godly Protestant public sphere that was the ideal audience of the 1570 edition has become the Elizabethan establishment. The conflicts embodied in the changes made between 1563 and 1570, the move from the prophetic to apocalyptic, are submerged and subsumed in 1583 within an image of a Protestant public sphere based on inclusiveness and stability. The growth in the size of Foxe's text, the simple effect of adding more letters, notes, accounts of examinations, stories of miraculous escapes and tales of God's punishments inflicted on persecutors, fed into this unifying agenda. *Acts and Monuments* in 1583 had a breadth and monumentality that reflected the sense of, admittedly embattled, permanency felt by later Elizabethan Protestantism.[18] In this context the besieged and imperilled but united and ultimately victorious example of La Rochelle became the perfect aspirational image of a godly community for late sixteenth-century English Protestants.

This understanding of the changing status of English Protestantism, and of the Elizabethan settlement, is also reflected in the work of late sixteenth-century English Catholic historians and polemicists. During

---

[16] This incitement of the reader to produce an understanding of recent events that places Protestant England within an explicitly European context remains a constant throughout the next hundred years. For a late seventeenth-century example of a text that incites a similar form of reading as does the last pages of *Acts and Monuments* in 1583 see Andrew Marvell, 'An account of the growth of popery and arbitrary government in England', in *State Tracts of the Reign of Charles II* (London, 1689), pp. 69–135.

[17] This structure is reproduced in the representation of Edward VI's reign in *Acts and Monuments* in which persecution is also placed firmly outside the realm.

[18] The status of Protestantism in the latter half of the sixteenth century in England is at the moment a matter of heated debate. For a balanced view see Diarmaid MacCulloch, *The Later Reformation in England: 1547–1603* (Basingstoke, 1990).

the 1560s it was still possible for Thomas Harding to imply that Elizabeth's stand on clerical vestments showed the queen was sympathetic to Catholicism. In *A Confutation of a Boke Intituled An Apologie of the Church of England*[19] Harding writes that:

> your good inclination towards the auncient and catholike religio[n], which the authors of that Apologie with an odious term do call papistre, encourageth me not a litle unto your Maiestie to offer this gyft and service.[20]

Harding's view of the queen relates directly to her refusal to give it to the 'preachers of hate' and their demands that she embark on a 'hasty and sharp persecution' of Catholics.[21]

By the time Nicolas Sanders wrote his *Rise and Growth of the Anglian Schism*[22] in 1585, such confidence had long since departed from Catholic views of Elizabeth. This text combines many of the elements found in Marian understandings of the Edwardian and Henrician Reformations. Like the earlier Catholic historians of Mary Tudor's reign, Sanders criticizes Protestantism as inherently private, feminine, disordered and heretical. He stresses the specifically corrupt and failed nature of English Protestantism writing that:

> But you, O king [Henry VIII], when you deserted the Roman Church, to what other Church did you go? Did you go to the Greek Church? Certainly not, for you have not denied the Possession of the Holy Ghost from the Son. Did you go to the Æthiopic Church? No, for you have not submitted to the rite of circumcision ... But at least, then, you went to Wicliffe, Luther, Zuinglius, or Calvin? Well, if you found any in your kingdom holding the errors of these men, you persecuted them with fire and sword. Whither, then, did you go when you went out of the Roman Church? Whither, indeed? It was to yourself.[23]

Sanders criticizes the Henrician Reformation, and by implication English Protestantism as a whole, on the basis that it was not sufficiently Protestant. This seems an incredible charge for a Catholic writer to make. It did, however, have polemical force in the later half of the sixteenth century. Certainly one of the main motivations of Foxe's historical agenda was to separate the English Reformation from the personal desires of Henry and to make it part of a far wider, religious movement. Indeed the

---

[19] Thomas Harding, *A Confutation of a Boke Intituled An Apologie of the Church of England* (Antwerp, 1565), STC 12762.

[20] Ibid., 2(v).

[21] Ibid., 3.

[22] Nicolas Sanders, *Rise and Growth of the Anglian Schism*, trans. David Lewis (London, 1877).

[23] Ibid., p. 106.

final pages of the 1583 edition of *Acts and Monuments* are perhaps designed to answer precisely this kind of critique of the English Church: to place it squarely within the European Protestant world.

For Sanders English Protestantism is a fraud, less worthy of respect than even such manifest heresies as Calvinism or Lutheranism. It is not an ordered coherent belief system but rather a perversion, a set of hollow practices and meaningless doctrines, a chaos of anti-beliefs. His attempt to separate English Protestantism from that of continental Europe is part of this agenda. Sanders's view of English Protestantism as heresy is a mirror image of Foxe's view of Catholicism as papistry. For these writers one's doctrinal opponents were not people holding religious beliefs similar but different from one's own. Instead, for writers like Foxe and Sanders, papistry and heresy are perversions of the truth: Catholics understood as papists and Protestants as heretics ape and mimic a religious truth that is beyond their understanding.[24] Despite this absolute rejection of the validity of each other's doctrinal positions, Sanders and Foxe manage to produce remarkably similar accounts of the Henrician Reformation. Sanders tells his Protestant adversaries that:

> [God] would not suffer these heresies of yours to come forth in any other way than through this incestuous marriage [Henry VIII and Anne Boleyn], thereby showing them to be the fruits of darkness, and that they could not be had but by deeds of darkness.[25]

Foxe also claimed that the obscurity of the relation between the English Reformation and Henry's matrimonial problems reflected God's purposes writing that:

> No ma[n] here doubeth, but that all this [Henry's divorce] was wrought not by mans desire, but by the secrete purpose of the Lord him selfe ... For as touchyng the kynges inte[n]t and purpose, hee neuer meant nor mynded any such thyng as to seke the ruine of [the] Pope, but rather fought all meanes contrary ...[26]

---

[24] The view that one's opponents' doctrinal position was a mimicry or parody of the truth was the norm in Tudor religious polemics. In *The Pedegrewe of Heretiques* papistry is equated with false teaching and the corruption of the Word of God while Thomas Stapleton claimed that:

> Calvin ... when he telleth some truthe, he stuffeth in a great deale of untruthe withall, and so saueth the swete and true doctrine, with the cancred venim of heresy, that he poysoneth pleasantly, and killeth craftely.

Thomas Stapleton, *A Fortresse of Faith* (Antwerp, 1565), STC 23232, g, and J. Barthlet, *The Pedegrewe of Heretiques. Wherein is truely and plainely set out, the first roote of Heretiques be-gon in the Church, since the time and passage of the Gospel, together with an example of the of-spring of the same* (London, 1566), STC 1534.

[25] Sanders, *Rise and Growth of the Anglian Schism*, p. 101.

[26] John Foxe, *The Ecclesiastical History, Contaynyng the Actes and Monumentes of*

In their understandings of the English Reformation Foxe and Sanders exploit the problematic relation between history and God's purpose to make opposing doctrinal points. Foxe argues that the truth of Protestantism is revealed by the impossibility of explaining in historical terms the relation between Henry's divorce and the Henrician Reformation. Sanders makes the identical historical argument to advance the opposite polemic point. Both writers place their labour as historians in the lacuna, the darkness, between Henry's intentions and God's purpose. They position themselves between history and the playing out of the divine will and claim an implicitly prophetic role based on their ability to relate the latter to the former. Sanders and Foxe can make the 'secrete purpose' of the Lord meaningful in their histories and in the process assert a privileged role for themselves within the commonwealth; while their histories are diametrically opposed their understanding of their status as historians is identical.

These parallels between Foxe and Sanders are not, however, unique since the texts of other Elizabethan Catholic historians and martyrologists are replete with textual motifs and patterns similar to those found in *Acts and Monuments*. For example, William Allan, in his *A briefe historie of the glorious martyrdom of XII priests*,[27] produces accounts of martyrdoms that would not have looked out of place in Foxe's work. There is the same motif of *imitatio Christi*, the same stoicism in the face of pain and emphasis on the certainty of election. Equally the persecutors in Allan's text, and those of his fellow Catholic polemicists, are symbolically identical to those found in Foxe; they are disordered, hasty, devious, violent, ultimately unsuccessful and often condemned by their own words. For example, in *An Abstracte of the Life and Martirdome of Mistres Margaret Clitherowe* a Protestant minister questions the status of the evidence given against Clitherowe and whether it was right to condemn someone to die on the words of one poor boy. The minister is told, however, by one of the judges that:

> The lawe doth warrante the doinge of it ... The Minister demanded what lawe. The judge replied the *queenes* law: That may be, (quoth the Minister) but I am assured, you cannot doe it by Gods lawe; And so he said no more.[28]

Thynges passed in euery Kynges tyme in this realme especially in the Church of England principally to be noted (London, 1570), STC 11223, p. 1195.

[27] William Allan, *A briefe historie of the glorious martyrdom of XII priests* (1582), STC 369.5.

[28] John Mush, *An Abstracte of the Life and Martirdome of Mistress Margaret Clitherowe* (1619), STC 18316.7, B.3.

This motif, in which a conflict between the law of God and that of the persecutors is revealed by the latter's own words, is constantly deployed in *Acts and Monuments* for identical polemical purposes. The world versus the Word is the meaning of martyrdom in the Elizabethan period for Catholics and Protestants. And it is the role of the historian to make this conflict explicit and public.

These similarities are not surprising since Elizabethan Catholics and Protestants were drawing on the same doctrinal and historical models in their martyrologies. Perhaps more surprisingly Allan's attitude to persecution as a process is remarkably similar to that of Foxe in 1563.[29] Allan asks of those persecuting Catholic priests,

> Do they not by othes, interrogatories, and other indevve meanes, purposly driue simple plaine meaning men, that neuer offended their lawes in word, deed, not thought, into the co[m]pass of their treaso[n]s?[30]

He goes on to suggest that, 'This is to make traitors and not to punish treasons'.[31] In the 1563 edition of *Acts and Monuments* John Foxe wrote that:

> neither is there any Article [of religion] which hath not his heresy annexed to him, as the shadow unto a body, insomuch that the matter is now come unto this point, that nothing can now be spoken of circumspectly, but that it shall tend to some snare of heresy, or at the least suspicion ... it were better that there were fewer Articles in the world and then the heresies would cease of their own accord.[32]

While Foxe had claimed that persecuting people for heresy inevitably produced heretics, Allan makes an almost identical point in terms of the productive relation between the laws of treason and the existence of traitors. What concerns both martyrologists is the problematic relation between beliefs, persons and the enforcement of orthodoxy: that to make heretics or traitors out of treasons and heresies is to relate words to people's deeds or beliefs in an inappropriate manner. This concern is potentially ironic, however, since Foxe's and Allan's historiographic agendas rely on just such a relation between words and beliefs – a martyr's beliefs, and their enactment, make his or her words authoritative. In these

---

[29] See pages 182–3 above for a discussion of Foxe's view of persecution as expressed in the 1563 edition of *Acts and Monuments*.

[30] Allan, *A briefe historie*, c.iiii(v).

[31] Ibid., c.iiii(v).

[32] John Foxe, *Actes and Monuments of these latter and perilous dayes, touching matters of the Church, wherein ar comprehended and described the great persecutions and horrible troubles* (London, 1563), STC 11222, p. 134.

terms the discourse of martyrdom and that of persecution have similar if not identical symbolic structures: to make heretics out of heresies is discursively the same as making martyrs out of martyrdom. The shadow of the act is all – whether it is attached by the historian or the persecutor.

The need to produce histories of the Reformation, to justify doctrine by turning to the past, was neither inevitable nor necessary in the sixteenth century. An obscure Protestant tract, written during the reign of Mary Tudor, illustrates the polemical potency but also the dangers of deploying a radical rejection of the role of history in matters of doctrine. *A trewe mirrour* claims that as the Church represented in the Acts of the Apostles does not have a history then its presence must be a sign of corruption.[33] This tract is written as a dialogue between Eusebius, a historian and Marian compromiser, and Theophilius, a Biblical figure and lover of God. The former uses the age of the Catholic Church to sustain the claim that it is the true Church. Protestant writers usually responded to this argument by producing their own counter history that proved Protestantism was of equal antiquity to Catholicism.[34] This move was not inevitable. A far more radical approach to answering this question is adopted in *A trewe mirrour* when Theophilius asks Eusebius:

> what thynke you of the Church of the Apostles, was not that a perfecte true Churche? Eusebius: Yes verely, and so perfect, as I bealeue there hath not been a perfecter. Theophilius: Very well, but I praye you, of what antiquitie were they? You graunt that Chryst was the begynner of that Churche beyng here a living man on earth. And then howe could they alledge for themselves antiquitie.[35]

Eusebius' response to this radical collapse of history as a source of authority in terms of the Church is to accuse his opponent of playing the sophist with him. Theophilius replies, however, that:

> Nay truly the reason is so playne that every ploweman maye well understande the same.[36]

The lover of God turns to the image of the honest plain-speaking ploughman to sustain his argument with the sophisticated worldly

---

[33] Laurence Saunders, *A trewe mirrour or glasse wherin we maye beholde the wofull state of thys our Realme of England, set forth in a Dialogue or communication betwene Eusebius and Theophilius* (1556), STC 21777.

[34] Indeed modern historians sometimes seem to assume that this was the only possible response to this Catholic claim. In a sense they are right, provided one is working within a magisterial understanding of sixteenth-century religious conflict.

[35] Saunders, *A trewe mirrour*, B.iii(3)–B.iii(3v).

[36] Ibid., B.iii(3v).

historian. Theophilius' truth, the one that a simple ploughman can easily understand, is that Christ has no need for history.

Tudor historians of the English Reformations, magisterial Protestants and Catholics, wrote to praise and condemn opposing events and persons; however, the historiographic discourses used by these writers to achieve their polemical aims display a homogeneity of imagery that suggests a shared set of concerns transcending their doctrinal differences. Catholic historians deployed an image of the untruth that must be driven from the public sphere as private, corrupting and textually disordered: an un- or anti-belief that aped and mimicked the Truth. In the process they reproduced an identical symbolic construction of the role of purge, purger and purged as that expressed in the texts of their Protestant opponents. The similarities between Catholic and Protestant constructions of each other reflect the extent to which the conflict reflected in mid-Tudor histories of the English Reformations is a magisterial one. The struggle enacted in these historical texts over the meaning of the various changes in official religion in England during the sixteenth century is based on a set of shared magisterial assumptions and norms. It is the status of these givens, of the unquestionable cultural right of a class or group, the *literati*, to determine, certify and judge religious beliefs and practices that the doctrinal conflicts of the sixteenth century justified and protected. *The* English Reformation, a simple struggle between two coherent and opposing doctrinal camps, Protestant and Catholic, was a result and not the cause of the social and cultural conflicts that were the English Reformations.

Bibliography

Primary texts

Acts of the Privy Council. Volume I, ed. J.R. Dascent (1890–1907).

Agrippa, Henri Cornelius, *A treatise of the nobilitie and excellencie of woman kynde*, trans. D. Clapham (London, 1542), STC 203.

Allan, William, *A briefe historie of the glorious martyrdom of XII priests* (1582), STC 369.5.

Bacon, Francis, *The History of the Reign of King Henry the Seventh*, ed. F.J. Levy (New York, 1972).

Bale, John, *Yet a course at the romyshe foxe* (Antwerp, 1543), STC 1309.

Bale, John, 'A Brief Chronicle concerning the examination and death of the Blessed Martyr of Christ, Sir John Oldcastle, Lord Cobham' (1544), in *Select Works*, ed. Henry Christmas (Cambridge, 1849), pp. 5–59, STC 1278.

Bale, John, 'The Image of Both Churches: Being an exposition of the most wonderful book of Revelation of St. John the Evangelist' (*c.* 1545), in *Select Works*, ed. Henry Christmas (Cambridge, 1849), pp. 249–640, STC 1296.5.

Bale, John, *A Mysterye of inyquyte* (Geneva, i.e. Antwerp, 1545), STC 1303.

Bale, John, *The first examinacyon of Anne Askewe* (Marpurg in the Lande of Hessen, i.e. Wesel, 1546), STC 848.

Bale, John, *A bryefe and plaine declaracion of certayne sente[n]ces in this litle boke foloing, to satifie the consciences of them that haue iudged me therby to be a fauorer of the Anabapistes* (1547).

Bale, John, *The Lattre examinacyon of Anne Askewe* (Marpurg in the Lande of Hessen, i.e. Wesel, 1547), STC 850.

Bale, John, *The Labouryouse Journey ... of Johan Leylande .. enlarged by John Bale* (1549), STC 15445.

Bale, John, ' The Vocacyon of Johan Bale to the Bishoprick of Ossorie in Irelande, his persecussions in the same, and final Delyverance' (1553), in *Harleian Miscellany* (12 vols, London, 1808), I, pp. 328–64, STC 1307.

Bale, John, *The first two partes of the Actes or unchaste examples of Englyshe Votaryes, gathered out of theyr owne legendes and Chronicles* (London, 1560), STC 1274.

Bale, John, 'King Johan', in *The Complete Plays of John Bale*, ed. Peter Happé, 2 vols (Cambridge, 1985), I.

Barlow, William, *A Dialogue Describing the Originall Ground of these Lutheran Faccyons, and Many of their Abuses* (1531), ed. John Robert Lum (London, 1897), STC 1461.

Barthlet, J., *The Pedegrewe of Heretiques. Wherein if truely and plainely set out, the first roote of Heretiques be-gon in the Church, since the time and passage of the Gospel, together with an example of the of-spring of the same* (London, 1566), STC 1534.

Baylor, Michael (ed.), *The Radical Reformation* (Cambridge, 1991).

Ballasus, Nicholas, *A True report of all the doyngs at the assembly co[n]cernyng matters of Religion, lately holden at Poyssy in France*, trans. J.D. (1561?), STC 6776.

Barnes, Robert, *A Supplicacion unto the most gracyons Prince Kinge Henry the eyght* (1531?), STC 1470.

A breuiat cronicle contaynynge all the kinges from brute to this daye (Canterbury, 1551?), STC 9968.

Brice, Thomas, *A compendius regester in metre, conteining the names, and suffryngs of the members of Jesus Christ* (London, 1559), STC 3726.

Brice, Thomas, *Against filthy writing and such like delighting* (London, 1562), STC 3725.

Brooks, James, *A sermon very notable, fructefull and godlie* (London, 1553), STC 3838.

Carion's Chronicle: The Thre Bokes of Chronicles and Carion gathered wyth great diligence of the beste athours: Whereunto is added an appendix by John Funcke, trans. G. Lynne (London, 1550), STC 4626.

Cavendish, George, *The Life and Death of Cardinal Wolsey*, ed. Richard S. Sylvester (EETS o.s. 243, London, 1961).

Cavendish, George, *Metrical Visions*, ed. A.S.G. Edwards (Columbia, 1980).

Champneys, John, *The harvest is at hand, wherin the tares shal be bound, and cast into the fyre and burnt* (London, 1548), STC 4956.

Christopherson, John, *An Exhortation to all Menne to ... Beware of Rebellion* (1554) (Amsterdam, 1973), STC 5207.

The Chronicle of Queen Jane and of two Years of Queen Mary, ed. John Gough Nichols (Camden Society, o.s. 48, 1850).

Chronicle of the Grey Friars of London, ed. John Gough Nichols (Camden Society, o.s. 53, 1852).

Cooper, Thomas, *Coopers Chronicle* (London, 1560), STC 15218.

Cranmer, Thomas, *A confutatio[n] of vnwritte[n] verities, both bi the holye scriptures and moste auncient autors*, trans. E.P. (Wesel?, 1556?), STC 5996.

Crowley, Robert, 'The Way to Wealth' (1550), in *The Select Works of*

Robert Crowley, ed. J.M. Cowper (EETS e.s. 15, London, 1872), pp. 129–76, STC 6096.

Crowley, Robert, 'The Printer to the Reader', *The Vision of Pierce Plowman, nowe the seconde tyme imprinted by Roberte Crowlye* (London, 1550), STC 19907.

Crowley, Robert, *Philargyrie of Greate Britayne* (1551), ed. John N. King, *ELR*, 10 (1980), pp. 46–75, STC 6089.5.

Crowley, Robert, *An Epitome of Cronicles ... continued to the Reigne of Quene Elizabeth by Robert Crowley, Thomas Cooper and Thomas Languet* (London, 1559), STC 15217.5.

The declaracyon of the procedyng of a conference, begon at Westminster the laste Marche, 1559. concerning certiane articles of religion and the breaking up of the sayde conference by default and contempt of certyane Byshops, parties of the sayd conference (London, 1560?), STC 25286.

Elyot, Sir Thomas, *Of the Knowledge which Maketh a Wise Man* (1533), ed. Edwin Johnston Howard (Oxford, Ohio, 1946), STC 7668.

Elyot, Sir Thomas, 'Pasquil the Playne' (1533), *Four Political Treatises* (Gainesville, Florida, 1967), pp. 41–100, STC 7672.

Certayne Questions Demanded and asked by the Noble Realme of Englande, of her true naturall chyldren and Subietes of the same, attributed to Myles Hogherde (Zurich?, 1555), STC 9981.

Fabyan, Robert, *The New Chronicles of England and France*, ed. Henry Ellis (London, 1811).

Fish, Simon, *The Supplication of the Beggars* (1529), ed. Edward Arber (London, 1878), STC 10883.

Fisher, John, *The English Works of John Fisher*, ed. John E.B. Mayor (EETS e.s. 27, New York, 1973).

The Life of Fisher, ed. Rev Ronald Bayne (EETS e.s. 117, London, 1921).

Foxe, John, *Actes and Monuments of these latter and perilous dayes, touching matters of the Church, wherein ar comprehended and described the great persecutions and horrible troubles ... Gathered and collected according to true copies and wrytinges certificatorie, as wel of the parties them selues that suffered, as also out of the Bishops Registers, which wer the doers therof* (London, 1563), STC 11222.

Foxe, John, *The Ecclesiastical History, Contaynyng the Actes and Monumentes of Thynges passed in euery Kynges tyme in this realme especially in the Church of England principally to be noted* (London, 1570), STC 11223.

Foxe, John, 'A Sermon of Christ Crucified' (1570), in *The English*

Sermons of John Foxe, ed. Warren Wooden (New York, 1978), STC 11242.

Foxe, John, *The Ecclesiastical History, Contaynyng the Actes and Monumentes of Thynges passed in euery Kynges tyme in this realme especially in the Church of England principally to be noted* (London, 1576), STC 11224.

Foxe, John, 'A Sermon preached at the Christening of a certaine Jew,' (1578), in *The English Sermons of John Foxe*, ed. Warren Wooden (New York, 1978), STC 11248.

Foxe, John, *Acts and Monuments of matters most speciall in the church. Newly reuised and reorganised, partly also augmented, and now for the fourth time published* (London, 1583), STC 11225.

Foxe, John, *Two Latin Comedies by John Foxe The Martyrologist; Titus et Gesippus, Christus Triumphans*, ed. intro. and trans. John Hazel Smith (Ithaca, 1973).

Gibson, T., *A breue Cronycle of the byshope of Romes blessynge* (1548?), STC 11842a.

'A Glasse of the Truthe' (1532), in *Records of the Reformation: the Divorce*, ed. Nicholas Pocock, 2 vols (London, 1870), vol. II, pp. 385–421, STC 11918.

The Grand Designs of the Papists, in the Reign of our Late Sovereign Charles the First, and now carried on against His present Majesty, his Government and the Protestant Religion (London, 1678).

Gwynnethe, John, *A Declaration of the state, wherin all heretickes dooe leade their lives* (London, 1554), STC 12558.

Halle, Edward, *The Union of the Two Noble and Illustre Families* (London, 1550), STC 12723.

Halle, Edward, *Halle's Chronicle*, collated with the editions of 1548 and 1550 (London, 1809).

Harding, Thomas, *A Confutation of a Boke Intituled An Apologie of the Church of England* (Antwerp, 1565), STC 12762.

Harpsfield, Nicholas, *Harpsfield's Life of More*, ed. Elsie Vaughan Hitchcock (EETS o.s. 186, London, 1963).

Heywood, John, *The Spider and the Fly* (1556), ed. John S. Farmer (London, 1908), STC 13308.

Hoccleve, Thomas, 'Address to Sir John Oldcastle', in *Hoccleve's Works: The Minor Poems*, ed. Frederick J. Furnivall and I. Gollancz (EETS e.s. 61 & 71, London, 1970), pp. 8–24.

Hogarde, Miles, *A Treatise entitled the Path waye to the towre of perfection* (London, 1554), STC 13561.

Hogarde, Miles, *The assault of the sacrame[n]t of the Altar* (London, 1554), STC 13556.

Hogarde, Miles, *A Mirrour of Loue* (1555), STC 13559.

Hogarde, Miles, *The Displaying of the Protestants* (London, 1556), STC 13557.

Joye, George, *A Present consolacion for the sufferers of persecucion for ryghtwysenes* (1544), STC 14828.

Lynne, Walter, *The beginning and endynge of all popery, or popishe kyngedome* (1548?), STC 17115.

Luther, Martin, 'The Burning of Brother Henry' (1525), trans. A.T.W. Steinhäuser, *Luther's Works*, ed. George W. Forell, 55 vols (Philadelphia, 1958), vol. 32, pp. 261–86.

Marvell, Andrew, 'An Account of the Growth of Popery and Arbitrary Government in England', in *State Tracts of the Reign of Charles II* (London, 1689), pp. 69–135.

More, Thomas, 'The History of Richard III, King of England', in *The Complete Works of St Thomas More*, ed. Daniel Kinney 15 vols (New Haven, 1986), vol. 15, pp. 313–485.

Morrison, Richard, 'A Remedy for Sedition Wherin Are Contained Many Things concerning the True and Loyal Obeisance That Commons Owe unto Their Lord Prince and Sovereign Lord the King' (1536), in *Humanist Scholarship and Public Order: Two Tracts against the Pilgrimage of Grace by Sir Richard Morrison*, ed. David Berkowitz (Washington, 1984), pp. 109–46, STC 18113.5.

Mush, John, *An Abstracte of the Life and Martirdome of Mistress Margaret Clitherowe* (1619), STC 18316.7.

A mustre of scimatyke byshoppes of Rome, otherwyse naming them selves popes, moche necessarye to be redde of al the kynges true subiectes (London, 1534?).

'A litel treatise ageynste the mutterynge of some papistes in corners' (1534), in *Records of the Reformation: the Divorce*, ed. Nicholas Pocock, 2 vols (London, 1870), vol. II, pp. 539–52, STC 19177.

Narratives of the Days of the Reformation, ed. John Gough Nichols (Camden Society, o.s. 77, 1859).

Origen, *Prayer, and Exhortation to Martyrdom*, trans. John J. O'Meara (London, 1954).

Original Letters relative to the English Reformation, ed. H. Robinson (Cambridge, 1846–47).

Parkyn, Robert, 'Robert Parkyn's Narrative of the Reformation', ed. A.G. Dickens, *EHR*, 62 (1947), pp. 58–83.

Parr, Catherine, 'The Lamentation or Complaint of a Sinner', in *The Harleian Miscellany*, 12 vols (London, 1808), vol. I, pp. 286–313.

Philippson, Joannes, *A briefe chronicle of the foure principal Empires*, trans. Stephan Wythers (London, 1563), STC 19849.

Pole, Reginald, *Pole's Defence of the Unity of the Church*, trans. Joseph C. Dwyer (Westminster, Maryland, 1965).

Proctor, John, *The historie of wyattes rebellion, with the order and maner of resisting the same* (London, 1554), STC 20407.

Proctor, John, 'The History of Wyat's Rebellion', in *An English Garner*, ed. Edward Arber, 8 vols (London, 1903), vol. 8.

Proctor, John, 'The Prologue to His Deer brethren and naturall countree men of Englande', *The waie home to Christ and truth leadinge from Antichrist and errour*, Vincent of Lerins (1556), S.T.C 24754.

'A Proper Dyalogue Betweene a Gentillman and a Husbandman: Eche complaynynge to other their miserable calamite through the ambicion of the clergye' (1529?), *English Reprints*, ed. E. Arber, 30 vols (London, 1871), vol. 28.

A proper dyaloge betwene a gentillman and a husbandma[n], eche complaynenge [about] the ambicion of the clergye (Marborow in the Lande of Hessen, i.e. Antwerp, 1530), STC 1462.5.

Sanders, Nicolas, *Rise and Growth of the Anglian Schism* (1585), trans. David Lewis (London, 1877).

Saunders, Laurence, *A trewe mirrour or glasse wherin we maye beholde the wofull state of thys our Realme of England, set forth in a Dialogue or communication betwene Eusebius and Theophilius* (1556), STC 21777.

Skelton, John, 'Magnyfycence', in *Four Morality Plays*, ed. Peter Happé (London, 1979), pp. 211–311.

Skelton, John, 'A Replycacion Agaynst Certayne Yong Scolers Adjured of Late', in *The Complete English Poems*, ed. John Scattergood (New Haven, 1983), pp. 373–86.

Smith, Thomas, *De Republica Anglorum: A Discourse on the Commonwealth of England*, ed. L. Alston (Cambridge, 1906).

A Speciall grace, appointed to haue been said after a banket at Yorke, upo[n] the good nues and proclamacion thear, of the entrance in to reign ouer us, of our soueraign lad Elizabeth (1558), STC 7599.

Stapleton, Thomas, *A Fortresse of Faith* (Antwerp, 1565), STC 23232.

Starkey, Thomas, *A Dialogue Between Reginald Pole and Thomas Lupset*, ed. Kathleen M. Burton (London, 1984).

The Sum of the Actes and decrees made by diverse bishops of rome, trans. T. Gydson (1538), STC 21307a.5.

The testament of master Wylliam Tracie esquier expounded both by William Tindall and Joh[n] Firth (Antwerp, 1535), STC 24167.

'The Testimony of William Thorpe' (1530?), in *Two Wycliffite Texts*, ed. Anne Hudson (EETS o.s. 301, Oxford, 1993), STC 24045.

Tudor, Elizabeth, 'The Glass of the Sinful Soul', in *Elizabeth's Glass*, ed. Marc Shell (Lincoln, 1993).

Tyndale, William, 'The Obedience of a Christian Man' (1528), in *Doctrinal Treatises and Introductions to Different Portions of the Holy*

Scriptures, ed. Henry Walter (Cambridge, 1848), pp. 127–344, STC 24446.

Tyndale, William, 'The Practice of Prelates' (1530), in *Expositions and Notes*, ed. Henry Walter (Cambridge, 1849), pp. 237–344, STC 24465.

Udall, Nicholas, *Respublica*, re-ed. W.W. Greg, (EETS o.s. 226, London, 1969).

Secondary sources

Aers, David, 'A whisper on the ear of Early Modernists; or, reflections on literary critics writing the "History of the Subject"', in David Aers (ed.), *Culture and History 1350–1600: Essays on English Communities, Identities and Writing* (Hemel Hempstead, 1992), pp. 177–202.

Aers, David, 'Altars of power: Reflections on Eamon Duffy's *The Stripping of the Altars: Traditional Religion in England 1400–1580*', *Literature and History*, n.s. 3/2 (1995), pp. 90–105.

Almsy, Rudolph P., 'Contesting voices in Tyndale's *The Practice of Prelates*', in John A.R. Dick and Ann Richardson (eds), *William Tyndale and the Law*, 'Sixteenth Century Essays and Studies' vol. 26 (1994), pp. 1–10.

Anderson, Judith, *Biographical Truth: The Representation of Historical Persons in Tudor and Stuart Writing* (New Haven, 1971).

Anglo, Sydney, 'An early Tudor programme for plays and other demonstrations against the Pope', *The Journal of the Warburg and Courtauld Institute*, 20 (1957), pp. 176–9.

Anglo, Sydney, *Spectacle, Pageantry and Early Tudor Policy* (Oxford, 1969).

Anglo, Sydney, *Images of Tudor Kingship* (Guildford, 1992).

Archambault, Paul, 'The analogy of the "body" in Renaissance political literature', *Bibliothéque D'Humanisme et Renaissance*, 29 (1967), pp. 21–53.

Aston, Margaret, 'Lollardy and the Reformation: survival or revival?', *History*, 49 (1964), pp. 149–70.

Aston, Margaret, *England's Iconoclasts: Laws against Images*, 2 vols (Oxford, 1988), vol.I.

Aston, Margaret, *Faith and Fire: Popular and Unpopular Religion, 1350–1600* (London, 1993).

Aston, Margaret, *The King's Bedpost: Reformation and Iconography in a Tudor Group Portrait* (Cambridge, 1993).

Aston, Margaret, 'Iconoclasm in England: official and clandestine', in Peter Marshall (ed.), *The Impact of the English Reformation, 1500–1640* (London, 1997), pp. 167–92.

Arnold, John, 'The historian as inquisitor: The ethics of interrogating subaltern voices', unpublished research article.

Ayers, P. K., 'The Protestant morality play and problems of dramatic structure', *Essays in Theatre*, 2 (1984), pp. 94–110.

Bakhtin, Mikhail, *Rabelais and His World*, trans. Hélène Iswolsky (Bloomington, 1984).

Barthes, Roland, 'Theory of the text', trans. Ian McLeod, in Robert Young (ed.), *Untying the Text: A Post-Structuralist Reader* (London, 1990), pp. 31–47.

Baskerville, E.J., *A Chronological Bibliography of Propaganda and Polemic Published in English between 1553 and 1558* (Philadelphia, 1979).

Bauckham, Richard, *Tudor Apocalypse* (Oxford, 1978).

Baylor, Michael, 'Introduction', in *The Radical Reformation* (Cambridge, 1991), pp. xi–xxvi.

Beckwith, Sarah, 'A very material mysticism: The Medieval mysticism of Margery Kempe', in David Aers (ed.), *Medieval Literature: Criticism, Ideology and History* (Brighton, 1986), pp. 34–57.

Beckwith, Sarah, *Christ's Body; Identity, Culture and Society in Late Medieval Writings* (London, 1993).

Beilin, Elaine, *Redeeming Eve: Women Writers of the English Renaissance* (Princeton, 1987).

Beilin, Elaine, 'Anne Askew's self-portrait in the Examinations', in Margaret Patterson (ed.), *Silent but for the Word: Tudor Women as Patrons, Translators and Writers of Religious Works* (Kent, 1985), pp. 77–91.

Beilin, Elaine, 'Anne Askew's dialogue with authority', in Marie Rose Logan (ed.), *Contending Kingdoms: Historical, Psychological and Feminist Approaches to the Literature of Sixteenth-Century England and France* (Detroit, 1991), pp. 313–22.

Bernard, G.W., *The Power of the Early Tudor Nobility: a Study of the Fourth and Fifth Earls of Shrewsbury* (Brighton, 1985).

Bernard, G.W., *Taxation and Rebellion in Early Tudor England: Henry VIII, Wolsey and the Amicable Grant* (Brighton, 1986).

Bernard, G.W., 'Politics and government in Tudor England', *HJ*, 31 (1988), pp. 159–82.

Bevington, David, *Tudor Drama and Politics: a Critical Approach to Topical Meaning* (Cambridge, Mass., 1966).

Black, Joseph, 'The rhetoric of reaction: The Martin Marprelate tracts (1588–89), anti-Martinism, and the uses of print in early modern England', *SCJ*, 28 (1997), pp. 707–25.

Blatt, T.B., *The Plays of John Bale* (Copenhagen, 1968).

Bill, Christopher Harper, 'Dean Colet's convocation sermon and the pre-Reformation Church in England', *History*, 73 (1988), pp. 191–210.

Bossy, John, *Christianity in the West: 1400–1700* (Oxford, 1985).

Bowker, Margaret, *The Henrician Reformation: the Diocese of Lincoln under John Langland 1521–1547* (Cambridge, 1981).

Bowler, Gerry, 'Marian Protestants and the idea of violent resistance to tyranny', in Peter Lake and Maria Dowling (eds), *Protestantism and the National Church in Sixteenth-Century England* (London, 1987), pp. 124–43.

Braddick, M., 'State formation and social change in early modern England: a problem stated and approaches suggested', *Social History*, 16 (1991), pp. 1–17.

Bradshaw, Christopher, 'David or Josiah? Old Testament kings as exemplars in Edwardian religious polemic', in Bruce Gordon (ed.), *Protestant History and Identity in Sixteenth-Century Europe: The Medieval Inheritance*, 2 vols (Aldershot, 1996), vol. I. pp. 77–90.

Breitenberg, Mark, 'The flesh made word: Foxe's *Acts and Monuments*', *Renaissance and Reformation/Renaissance et Réforme*, 15 (1989), pp. 381–407.

Brigden, Susan, *London and the Reformation* (Oxford, 1994).

Britnell, R.H., 'Penitence and prophecy: George Cavendish on the late state of Cardinal Wolsey', *JEH*, 48 (1997), pp. 263–81.

Cameron, Euan, *The European Reformation* (Oxford, 1991).

Calhoun, Craig, 'Introduction: Habermas and the public sphere', in Craig Calhoun (ed.), *Habermas and the Public Sphere* (Cambridge, Mass., 1993), pp. 1–48.

Certeau, De Michel, *The Writing of History*, trans. Tom Conley (New York, 1988).

Chester, Joseph L., *John Rogers: The Compiler of the First Authorised English Bible: The Pioneer of the English Reformation and its First Martyr* (London, 1861).

Christian, Margaret, 'Elizabeth's preachers and the government of women: defining and correcting a Queen', *SCJ*, 24 (1993), pp. 561–76.

Christianson, Paul, *Reformers and Babylon: English Apocalyptic Visions from the Reformation to the Eve of the Civil War* (Toronto, 1978).

Coats, Catherine Randall *(Em)bodying the Word: Textual Resurrections in the Martyrological Narratives of Foxe, Crespin, de Beze and d'Aubigne* (New York, 1992).

Cohn, Norman, *The Pursuit of the Millennium: Revolutionary Millenarians and Mystical Anarchists of the Middle Ages* (London, 1993).

Collinson, Patrick, *The Religion of the Protestants: The Church in English Society, 1559–1625* (Oxford, 1988).

Collinson, Patrick, *From Iconoclasm to Iconophobia: the Cultural Impact of the Second English Reformation* (Reading, 1988).

Collinson, Patrick, *The Elizabethan Puritan Movement* (Oxford, 1990).

Collinson, Patrick, *The Birthpangs of Protestant England: Religious and Cultural Change in Sixteenth and Seventeenth Centuries* (London, 1991).

Collinson, Patrick, 'Truth and legend: the veracity of John Foxe's *Book of Martyrs*', in *Elizabethan Essays* (London, 1994), pp. 151–77.

Collinson, Patrick, '*De Republica Anglorum*: or; History with the politics put back', in *Elizabethan Essays* (London, 1994), pp. 1–29.

Collinson, Patrick, 'The monarchical republic of Queen Elizabeth I', in *Elizabethan Essays* (London, 1994), pp. 31–57.

Collinson, Patrick, 'England', in Bob Scribner, Roy Porter and Mikiláš Teich (eds), *The Reformation in National Context* (Cambridge, 1994), pp. 80–94.

Collinson, Patrick, 'William Tyndale and the course of the English Reformation', *Reformation*, 1 (1996), pp. 72–97.

Collinson, Patrick, 'Biblical rhetoric: the English nation and national sentiment in the prophetic mode', in Claire McEachern and Debora Shuger (eds), *Religion and Culture in Renaissance England* (Cambridge, 1997), pp. 15–45.

Conrad, F.W., 'The problem of counsel reconsidered: the case of Sir Thomas Elyot', in Paul A. Fideler and T.F. Mayer (eds), *Political Thought and the Tudor Commonwealth: Deep Structure, Discourse and Disguise* (London, 1992), pp. 75–107.

Cross, Claire, 'An Elizabethan martyrologist and his martyr: John Mush and Margaret Clitherow', in Diane Wood (ed.), *Martyrs and Martyrologists: Studies in Church History*, 33 vols (Oxford, 1993), vol. 30, pp. 271–81.

Davis, Catherine and Facey, Jane, 'A Reformation dilemma: John Foxe and the problem of discipline', *JEH*, 39 (1988), pp. 37–65.

Davis, J.C., 'A short course of discourse: Studies in early modern conscience, duty and the "English Protestant interest"', *JEH*, 46 (1995), pp. 302–9.

Davis, John, 'Joan of Kent, Lollardy and the English Reformation', *JEH*, 33 (1982), pp. 225–33.

Davis, J.F., 'Lollardy and the Reformation in England', *Archiv für Reformationsgeschicte*, 73 (1982), pp. 217–36.

Davis, W.T., 'A bibliography of John Bale', *Oxford Bibliographical Society Proceedings and Papers*, V (1939), pp. 201–79.

Dawson, Jane, 'Revolutionary conclusions: the case of the Marian exiles', *History of Political Thought*, 11 (1990), pp. 257–72.

O'Day, Rosemary, *The Debate on the English Reformation* (London, 1986).

O'Day, Rosemary, 'Hugh Latimer: prophet of the kingdom', *Historical Research*, 65 (1992), pp. 258–76.

Debax, J.P. , ' The diversity of morality plays', *Cahiers Elizabethains*, 28 (1985), pp. 3–15.

Deakins, Roger, 'The Tudor prose dialogue: genre and anti-genre', *SEL*, 20 (1980), pp. 5–23.

Devereux, E.J., 'Empty tuns and unfruitful grafts: Richard Grafton's historical publications', *SCJ*, 21 (1990), pp. 33–56.

Dickens, A.G., 'The early expansion of Protestantism in England 1520–1558', *Archiv für Reformationsgeschicte*, 78 (1987), pp. 187–221.

Dickens, A.G., *The English Reformation* (London, 1989).

Dickens, A.G. and Tonkin, J.M., *The Reformation in Historical Thought* (Oxford, 1985).

Doran, Susan, 'Religion and politics at the court of Elizabeth 1: the Habsburg marriage negotiations of 1559–1567', *EHR*, 104 (1989) pp. 908–26.

Dubrow, Heather and Strier, Richard (eds), *The Historical Renaissance: New Essays on Tudor and Stuart Literature and Culture* (Chicago, 1988).

Duffy, Eamon, *The Stripping of the Altars: Traditional Religion in England, 1400–1580* (New Haven, 1992).

Duffy, Eamon, 'The spirituality of John Fisher', in Brendan Bradshaw and Eamon Duffy (eds), *Humanism, Reform and Reformation: The Career of Bishop John Fisher* (Cambridge, 1989), pp. 205–31.

Duffy, Eamon, 'Cranmer and popular religion', in Paul Ayris and David Selwyn (eds), *Thomas Cranmer: Churchman and Scholar* (Woodbridge, Suffolk, 1993), pp. 199–215.

Duncan, Robert, 'The play as Tudor propaganda: Bale's King John and the authority of kings', *University Drayton Review*, 16 (1983–84), pp. 67–74.

Eagleton, Terry, ' History, narrative and Marxism', in James Phelan (ed.), *Reading Narrative: Form, Ethics, Ideology* (Columbus, 1989), pp. 272–82.

Eisenstein, Elizabeth L., *The Printing Press as an Agent of Change* (Cambridge, 1994).

Elshtain, Jean Bethke, *Public Men, Private Woman: Women in Social and Political Thought* (Oxford, 1981).

Elton, Geoffrey, *Policy and Police: the Enforcement of the Reformation in the Age of Thomas Cromwell* (Cambridge, 1972).

Elton, Geoffrey, *The Tudor Constitution* (Cambridge, 1972).

Elton, Geoffrey, *Reform and Reformation: England 1509–1558* (London, 1977).

Elton, Geoffrey, 'Tudor government: the points of contact', in *Studies in Tudor and Stuart Politics and Government*, 4 vols (Cambridge, 1983), vol. III, pp. 3–57.

Evans, G.R., *Problems of Authority in the Reformation Debates* (Cambridge, 1992).

Facey, Jane, 'John Foxe and the defence of the English Church', in Peter Lake and Maria Dowling (eds), *Protestantism and the National Church in Sixteenth Century England* (London, 1987), pp. 162–92.

Fairfield, Leslie P., 'John Bale and the development of Protestant hagiography in England', *JEH*, 24 (1973), pp. 145–60.

Fairfield, Leslie P., *John Bale: Mythmaker of the English Reformation* (Indiana, 1976).

Ferguson, Arthur B., *The Articulate Citizen and the English Renaissance* (Durham, 1965).

Ferguson, Margaret W., 'Saint Augustine's region of unlikeness: the crossing of exile and language', *Georgia Review*, 29 (1975), pp. 844–64.

Ferguson, Margaret W., 'Moderation and its discontents: recent work on Renaissance women', *Feminist Studies*, 20 (1994), pp. 349–66.

Fichte, J.O., 'New wine in old bottles: the Protestant adaptation of the morality play', *Anglia Zeitschrift Englische Philologie*, 110 (1992), pp. 65–84.

Fifield, Merle, 'Methods and modes: the application of genre theory to descriptions of moral plays', in Donald Gilman (ed.), *Everyman & Company: Essays on the Theme and Structure of the European Moral Play* (New York, 1989), pp. 7–74.

Firth, Katherine R., *The Apocalyptic Tradition in Reformation Britain: 1530–1645* (Oxford, 1979).

Foucault, Michel, 'What is an author', trans. Josué V. Harari, in Paul Rabinow (ed.), *The Foucault Reader* (London, 1991), pp. 101–20.

Foucault, Michel, 'Nietzsche, genealogy, history', trans. Donald F. Bouchard and Sherry Simon, in Paul Rabinow (ed.), *The Foucault Reader* (London, 1991), pp. 76–100.

Fox, Alistair and Guy, John (eds), *Reassessing the Henrician Age: Humanism, Politics and Reform 1500–1550* (Oxford, 1986).

Fox, Alistair, 'John Foxe's *Acts and Monuments* as polemical history', *Parergon*, 14 (1976), pp. 43–51.

Fox, Alistair, 'Sir Thomas Elyot and the humanist dilemma', in Alistair Fox and John Guy (eds), *Reassessing the Henrician Age: Humanism, Politics and Reform 1500–1550* (Oxford, 1986), pp. 52–73.

torical Scholarship in the Sixteenth and
on, 1956).

public sphere: a contribution to the
ung democracy', in Craig Calhoun (ed.),
blic Sphere (Cambridge, Mass., 1993), pp. 109–

omas S., '*A solemne contestation of diverse Popes*: A work
n Foxe?', *English Language Notes*, 31 (1994), pp. 35–41.

man, Thomas S., 'Research, rumour and propaganda: Anne Boleyn in Foxe's "Book of Martyrs"', *HJ*, 38 (1995), pp. 797–819.

Freeman, Thomas S., ' "The reik of Maister Patrick Hammylton": John Foxe, John Winram and the Martyrs of the Scottish Reformation', *SCJ*, 27 (1996), pp. 43–60.

Fritze, Ronald H., 'Root or link? Luther's position in the historical debate over the legitimacy of the Church of England, 1558–1625', *JEH*, 37 (1986), pp. 288–302.

Fussner, F.S., *The Historical Revolution: English Historical Writing and Thought, 1580–1640* (London, 1962).

Fussner, F.S., *Tudor History and Historians* (New York, 1970).

Genet, J.P. , 'Which state rises?', *Historical Research*, 65 (1992), pp. 119–33.

Gilman, Ernest B., *Iconoclasm and Poetry in the English Reformation: Down went Dagon* (Chicago, 1986).

Ginsburg, David, 'Ploughboys versus prelates: Tyndale and More and the politics of Biblical translation', *SCJ*, 14 (1988), pp. 45–58.

Gordon, Bruce (ed.), *Protestant History and Identity in Sixteenth-Century Europe*, 2 vols (Aldershot, 1996).

Gordon, Bruce, 'The changing face of Protestant history and identity in the sixteenth century', in Bruce Gordon (ed.), *Protestant History and Identity in Sixteenth-Century Europe: The Medieval Inheritance*, 2 vols (Aldershot, 1996), vol. I, pp. 1–22.

Gransden, Antonia, *Historical Writing in England Vol. 2: 1307 to the Early Sixteenth Century* (London, 1982).

Gransden, Antonia, 'Politics and historiography during the Wars of the Roses', in D.O. Morgan (ed.), *Medieval Historical Writing in the Christian and Islamic Worlds* (London, 1982), pp. 125–48.

Greaves, Richard L., 'Concepts of political obedience in late Tudor England: conflicting perspectives', *Journal of British Studies*, 22 (1982), pp. 23–34.

Greengrass, Mark, *The French Reformation* (Oxford, 1987).

Guy, John, 'The King's Council and political participation', in Alistair Fox and John Guy (eds), *Reassessing the Henrician Age: Humanism, Politics and Reform 1500–1550* (Oxford, 1986), pp. 121–47.

Guy, John, *Tudor England* (Oxford, 1991).

Guy, John, 'The Henrician age', in J.G.A. Pocock, assisted by Gor Schochet and Lois G. Schwerver (eds), *Varieties of British Poli* *Thought 1500–1800* (Cambridge, 1993), pp. 13–46.

Guy, John, 'The rhetoric of counsel in early modern England', in Dal Hoak (ed.), *Tudor Political Culture* (Cambridge, 1995), pp. 292–310.

Guy, John (ed.), *The Tudor Monarchy* (London, 1997).

Guy, John, 'Tudor monarchy and its critiques', in John Guy (ed.), *Tudor* *Monarchy* (London, 1997), pp. 78–109.

Haas, Steven W., 'Henry VIII's Glasse of Truthe', *History*, 64 (1979), pp. 353–62.

Habermas, Jürgen, *Legitimation Crisis*, trans. Thomas McCarthey (Cam- bridge, 1992).

Habermas, Jürgen, *The Structural Transformation of the Public Sphere:* *An Inquiry into a Category of Bourgeois Society*, trans. Thomas Burger, with the assistance of Frederick Lawrence (Cambridge, 1992).

Habermas, Jürgen, 'Concluding remarks', in Craig Calhoun (ed.), *Habermas and the Public Sphere* (Cambridge, Mass., 1993), pp. 462– 79.

Hadfield, Andrew, *Literature, Politics and National Identity: Reforma-* *tion to Renaissance* (Cambridge, 1994).

Hageman, Elizabeth H., 'John Foxe's Henry VIII as "Justitia"', *SCJ*, 10 (1979), pp. 35–43.

Haigh, Christopher (ed.), *The English Reformation Revised* (Cambridge, 1987).

Haigh, Christopher, 'The English Reformation: a premature birth, a difficult labour and a sickly child', *HJ*, 33 (1990), pp. 449–59.

Haigh, Christopher, 'Anticlericalism and the English Reformation', in Christopher Haigh (ed.), *The English Reformation Revised* (Cam- bridge, 1992), pp. 56–74.

Haigh, Christopher, *English Reformations: Religion, Politics, and Soci-* *ety under the Tudors* (Oxford, 1993).

Hale, J.R., *The Evolution of British Historiography: from Bacon to* *Namier* (Ohio, 1964).

Hall, Basil, 'The early rise and gradual decline of Lutheranism in Eng- land (1520–1600)', in Derek Baker (ed.), *Reform and Reformation:* *England and the Continent: c.1500–c.1750: Studies in Church His-* *tory*, 33 vols (Oxford, 1979), vol. II, pp. 103–31.

Haller, W., *Foxe's Book of Martyrs and the Elect Nation* (London, 1963).

Hanson, Elizabeth, 'Torture and truth in Renaissance England', *Repre-* *sentations*, 34 (1991), pp. 53–84.

Happé, Peter, 'Properties and costumes in the Plays of John Bale', *Medieval English Theatre*, 2 (1980), pp. 55–65.

Happé, Peter, 'The Protestant adaptation of the saint play', in Clifford Davidson (ed.), *The Saint Play in Medieval Europe* (Kalamazoo, 1986), pp. 205–40.

Harvey, Elizabeth D., *Ventriloquized Voices: Feminist Theory and English Renaissance Texts* (London, 1992).

Hay, Denys, *Annalists and Historians: Western Historiography from the Eighth to the Eighteenth Centuries* (London, 1977).

Hay, Denys, *Polydore Vergil: Renaissance Historian and Man of Letters* (Oxford, 1952).

Hay, Denys, 'History and historians in France and England during the fifteenth century', *BIHR*, 35 (1962), pp. 111–27.

Headley, John M., 'The Reformation as crisis in the understanding of tradition', *Archiv Für Reformationsgeschicte*, 78 (1987), pp. 5–23.

Heath, James, *Torture and English Law: An Administrative and Legal History from the Plantagenets to the Stuarts* (Westport, Connecticut, 1982).

Helgerson, Paul, *Forms of Nationhood: The Elizabethan Writing of England* (Chicago, 1992).

House, Seymour Baker, 'Cromwell's message to the regulars: the Biblical trilogy of John Bale, 1537', *Renaissance and Reformation/ Renaissance et Reforme*, 16 (1991), pp. 123–38.

Houston, Julia, 'Transubstantiation and the sign: Cranmer's drama of the Lord's Supper', *JMRS*, 24 (1994), pp. 113–30.

Howard, Jean, 'Feminism and the question of history: resituating the debate', *Women's Studies: An Interdisciplinary Journal*, 19 (1991), pp. 149–57.

Hoyle, R.W., 'The origins of the dissolution of the monasteries', *HJ*, 38 (1995), pp. 275–305.

Hudson, Anne, '"No Newe Thyng": the printing of medieval texts in the early Reformation period', in *Lollards and Their Books* (London, 1985), pp. 227–48.

Hudson, Anne, *The Premature Reformation: Wycliffite Texts and Lollard History* (Oxford, 1988).

Hudson, Anne, 'William Thorpe and the question of authority', in G.R. Evans (ed.), *Christian Authority: Essays in Honour of Henry Chadwick* (Oxford, 1988), pp. 127–37.

Jansen, Sharon L., *Political Protest and Prophecy under Henry VIII* (Woodbridge, Suffolk, 1991).

Jenkins, Keith (ed.), *The Postmodern History Reader* (London, 1997).

Jones, N.L., *Faith by Statute: Parliament and the Settlement of Religion 1559* (London, 1982).

Jordan, W.K., *Edward VI: The Young King: the Protectorship of the Duke of Somerset* (London, 1968).

Jordan, W.K., *Edward VI: The Threshold of Power: the Dominance of the Duke of Northumberland* (London, 1970).

Justice, Steven, 'Inquisition, speech, and writing: a case from late-medieval Norwich', *Representations*, 48 (1994), pp. 1–29.

Kastan, David Scott, '"Holy Wordes" and "Slypper Wit": John Bale's *King Johan* and the poetics of propaganda', in Peter C. Herman (ed.), *Rethinking the Henrician Era: Essays on Early Tudor Texts and Contexts* (Urbanna, 1994), pp. 267–82.

Kaufman, Peter Iver, *'The Polytygue Churche': Religion and Early Tudor Political Culture: 1485–1516* (Macon, GA, 1986).

Kelen, Sarah A., '"It is dangerous (gentle reader)": censorship, Holinshed's Chronicle, and the politics of control', *SCJ*, 27 (1996), pp. 705–20.

Kelly, R.L., 'Hugh Latimer as Piers Plowman', *SEL*, 17 (1977), pp. 13–26.

Kendall, D., *The drama of dissent: the radical poetics of nonconformity, 1380–1590* (Chapel Hill, 1986).

Kendrick, T.D., *British Antiquity* (London, 1950).

Kenyon, John, *The History Men: the Historical Profession in England since the Renaissance* (London, 1983).

King, John N., 'Robert Crowley's editions of Piers Plowman: a Tudor apocalypse', *MP*, 73 (1976), pp. 342–52.

King, John N., *English Reformation Literature: The Tudor Origins of the Protestant Tradition* (Princeton, 1982).

King, John N., *Tudor Royal Iconography: Literature and Art in an Age of Religious Crisis* (Princeton, 1989).

King, John N., 'Recent studies in Protestant poetics', *ELR*, 21 (1991), pp. 283–307.

Knott, John R., *Discourses of Martyrdom in English Literature, 1563–1694* (Cambridge, 1993).

Kolb, Robert, *For All the Saints: Changing Perceptions of Martyrdom and Sainthood in the Lutheran Reformation* (Macon, GA, 1987).

Kolb, Robert, 'God's gift of martyrdom: the early Reformation understanding of dying for the faith', *Church History*, 64 (1995), pp. 399–411.

Krontiris, Tina, *Oppositional Voices: Women as Writers and Translators of Literature in the English Renaissance* (London, 1992).

Laclau, Ernesto, 'Introduction', in Ernesto Laclau (ed.), *The Making of Political Identities* (London, 1994), pp. 1–8.

Lake, Peter, 'Presbyterianism, the idea of a national church and the argument from divine right', in Peter Lake and Maria Dowling (eds),

Protestantism and the National Church in Sixteenth Century England (London, 1987), pp. 193–224.

Lake, Peter, 'Anti-popery: the structure of a prejudice', in Richard Cust and Ann Hughes (eds), *Conflict in Early Stuart England: Studies in Religion and Politics, 1603–1642* (London, 1989), pp. 72–106.

Lander, Jesse, 'Foxe's Books of Martyrs: printing and popularising the Acts and Monuments', in Claire McEachern and Debora Shuger (eds), *Religion and Culture in Renaissance England* (Cambridge, 1997), pp. 69–92.

Lawton, David, 'Lollardy and the "Piers Plowman" tradition', *MLR*, 76 (1981), pp. 780–93.

Lawton, David, 'Dullness and the fifteenth century', *ELH*, 54 (1987), pp. 761–99.

Lawton, David, *Faith, Text and History: the Bible in English* (Hemel Hempstead, 1990).

Levin, Carole, 'Women in the Book of Martyrs as models of behaviour in Tudor England', *International Journal of Women's Studies*, 2 (1981), pp. 196–207.

Levin, Carole, 'John Foxe and the responsibilities of queenship', in Mary Beth Rose (ed.), *Women in the Middle Ages and the Renaissance: Literary and Historical Perspectives* (Syracuse, 1986), pp. 113–33.

Levine, Joseph M., 'Method in the history of ideas: More, Machiavelli and Quentin Skinner', *Annals Scholarship*, 3 (1986), pp. 37–60.

Levine, Joseph M., *Humanism and History: Origins of Modern Historiography* (Ithaca, 1987).

Levy, F.J., *Tudor Historical Thought* (San Marino, California, 1967).

Loach, Jennifer and Tittler, Robert, *Mid-Tudor Polity, 1540–1560* (London, 1980).

Loades, David, *Two Tudor Conspiracies* (Cambridge, 1965).

Loades, David, *The Reign of Mary Tudor: Politics, Government and Religion in England 1553–1558* (London, 1991).

Loades, David, *The Mid-Tudor Crisis 1545–1565* (Basingstoke, 1992).

Loades, David, *The Oxford Martyrs* (Bangor, 1992).

Loades, David (ed.), *John Foxe and the English Reformation* (Aldershot, 1997).

MacCulloch, Diarmaid, *The Later Reformation in England: 1547–1603* (Basingstoke, 1990).

MacCulloch, Diarmaid, 'The myth of the English Reformation', *Journal of British Studies*, 30 (1991), pp. 1–19.

MacCulloch, Diarmaid (ed.), *The Reign of Henry VIII: Politics, Policy and Piety* (Basingstoke, 1995).

MacCulloch, Diarmaid, *Thomas Cranmer: A Life* (New Haven, 1996).

Macek, Ellen, 'The emergence of a feminine spirituality in "The Book of Martyrs"', *SCJ*, 19 (1988), pp. 63–80.

Macherey, Pierre, 'The problem of reflection', *Substance*, 15 (1976), pp. 6–20.

Maclean, Ian, *The Renaissance Notion of Woman: a Study in the Fortunes of Scholasticism and Medieval Science in European Intellectual Life* (Cambridge, 1980).

Markus, R.A., *Saeculum: History and Society in the Theology of St Augustine* (London, 1970).

Martin, J.W., *Religious Radicals in Tudor England* (London, 1989).

Mason, H.A., *Humanism and Poetry in the Early Tudor Period* (London, 1959).

Mayer, T.F., *Thomas Starkey and the Commonweal; Humanist Politics and Religion in the Reign of Henry VIII* (Cambridge, 1989).

McEachern, Claire, '"A whore at the first blush seemth only a woman": John Bale's *Image of Both Churches* and the terms of religious difference in the early English Reformation', *JMRS*, 25 (1995), pp. 243–69.

McGrath, Alister, *The Intellectual Origins of the European Reformation* (Oxford, 1987).

McGrath, Alister, *Reformation Thought: An Introduction* (Oxford, 1993).

McKisack, Mary, *Medieval History in the Tudor Age* (Oxford, 1971).

McLevan, A.N., 'Delineating the Elizabethan body politic: Knox, Aylmer and the definition of counsel 1558–88', *History of Political Thought*, 17 (1996), pp. 224–52.

McNiel, John T., 'John Foxe: historiographer, disciplinarian, tolerationist', *Church History*, 43 (1974), pp. 216–29.

McNiven, Peter, *Heresy and Politics in the Reign of Henry IV: The Burning of John Badby* (Woodbridge, Suffolk, 1987).

McQuade, Paula, '"Except that they had offended the Lawe": Gender and Jurisprudence in *The Examinations of Anne Askew*', *Literature and History*, n.s. 3/2 (1994), pp. 1–14.

Miller, E.S., 'The Roman rite in Bale's King John', *PMLA*, 64 (1949), pp. 802–22.

Moore, R.I., *The Formation of a Persecuting Society; Power and Deviance in Western Europe, 950–1250* (Oxford, 1994).

Mozley, J.F., *John Foxe and His Book* (London, 1940).

Mueller, Janel, *The Native Tongue and the Word: Developments in English Prose Style, 1380–1580* (Chicago, 1984).

Mueller, Janel, 'A Tudor queen finds voice: Katherine Parr's Lamentation of a Sinner', in Heather Dubrow and Richard Strier (eds), *The Historical Renaissance: New Essays on Tudor and Stuart Literature and Culture* (Chicago, 1988), pp. 15–47.

Muir, Edward, *Ritual in Early Modern Europe* (Cambridge, 1997).

Murphy, Virginia, 'The literature and propaganda of Henry VIII's first divorce', in Diarmaid MacCulloch (ed.), *The Reign of Henry VIII: Politics, Policy and Piety* (London, 1995), pp. 135–58.

Nicholls, David, 'The theatre of martyrdom in the French Reformation'. *P & P*, 121 (1988), pp. 49–73.

Nicholls, David J., 'The nature of popular heresy in France', *HJ*, 26 (1983), pp. 261–75.

Nicholson, G.D., 'The nature of and functions of historical argument in the Henrician Reformation', Phd Thesis (Cambridge, 1977).

Norbrook, David, *Poetry and Politics in the English Renaissance* (London, 1984).

Nussbaum, Damien, 'The later editions of Acts and Monuments', unpublished paper given at the John Foxe Colloquium (Cambridge, 1995).

Nussbaum, Damien, 'Appropriating martyrdom: fears of renewed persecution and the 1632 edition of Acts and Monuments', in David Loades (ed.), *John Foxe and the English Reformation* (Aldershot, 1997), pp. 178–91.

Oakley, Francis, 'Legitimation by consent: the question of the medieval roots', *Viator*, 14 (1983), pp. 303–35.

Oakley, Francis, 'Christian obedience and authority, 1520–1550', in J.H. Burns, with the assistance of Mark Goldie (ed.), *The Cambridge History of Political Thought, 1450–1700* (Cambridge, 1994), pp. 159–92.

Olsen, Palle J., 'Was John Foxe a millenarian?', *JEH*, 45 (1994), pp. 600–624.

Olsen, V.N., *John Foxe and the Elizabethan Church* (Berkeley, 1973).

Orlin, Lena Cowen, *Private Matters and Public Culture in Post-Reformation England* (Ithaca, 1994).

Parker, Douglas H., 'A proper dyalogue betwene a gentillman and a husbandman: the question of authorship', *Bulletin of the John Rylands Library*, 78 (1996), pp. 63–75.

Partner, Nancy F., 'Making up lost time: writing on the writing of history', *Speculum*, 61 (1986), pp. 90–117.

Patterson, Annabel, *Censorship and Interpretation: The Conditions of Writing and Reading in Early Modern England* (Wisconsin, 1984).

Patterson, Annabel, 'Rethinking Tudor historiography', *South Atlantic Quarterly*, 92 (1993), pp. 185–208.

Patterson, Annabel, *Reading Holinshed's Chronicles* (Chicago, 1994).

Patterson, Lee, *Negotiating the Past: the Historical Understanding of Medieval Literature* (Wisconsin, 1987).

Patterson, Lee, 'Critical historicism and medieval studies', in Lee

Patterson (ed.), *Literary Practice and Social Change in Britain, 1380–1530* (Berkeley, 1990), pp. 1–14.

Patterson, Lee, 'On the margin: postmodernism, ironic history, and medieval studies', *Speculum*, 65 (1990), pp. 87–108.

Pettegree, Andrew, *Marian Protestantism: Six Studies* (Aldershot, 1996).

Pineas, Rainer, 'The English morality play as a weapon of religious controversy', *SEL*, 2 (1962), pp. 157–80.

Pineas, Rainer, 'William Tyndale's use of history as a weapon of religious controversy', *Harvard Theological Review*, 55 (1962), pp. 121–41.

Pineas, Rainer, 'John Bale's nondramatic works of religious controversy', *Studies in the Renaissance*, 9 (1962), pp. 218–33.

Pineas, Rainer, 'Some polemical techniques in the nondramatic works of John Bale', *Bibliotheque d'Humanisme et Renaissance*, 24 (1962), pp. 583–8.

Pineas, Rainer, 'William Tyndale's influence on John Bale's polemical use of history', *Archiv für Reformationsgeschichte*, 53 (1962), pp. 79–96.

Pineas, Rainer, 'More versus Tyndale: a study of controversial technique', *MLQ*, 24 (1963), pp. 144–50.

Pineas, Rainer, 'Robert Barnes's polemical use of history', *Bibliotheque d'Humanisme et Renaissance*, 26 (1964), pp. 55–69.

Pineas, Rainer, *Tudor and Early Stuart Anti-Catholic Drama* (Nieuwkroop, 1972).

Pineas, Rainer, 'Polemical use of the Scriptures in the plays of John Bale', *Nederlands Archief vour Kerkgeschiedew*, 66 (1986), pp. 180–89.

Pineas, Rainer, 'The polemical drama of John Bale', in W.R. Elton and William B. Lang (eds), *Shakespeare and Dramatic Tradition: Essays in Honour of S.F. Johnson* (Newark, 1989), pp. 194–210.

Pocock, J.G.A., *The Machiavellean Moment: Florentine Political Thought and the Atlantic Republican Tradition* (Princeton, 1975).

Pocock, J.G.A., 'A discourse of sovereignty: observations on the work in progress', in Nicholas Phillipson and Quentin Skinner (eds), *Political Discourse in Early Modern Britain* (Cambridge, 1993), pp. 377–428.

Preston, Joseph, 'Was there an historical revolution?', *Journal of the History of Ideas*, 38 (1977), pp. 353–64.

Potter, Robert, *The English Morality Play: Origins, History and Influence of a Dramatic Tradition* (London, 1975).

Potter, Robert, 'Afterword', in Donald Gilman (ed.), *Everyman & Company: Essays on the Theme and Structure of the European Moral Play* (New York, 1989), pp. 329–34.

Quilligan, Maureen, *The Language of Allegory: Defining the Genre* (Ithaca, 1979).

Redworth, G., *In Defence of the Catholic Church: The Life of Stephen Gardiner* (Oxford, 1990).

Rex, Richard, 'The crisis of obedience: God's Word and Henry's Reformation', *HJ*, 39 (1996), pp. 863–94.

Riley, Denise, *'Am I That Name?': Feminism and the Category of 'Women' in History* (London, 1988).

Rose, Mary Beth (ed.), *Women in the Middle Ages and the Renaissance: Literary and Historical Perspectives* (Syracuse, 1986).

Ross, Trevor, 'Dissolution and the making of the English literary canon: the catalogues of Leland and Bale', *Renaissance and Reformation/ Renaissance et Réforme*, 16 (1991), pp. 57–80.

Rubin, Miri, 'Choosing death? Experiences of martyrdom in late medieval Europe', in Diane Wood (ed.), *Martyrs and Martyrologies; Studies in Church History*, 33 vols (Oxford, 1993), vol. 30. pp. 153–83.

Rutledge, Douglas F., 'Respublica: rituals of status elevation and the political mythology of Mary Tudor', *Medieval and Renaissance Drama in England: An Annual Gathering of Research*, 5 (1991), pp. 55–68.

Ryrie, Alec, 'The problems of legitimacy and precedent in English Protestantism, 1539–47', in Bruce Gordon (ed.), *Protestant History and Identity in Sixteenth-Century Europe: The Medieval Inheritance*, 2 vols (Aldershot, 1996), vol. I, pp. 78–92.

Scarisbrick, J.J., *The Reformation and the English People* (Oxford, 1984).

Scarisbrick, J.J., *Henry VIII* (London, 1988).

Skinner, Quentin, *The Foundations of Modern Political Thought. The Renaissance*, 2 vols (Cambridge, 1990), vol. I.

Skinner, Quentin, *The Foundations of Modern Political Thought. The Age of Reformation*, 2 vols (Cambridge, 1992), vol.II.

Slavin, Arthur J., 'Telling the story: G.R. Elton and the Tudor Age', *SCJ*, 21 (1990), pp. 151–69.

Smart, Stefan J., 'John Foxe and the story of Richard Hun, Martyr', *JEH*, 37 (1986), pp. 1–4.

Smart, Stefan J., '"Favourers of God's Word?" John Foxe's Henrician martyrs', PhD Thesis (Southampton, 1988).

Southern, R.W., 'Presidential address: aspects of the European tradition of historical writing. 1. The Classical tradition from Einhard to Geoffrey of Monmouth', *TRHS*, 20 (1970), pp. 173–96.

Stallybrass, Peter, and White, Allon, *The Politics and Poetics of Transgression* (London, 1986).

Stallybrass, Peter, '"Drunk with the Cup of Liberty": Robin Hood, the carnivalesque, and the rhetoric of violence in early modern England', in Nancy Armstrong and Leonard Tennenhouse (eds), *The Violence of Representation: Literature and the History of Violence* (London, 1989), pp. 45–76.

Starkey, David, 'Intimacy and innovation: the rise of the Privy Chamber, 1485–1547', in David Starkey, D.A.L. Morgan et al. (eds), *The English Court: from the Wars of the Roses to the Civil War* (London, 1987), pp. 71–118.

Stewart, Alan, *Close Readers: Humanism and Sodomy in Early Modern England* (New Jersey, 1997).

Strauss, Gerald, 'The idea of order in the German Reformation', in *Enacting the Reformation in Germany: Essays on Institution and Reception* (Aldershot, 1993), pp. 1–16.

Strype, John, *Ecclesiastical Memorials*, 3 vols (Oxford, 1822), vol. II.i.

Thomas, Keith, *The Perception of the Past in Early Modern England* (London, 1983).

Thompson, J.W., *A History of Historical Writing* (Gloucester, Mass., 1967).

Thomson, John A.F., *The Later Lollards* (London, 1965).

Trueman, Carl R., *Luther's Legacy: Salvation and the English Reformers, 1525–1556* (Oxford, 1994).

Vanhoutte, Jacqueline A., 'Engendering England: the restructuring of allegiance in the writings of Richard Morison and John Bale', *Renaissance and Reformation/Renaissance et Réforme*, 20 (1996), pp. 49–77.

Wabuda, Susan, 'Equivocation and recantation during the English Reformation: the "subtle shadows" of Dr Edward Crone', *JEH*, 44 (1993), pp. 224–42.

Wabuda, Susan, 'Henry Bull, Miles Coverdale and the making of Foxe's Book of Martyrs', in Diane Wood (ed.), *Martyrs and Martyrologies; Studies in Church History*, 33 vols (Oxford, 1993), vol. 30, pp. 245–58.

Walker, Greg, *John Skelton and the Politics of the 1520s* (Cambridge, 1988).

Walker, Greg, *Plays of Persuasion: Drama and Politics at the Court of Henry VIII* (Cambridge, 1991).

Walker, Greg, 'Heretical sects in pre-Reformation England', *History Today*, 43 (May 1993), pp. 42–8.

Walter, John and Wrightson, Keith, 'Dearth and social order in early modern England', *P & P*, 71 (1976), pp. 22–42.

Wasson, John, 'The morality play: ancestor of Elizabethan drama', in Clifford Davidson, C.J. Gianakaris and John H. Stroupe (eds), *The Drama of the Middle Ages: Comparative and Critical Essays* (New York, 1982), pp. 316–27.

Watson, Nicholas, 'Censorship and cultural change in late-medieval

England: vernacular theology, the Oxford Translation Debate, and Arundel's Constitutions of 1409', *Speculum*, 70 (1995), pp. 822–64.

White, Hayden, 'The question of narrative in contemporary theory', *History and Theory*, 23 (1984), pp. 1–33.

White, Hayden, 'The value of narrativity in the representation of reality', in *The Content of the Form: Narrative Discourse and Historical Representation* (Baltimore, 1987), pp. 1–25.

White, Helen C., *Social Criticism in Popular Literature of the Sixteenth Century* (New York, 1944).

White, Helen C., *Tudor Books of Saints and Martyrs* (Madison, 1963).

Whitehead, Lydia, 'A Poena et Culpa: Penitence, Confidence and the Miserere in Foxe's Acts and Monuments', *Renaissance Studies: Journal of the Society for Renaissance Studies*, 4 (1990), pp. 287–99.

White, Paul Whitfield, *Theatre and Reformation: Protestantism, Patronage and Playing in Tudor England* (Cambridge, 1993).

Whiting, Robert, *The Blind Devotion of the People: Popular Religion and the English Reformation* (Cambridge, 1989).

Williams, George Huntston, *The Radical Reformation* (London, 1962).

Williams, Glanmor, *Reformation Views of Church History* (London, 1970).

Wilson, Derek, *A Tudor Tapestry: Men, Women and Society in Reformation England* (London, 1972).

Wilson, K.J., *Incomplete Fictions: The Formation of English Renaissance Dialogue* (Washington, 1985).

Wilson, John F., *Pulpit in Parliament: Puritanism during the English Civil War, 1640–1648* (Princeton, 1969).

Womack, Peter, 'Imagining communities: theatre and the English nation in the sixteenth century', in David Aers (ed.), *Culture and History 1350–1600: Essays on English Communities, Identities and Writing* (New York, 1992), pp. 91–145.

Womersley, David, 'Sir Thomas More's History of King Richard III: a new theory of the English texts', *Renaissance Studies*, 7 (1993), pp. 272–90.

Wooden, Warren, *John Foxe* (Boston, 1983).

Wooden, Warren, 'Recent studies in Foxe', *ELR*, 11 (1981), pp. 224–32.

Woolf, D.R., 'Genre into artifact: the decline of the English chronicle in the sixteenth century', *SCJ*, 19 (1988), pp. 321–54.

Woolf, D.R., 'The power of the past: history, ritual and political authority in Tudor England', in Paul A. Fideler and T.F. Mayer (eds), *Political Thought and the Tudor Commonwealth: Deep Structure, Discourse and Disguise* (London, 1992), pp. 19–49.

Woolf, D.R., 'The rhetoric of martyrdom: generic contradiction and narrative strategy in John Foxe's Acts and Monuments', in Thomas F. Mayer and D.R. Woolf (eds), *The Rhetorics of Life Writing in Early Modern Europe: Forms of Biography from Canandra Fedde to Louis XIV* (Michigan, 1995), pp. 243–82.

Wriedt, Markus, 'Luther's concept of history and the formation of an evangelical identity', in Bruce Gordon (ed.), *Protestant History and Identity in Sixteenth-Century Europe: The Medieval Inheritance*, 2 vols (Aldershot, 1996), vol. I, pp. 31–45.

Wrightson, Keith, *English Society, 1580–1680* (London, 1982).

Yates, Francis, *Astraea: The Imperial Theme in the Sixteenth Century* (London, 1975).

Yates, Frances, 'Foxe as propagandist', *Encounter*, 27 (1966), pp. 78–86.

Zakai, Avihu, 'Reformation, history, and eschatology in English Protestantism', *History and Theory*, 26 (1987), pp. 300–318.

Zaret, David, 'Religion, science and printing in the public spheres in seventeenth-century England', in Craig Calhoun (ed.), *Habermas and the Public Sphere* (Cambridge, Mass., 1993), pp. 212–35.

Žižek, Slavoj, *For they know not what they do: Enjoyment as a Political Factor* (London, 1991).

Žižek, Slavoj, 'Identity and its vicissitudes: Hegel's "Logic of Essence" as a theory of ideology', in Ernesto Laclau (ed.), *The Making of Political Identities* (London, 1994), pp. 40–75.

Žižek, Slavoj, *The Plague of Fantasies* (London, 1997).

Index